WASTEWATER TREATMENT PLANT DESIGN HANDBOOK

2012

Water Environment Federation
601 Wythe Street
Alexandria, VA 22314-1994 USA

Wastewater Treatment Plant Design Handbook

About WEF

Formed in 1928, the Water Environment Federation® (WEF®) is a not-for-profit technical and educational organization with members from varied disciplines who work towards WEF's vision to preserve and enhance the global water environment.

For information on membership, publications, and conferences, contact

Water Environment Federation
601 Wythe Street
Alexandria, VA 22314-1994 USA
(703) 684-2400
http://www.wef.org

Prepared by the **Wastewater Treatment Plant Design Handbook** Task Force of the **Water Environment Federation**

Hannah T. Wilner, P.E., *Chair*

James S. Bays
Lucas Botero, P.E., BCEE
Peter Burrowes, P.Eng.
Mary Kay Camarillo, Ph.D., P.E.
Peter V. Cavagnaro, P.E., BCEE
Rhodes R. Copithorn, P.E., BCEE
Timur Deniz, Ph.D., P.E.
Leon S. Downing, Ph.D., P.E.
Sarah Hubbell
Thomas E. Jenkins, P.E.
Samuel S. Jeyanayagam, Ph.D., P.E., BCEE
Kenneth Knickerbocker, P.E., R.L.S.
Terry L. Krause, P.E., BCEE

Ting Lu, Ph.D.
Eric Lynne
Maritza A. Macias-Corral, Ph.D.
William C. McConnell, P.E.
Heather M. Phillips, P.E.
Christopher Pizarro
Joseph C. Reichenberger, P.E., BCEE
Nalin Sahni, E.I., LEED Green Assoc.
Julian Sandino, P.E., Ph.D.
Paul J. Schuler, P.E.
Stephanie L. Spalding, P.E.
K.C. "Kumar" Upendrakumar, P.E., BCEE
Thor Young, P.E., BCEE

Under the Direction of the **Municipal Design Subcommittee** of the **Technical Practice Committee**

2012

Water Environment Federation
601 Wythe Street
Alexandria, VA 22314–1994 USA
http://www.wef.org

Manuals of Practice of the Water Environment Federation®

The WEF Technical Practice Committee (formerly the Committee on Sewage and Industrial Wastes Practice of the Federation of Sewage and Industrial Wastes Associations) was created by the Federation Board of Control on October 11, 1941. The primary function of the Committee is to originate and produce, through appropriate subcommittees, special publications dealing with technical aspects of the broad interests of the Federation. These publications are intended to provide background information through a review of technical practices and detailed procedures that research and experience have shown to be functional and practical.

Contents

List of Figures

List of Tables

Preface

This handbook is intended to complement several recognized wastewater treatment design references. It facilitates access to those design guides by providing concise information from them and enabling the reader to quickly locate additional information by following direct references. This handbook is organized similarly to the *Design of Municipal Wastewater Treatment Plants* (Water Environment Federation Manual of Practice No. 8; 5th Edition; 2009) publication so that cross references may be more easily found.

This reference is written for students and design professionals familiar with wastewater treatment concepts, the design process, plant operations, and the regulatory basis of water pollution control. It is not intended to be a primer for either the inexperienced or the generalist but still a tool for them as well, allowing them to quickly identify where they can find more information for unfamiliar subjects. As such, the authors of this handbook are industry professionals who have used their experience as both students and design professionals to identify the most critical information to present in tables and figures. It is highly recommended that the reader does not rely solely on information, such as design criteria, identified by this handbook as it is not inclusive. A thorough understanding of the principles behind these summary chapters is necessary for the correct application and use of all information contained in this handbook.

This publication was produced under the direction of Hannah T. Wilner, P.E., *Chair*.

The principal authors of this publication are as follows:

Chapter 1	Hannah T. Wilner, P.E.
Chapter 2	Hannah T. Wilner, P.E.
Chapter 3	Hannah T. Wilner, P.E.
Chapter 4	Hannah T. Wilner, P.E.
Chapter 5	Sarah Hubbell
Chapter 6	Stephanie L. Spalding, P.E.
Chapter 7	Sarah Hubbell
Chapter 8	Eric Lynne
Chapter 9	Stephanie L. Spalding, P.E.
Chapter 10	Hannah T. Wilner, P.E.

Chapter 11   Eric Lynne
Chapter 12   Sarah Hubbell
Chapter 13   Hannah T. Wilner, P.E.
Chapter 14   Eric Lynne
Chapter 15   Eric Lynne
Chapter 16   Stephanie L. Spalding, P.E.
Chapter 17   Hannah T. Wilner, P.E.
Chapter 18   Hannah T. Wilner, P.E.

Authors' and reviewers' efforts were supported by the following organizations:

Black & Veatch Corporation, Kansas City, Missouri
CDM Smith, Cambridge, Massachusetts
CH2M HILL, Chicago, Illinois; Cincinnati and Columbus, Ohio; Englewood, Colorado; Overland Park, Kansas; Tampa, Florida; and Kitchener, Ontario, Canada
Donohue and Associates, Sheboygan, Wisconsin
Entex Technologies Inc., Chapel Hill, North Carolina
GE Power & Water, Portland, Oregon
GHD, Bowie, Maryland
Hatch Mott MacDonald, Millburn, New Jersey
JenTech Inc., Milwaukee, Wisconsin
Johnson Controls, Inc., Milwaukee, Wisconsin
Loyola Marymount University, Los Angeles, California
Malcolm Pirnie, the Water Division of ARCADIS, Newport News, Virginia
Metropolitan Sewer District of Greater Cincinnati, Cincinnati, Ohio
Molzen Corbin, Albuquerque, New Mexico
University of the Pacific, Stockton, California
Veolia Water North America, Indianapolis, Indiana
Wood, Patel & Assoc., Phoenix, Arizona

Chapter 1

Introduction

1.0   OVERVIEW

The intent of this handbook is to complement *Design of Municipal Wastewater Treatment Plants* (WEF et al., 2009) and other pertinent and recognized wastewater treatment design guidance documents, including

- *Wastewater Engineering: Treatment and Reuse* (Metcalf and Eddy, 2003);

- *Wastewater Treatment Plants: Planning, Design and Operation* (Qasim, 1999); and

- *Wastewater Treatment Plant Design* (Vesilind [Ed.], 2003).

At times, other references were consulted for various chapters in this handbook; these specific references are listed to direct the reader to additional information. The purpose of this handbook is to provide the information a designer needs directly at his or her fingertips or to allow them to simply and immediately determine which reference to review for that information. This handbook includes numerous tables and bulleted lists containing the most critical information found in these design resources and directs the reader to the source for more detailed information. It is highly recommended that the reader not rely solely on information identified by this handbook, such as design criteria, because it is not inclusive. A thorough understanding of the principles behind these summary chapters is necessary for the correct application and usage of all information contained in this handbook.

This reference is written for design professionals familiar with wastewater treatment concepts, the design process, plant operations, and the regulatory basis of water pollution control. It is not intended to be a primer for either the inexperienced or the generalist. The organization and structure of this handbook is similar to *Design of Municipal Wastewater Treatment Plants* (WEF et al., 2009), although some chapters have been consolidated for brevity.

Each chapter of this handbook is organized to capture the minimum required knowledge for designing the relevant unit process for that chapter. The unit process is described in an introductory section immediately followed by a list describing the sections of other reference material, including *Design of Municipal Wastewater Treatment Plants* (WEF et al., 2009), that should be consulted. Individual chapters for *Design of Municipal Wastewater Treatment Plants* (WEF et al., 2009) are available through the Water Environment Federation, and this handbook allows the user to identify exactly which chapters and sections he or she need. Key design information is then presented with various tables, figures, formulas and equations, and citations as warranted. References are listed at the end of each chapter.

A history of wastewater treatment and a description of the designer's role in a wastewater treatment project are provided in the first chapter of *Design of Municipal Wastewater Treatment Plants* (WEF et al., 2009).

2.0   REFERENCES

Metcalf and Eddy, Inc. (2003) *Wastewater Engineering: Treatment and Reuse*, 4th ed.; McGraw-Hill: New York.

Qasim, S. (1999) *Wastewater Treatment Plants: Planning, Design and Operation*, 2nd ed.; CRC Press: Boca Raton, Florida.

Vesilind, P. A., Ed. (2003) *Wastewater Treatment Plant Design*; Water Environment Federation: Alexandria, Virginia.

Water Environment Federation; American Society of Civil Engineers; Environmental & Water Resources Institute (2009) *Design of Municipal Wastewater Treatment Plants*, 5th ed.; WEF Manual of Practice No. 8; ASCE Manuals and Reports on Engineering Practice No. 76; McGraw-Hill: New York.

Chapter 2

Raw Wastewater Characterization and Hydraulics

1.0 INTRODUCTION

There are numerous overall design factors and considerations for designing a municipal wastewater treatment plant (WWTP) that lead to the selection of specific technologies and treatment processes. Many of these factors and considerations are focused on unit processes or individual facilities, but others are more broad, such as mass balances that are used to determine whether a particular treatment will indeed be adequate. This section of the handbook introduces the reader to only a few significant broad considerations, that is, raw wastewater characteriziation and hydraulics of the WWTP, both of which are pertinent for a thorough materials balance. It is a combination of several key sections from Volume 1 of *Design of Municipal Wastewater Treatment Plants* (WEF et al., 2009).

Suggested reading material for additional information includes the following:

- *Design of Municipal Wastewater Treatment Plants* (WEF et al., 2009) (Chapter 2, "Municipal Wastewater Characteristics: Source and Phase", Chapter 3, "Facility Design Requirements", Chapter 6, "Plant Hydraulics and Pumping", and Chapter 21, "Solids Storage and Transport");

- *Wastewater Engineering: Treatment and Reuse* (Metcalf and Eddy, 2003) (Chapter 1, "Wastewater Engineering: An Overview");

- *Wastewater Treatment Plants Planning Design and Operation* (Qasim, 1999) (Chapter 2, "Basic Design Considerations", Chapter 3, "Wastewater Characteristics", and Chapter 9, "Pumping Station");

- *Wastewater Treatment Plant Design* (Vesilind [Ed.], 2003) (Chapter 2, "The Design Process", and Chapter 3, "Plant Hydraulics");

- *Recommended Standards for Wastewater Facilities* (GLUMRB, 2004); and

- *Water and Wastewater Engineering: Design Principles and Practices* (Davis, 2010) (Chapter 18, "General Wastewater Collection and Treatment Design Considerations").

An Introduction to Process Modeling for Designers (WEF, 2009) is suggested for more information regarding conducting mass balances for individual facilities and whole-plant treatment processes.

2.0   RAW WASTEWATER CHARACTERIZATION

The wastewater quality and quantity characteristics of a plant's influent typically reflect the nature and demographics of the contributing area, water uses, and conditions of the conveyance system. In general, the design professional determines the wastewater characteristics and develops an end-of-pipe solution responsive to discharge compliance standards and other wastewater management objectives.

2.1   Flow Projections

Population and flow projections including nonpermanent residents, and seasonal changes in populations must be considered. The sum of the nonpermanent and the permanent population is considered the functional population and is the basis for WWTP flow.

Most public wastewater treatment systems are designed with a phased approach, often using a minimum of 20 years of service life before an expansion is needed. However, in addition to effects of lower startup flows, the designer should also consider potential additional future facility and site requirements, in particular, in instances where the sewer system service area is not expected to reach ultimate build-out levels within the design period adopted for the project.

Consideration of existing conditions and service area characteristics should be included when estimating flow per capita. When available, water consumption for an area should be used to estimate wastewater flow generation. At least 60 to 90% of the water consumption typically reaches the sewer system (the lower percentage is applicable in semiarid regions) (WEF et al., 2009). If water consumption data are not available or an area is undeveloped, an estimation of flow per capita can be used to generate expected wastewater flow. Flow per capita estimates can be obtained from several available references. One of these, which considers increased uses of water-conserving devices and appliances, is shown in Table 2.7 of *Wastewater Engineering: Treatment and Reuse* (Metcalf and Eddy, 2003). Infiltration and inflow should also be considered, especially in areas with older sewer systems. This is discussed in the following section (Section 2.2, "Characteristics").

Some U.S. state regulatory agencies use *Recommended Standards for Wastewater Facilities* (GLUMRB, 2004), which recommends 380 L/cap·d (100 gal/cap·d) for use as an average design flow. Tables 2.8 and 2.9 in *Design of Municipal Wastewater Treatment Plants* (WEF et al., 2009) show estimates of typical wastewater flowrates from commercial and institutional sources, respectively.

The most consistent component of municipal wastewater is the character of its domestic wastes. These wastes reflect the demographic makeup, character, and practices of the served population. Flowrates and concentrations will vary hourly in municipal systems, with typical values as shown in Figure 2.2 of *Design of Municipal Wastewater Treatment Plants* (WEF et al., 2009). Generally, the smaller the system, the more variable the waste flowrates and concentrations, while larger systems may have smaller diurnal variations. Peaking factors are established and used in performance projections to evaluate the effects of higher flowrates, such as peak hourly and maximum day, especially during dry or wet weather conditions. These must be considered carefully both in terms of hydraulic loadings and pollutant loadings because treatment performance may be adversely affected with serious consequences such as exceeding effluent permit limitations.

2.2   Characteristics

Table 2.1 of this handbook delineates the typical pollutant composition of domestic wastewater and Table 2.2 shows other characteristics typical of domestic wastewater.

Recent trends of water-saving efforts and water reuse have increased some biochemical oxygen demand, total suspended solids (TSS), ammonia, and organic nitrogen concentrations in municipal WWTP influent. The design professional is cautioned to include consideration of these low-flow systems, where applied, and their effect on influent characteristics. It is recommended to analyze the influent for specific characteristics and concentrations, if possible, rather than relying on historical data, and to consider the mass loadings in influent and concentrations. Additionally, the user should consider the effect of domestic water use, such as total dissolved solids in the local water supply. More information is presented in Table 2.13 of *Design of Municipal Wastewater Treatment*

TABLE 2.1   Daily quantity of waste discharged by individuals on a dry-weight basis (from Metcalf & Eddy, *Wastewater Engineering: Treatment and Reuse*, 4th ed. Copyright © 2003, The McGraw-Hill Companies, New York, N.Y., with permission).

Constituent*	Value, lb/capita·d			Value, g/capita·d		
	Range	Typical without ground-up kitchen waste	Typical with ground-up kitchen waste	Range	Typical without ground-up kitchen waste	Typical with ground-up kitchen waste
BOD$_5$	0.11 to 0.26	0.180	0.220	50 to 120	80	100
COD	0.30 to 0.65	0.420	0.480	110 to 295	190	220
TSS	0.13 to 0.33	0.200	0.250	60 to 150	90	110
NH$_3$ as N	0.011 to 0.026	0.017	0.018	5 to 12	7.6	8.4
Organic N as N	0.009 to 0.022	0.012	0.013	4 to 10	5.4	5.9
TKN as N	0.020 to 0.048	0.029	0.032	9 to 21.7	13	14.3
Organic P as P	0.02 to 0.004	0.0026	0.0028	0.9 to 1.8	1.2	1.3
Inorganic P as P	0.004 to 0.006	0.0044	0.0048	1.8 to 2.7	2.0	2.2
Total P as P	0.006 to 0.010	0.0070	0.0076	2.7 to 4.5	3.2	3.5
Oil and grease	0.022 to 0.088	0.0661	0.075	10 to 40	30	34

*BOD$_5$ = 5-day biochemical oxygen demand, COD = chemical oxygen demand, TSS = total suspended solids, N = nitrogen, NH$_3$ = ammonia, TKN = total Kjeldahl nitrogen, and P = phosphorus.

Plants (WEF et al., 2009) and Table 3.16 of *Wastewater Engineering: Treatment and Reuse* (Metcalf and Eddy, 2003).

Flow and conventional pollutant load contributions from commercial sources generally are considered within the allowance for domestic sources. This consideration becomes less appropriate for smaller service areas where commercial operations such as laundromats, car washes, and sports events may substantially affect the character of an area's wastewater. These need to be considered in the design of the treatment system, and tables of estimated values for these and other contributors should be used as a reference for design values.

Some typical flowrates from institutional facilities, essentially domestic in characteristics, are shown in Table 2.9 of *Design of Municipal Wastewater Treatment Plants* (WEF et al., 2009). Flowrates for these wastes also vary by region, climate, and type of facility. The actual flow records from the institutions are the best source of flow data for design purposes.

A municipal WWTP may also receive septic tank waste (septage) generated in the surrounding, unsewered areas from septic tank cleaning contractors and solids from sewer cleanings. Sewer cleanings are expected to exhibit highly variable characteristics of organically enriched grit. Sewer cleaning also can include

TABLE 2.2 Typical composition of untreated domestic wastewater (from Metcalf & Eddy, *Wastewater Engineering: Treatment and Reuse*, 4th ed. Copyright © 2003, The McGraw-Hill Companies, New York, N.Y., with permission).

Contaminants	Unit	Concentration[a]		
		Low strength	Medium strength	High strength
Solids, total (TS)	mg/L	390	720	1 230
Dissolved, total (TDS)	mg/L	270	500	860
Fixed	mg/L	160	300	520
Volatile	mg/L	110	200	340
Suspended solids, total (TSS)	mg/L	120	210	400
Fixed	mg/L	25	50	85
Volatile	mg/L	95	160	315
Settleable solids	mL/L	5	10	20
Biochemical oxygen demand, 5–d, 20° C (BOD$_5$, 20° C)	mg/L	110	190	350
Total organic carbon (TOC)	mg/L	80	140	260
Chemical oxygen demand (COD)	mg/L	250	430	800
Nitrogen (total as N)	mg/L	20	40	70
Organic	mg/L	8	15	25
Free ammonia	mg/L	12	25	45
Nitrites	mg/L	0	0	0
Nitrates	mg/L	0	0	0
Phosphorus (total as P)	mg/L	4	7	12
Organic	mg/L	1	2	4
Inorganic	mg/L	3	5	10
Chlorides[b]	mg/L	30	50	90
Sulfate[b]	mg/L	20	30	50
Oil and grease	mg/L	50	90	100
Volative organic compounds (VOCs)	mg/L	<100	100 to 400	>400
Total coliform	No./100 mL	10^6 to 10^8	10^7 to 10^9	10^7 to 10^{10}
Fecal coliform	No./100 mL	10^3 to 10^5	10^4 to 10^6	10^5 to 10^8
Cryptosporidum oocysts	No./100 mL	10^{-1} to 10^0	10^{-1} to 10^1	10^{-1} to 10^2
Giardia lamblia cysts	No./100 mL	10^{-1} to 10^1	10^{-1} to 10^2	10^{-1} to 10^3

[a]Low strength is based on an approximate wastewater flowrate of 750 L/cap·d (200 gal/cap·d). Medium strength is based on an approximate wastewater flowrate of 460 L/cap·d (120 gal/cap·d). High strength is based on an approximate wastewater flowrate of 240 L/cap·d (60 gal/cap·d).

[b]Values should be increased by amount of constituent present in domestic water supply.

Note: mg/L = g/m^3.

high quantities of grease, rags, trash, and other debris. Management and treatment of the grease from sewer or wet well cleaning needs special consideration in the design of the treatment system and its components.

Waste solids from a water treatment plant can be expected to exhibit the characteristics of TSS in the raw water supply before water treatment and any solid (i.e., powdered activated carbon) or solid-forming material (i.e., alum addition and the resultant hydroxide precipitate) are added during the course of treatment.

Some of the most significant components of wastewater received at a treatment plant include *infiltration*, which refers to unintentional water seepage or leaks through collection system pipes, house laterals, and manholes; and *inflow*, which refers to surface and subsurface stormwater allowed to enter the collection system (mirroring the character of the precipitation event). Inflow can be high in communities with older or combined sewer systems. Although combined sewer service may represent only a small fraction of the influent service area, inflow derived from the combined sewer service area often will dominate design and operation of the treatment works. The reader is referred to Section 8.2, "Extraneous Flows", of Chapter 2 in *Design of Municipal Wastewater Treatment Plants* (WEF et al., 2009) for more information.

Similar to flow variations, influent pollutant loadings also vary throughout the day and must be considered by the designer when sizing treatment facilities. Peaking factors are often used; these are discussed in more detail in Section 4.1, "Definition of Plant Capacity", in Chapter 3 of *Design of Municipal Wastewater Treatment Plants* (WEF et al., 2009).

3.0   PLANT HYDRAULICS

After a treatment concept has been selected and a preliminary site layout has been determined, the next step is to determine the hydraulic profile (water surface profile or hydraulic grade line) for a WWTP and its unit processes. The objective is to ensure there is adequate head available to allow the wastewater to flow from one unit process to another and to establish the appropriate control weir elevations and water surface elevations within each unit process to ensure that adequate freeboard is provided. The designer must also consider the contributions of recycle and return flows from equipment and processes. Additionally, hydraulic consideration must include performance issues such as maintaining flow velocities to keep solids in suspension, thus avoiding future operation and maintenance (O&M) problems. This may include making conduits and channels large enough to meet future expansion beyond the capacity required during the design year. Sufficient hydraulic head should be provided to permit good distribution of the plant flow to all treatment processes over the range of expected flow conditions, without being excessive. During calculation of the hydraulic

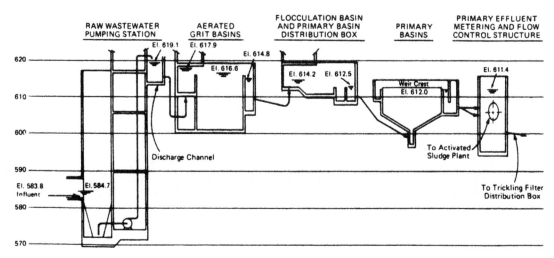

FIGURE 2.1 Typical hydraulic profile for influent pumping and primary treatment (WEF et al., 2009).

profile, the economics of building deeper plant structures should be considered as an alternative to pumping. Pumping stations result in higher O&M costs and reduced reliability. Depending on the process or processes selected, intermediate pumping may be required. This is common upstream of biotowers, trickling filters, and tertiary processes.

A hydraulic profile is generated to determine the water level required at each treatment process for the wastewater to flow through the plant. The resulting water surface profile elevations typically are presented graphically on a drawing sheet in the WWTP construction drawings. Figures 2.1 through 2.3 show examples of hydraulic profiles.

Chapter 6 of *Design of Municipal Wastewater Treatment Plants* (WEF et al., 2009) describes the procedures for generating the hydraulic profile, including

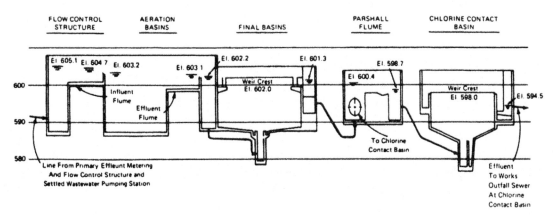

FIGURE 2.2 Typical hydraulic profile for an activated sludge plant (WEF et al., 2009).

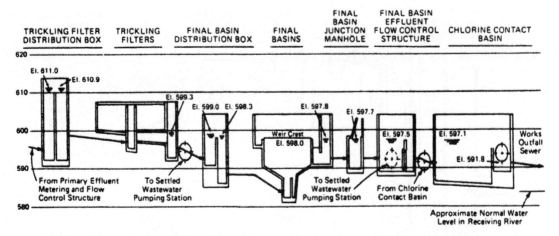

FIGURE 2.3   Typical hydraulic profile for a trickling filter plant (WEF et al., 2009).

head loss equations and flow splitting strategies, assuming the reader has an understanding of basic fluid hydraulic principles. Texts are suggested to provide the reader with that fundamental hydraulic information.

Pumping is also an important part of overall WWTP design. Table 2.3 provides a description of the types of pumps and their application in various parts of the WWTP.

Understanding pump performance curves and the system is required to select an appropriately sized pump. In *Design of Municipal Wastewater Treatment Plants* (WEF et al., 2009), Section 5 of Chapter 6 describes pump curves and other considerations for designing pump systems (such as controls and power requirements); design examples are provided for generating a hydraulic profile.

4.0   REFERENCES

Davis, M. (2010) *Water and Wastewater Engineering: Design Principles and Practice*; McGraw-Hill: New York.

Great Lakes–Upper Mississippi River Board of State and Provincial Public Health and Environment Managers (2004) *Recommended Standards for Wastewater Facilities*; Health Research Inc.: Albany, New York.

Metcalf and Eddy, Inc. (2003) *Wastewater Engineering: Treatment and Reuse*, 4th ed.; McGraw-Hill: New York.

Qasim, S. (1999) *Wastewater Treatment Plants: Planning, Design and Operation*, 2nd ed.; CRC Press: Boca Raton, Florida.

Vesilind, P. A., Ed. (2003) *Wastewater Treatment Plant Design*; Water Environment Federation: Alexandria, Virginia.

TABLE 2.3   Pump classification and applications in the wastewater industry (RAS = return activated sludge) (WEF et al., 2009).

Major classification	Pump type	Pump description	Major pumping applications
Kinetic	Centifugal (volute)	– Separately coupled – Close coupled – Submersible – Axial split – Radial split	– Raw wastewater – RAS and waste activated sludge (WAS) (non-clog) – Settled primary and thickened sludge – Secondary or tertiary effluent
	Peripheral (torque-flow)	– Separately coupled – Close coupled – Radial flow – Recessed impeller	– Raw wastewater – Scum – RAS and WAS – Dilute sludge – Dilute digested sludge
	Vertical (turbine)	– Lineshaft – Submersible – Horizontally mounted axial flow – Vertical turbine solids handling (VTSH*)	– Screened wastewater (VTSH) – Primary effluent (VTSH) – Secondary or tertiary effluent
Positive displacement	Reciprocating	– Plunger – Piston	– Scum – Primary, secondary, and settled sludges – Digested sludge – Thickened sludge – Chemical solutions
		– Diaphragm	– Scum – RAS and WAS – Digested sludge – Thickened sludge – Chemical solutions
	Rotary	– Lobe – Screw	– Raw wastewater – Digested sludge (rotary-lobe) – Thickened sludge – Chemical solutions
		– Progressive cavity	– Scum – Sludge (when pumping primary sludge grinder typically precedes pump) – Digested sludge – Thickened sludge
	Screw	– Spiral crew	– Raw wastewater – Settled primary and secondary sludges – Thickened sludge
	Pneumatic	– Airlift – Ejector	– RAS and WAS – Raw wastewater at small installations – Scum

*VTSH is a proprietary patented design (Fairbanks Morse, Kansas City, Kansas).

Water Environment Federation (2009) *An Introduction to Process Modeling for Designers*; WEF Manual of Practice No. 31; McGraw-Hill: New York.

Water Environment Federation; American Society of Civil Engineers; Environmental & Water Resources Institute (2009) *Design of Municipal Wastewater Treatment Plants*, 5th ed.; WEF Manual of Practice No. 8; ASCE Manuals and Reports on Engineering Practice No. 76; McGraw-Hill: New York.

Chapter 3

Preliminary Treatment

1.0 INTRODUCTION

Preliminary treatment consists of physical unit operations to remove, reduce, or modify wastewater constituents in the raw influent that can cause operational problems with downstream processes or increase maintenance of downstream equipment. Preliminary treatment is often considered the headworks of a plant and typically includes screening and grit removal.

This chapter also addresses handling of hauled-in septic tank waste (septage) and attenuation of high flows and pollutant loading that can disrupt the performance of downstream processes (equalization).

Suggested reading material for additional information includes the following:

- *Design of Municipal Wastewater Treatment Plants* (WEF et al., 2009) (Chapter 11, "Preliminary Treatment");

- *Wastewater Engineering: Treatment and Reuse* (Metcalf and Eddy, 2003) (Chapter 5, "Physical Unit Operations");

- *Wastewater Treatment Plants: Planning, Design and Operation* (Qasim, 1999) (Chapter 8, "Screening", and Chapter 11, "Grit Removal");

- *Wastewater Treatment Plant Design* (Vesilind [Ed.], 2003) (Chapter 4, "Preliminary Treatment"); and

- *Water and Wastewater Engineering: Design Principles and Practices* (Davis, 2010) (Chapter 20, "Headworks and Preliminary Treatment").

2.0   SCREENING

2.1   Screen Sizes

Screening of wastewater can be categorized according to screen opening size, as follows:

- Trash racks and bypass screens—greater than 36-mm (1.5-in.) openings,
- Coarse screens—greater than 6- to 36-mm (0.25- to 1.5-in.) openings,
- Fine screens—greater than 0.5- to 6-mm (0.25-in.) openings, and
- Microscreens—10- to 0.5-mm openings.

There are different types of screens available based on the size needed.

2.2   Types of Screens

Table 3.1 summarizes the various types of screens most commonly used in wastewater treatment.

There are four types of screening media that are typically used: bars, wedge wire, perforated plate, and mesh.

In addition to space constraints, headloss is a governing criteria in the design of a screenings facility. Table 3.2 describes the governing headloss equations typically used.

Typical headloss through a coarse screen is 15 cm (6 in.). A benefit of moving screens is lower headloss, although bar screens can be equipped with a mechanical rake or scraper mechanism that removes accumulated debris out of the channel for disposal. This helps prevent clogging and minimizes headloss.

Headloss and influent levels should be monitored continuously to alert operators of clogged screens. Additionally, screens are often programmed such that when a set water elevation is reached, the cleaning cycle of the mechanical screen is automatically initiated.

3.0   GRIT REMOVAL

Grit materials include particles of sand, gravel, other mineral matter, and minimally putrescible organics such as coffee grounds, eggshells, fruit rinds, and seeds. There are three general types of grit chambers; these are summarized in Table 3.3.

TABLE 3.1   Types of screens.

Screen type	Screen size	Screen media	Function	References
Bar rack	Coarse	Stainless steel bars	Protect pumps, valves, pipelines, and other appurtenances from damage or clogging.	Chapter 5, Section 1 (Metcalf and Eddy, 2003) Chapter 11, Section 2.5.1 (WEF et al., 2009) Chapter 8, Section 2.1 (Qasim, 1999) Chapter 4 (Vesilind [Ed.], 2003)
Inclined (fixed)	Fine	Stainless steel wedge wire screen through.	Offer more surface area for wastewater to pass	Chapter 5, Section 1 (Metcalf and Eddy, 2003) Chapter 11, Section 2.5.3 (WEF et al., 2009) Chapter 8, Section 2.2 (Qasim, 1999) Chapter 4 (Vesilind [Ed.], 2003)
Drum (rotary)	Fine	Stainless steel wedge wire screen, stainless steel, and polyester screen cloths	Influent flows through a rotating screen. Shearing action helps separate solids from water.	Chapter 5, Section 1 (Metcalf and Eddy, 2003) Chapter 11, Section 2.5.3 (WEF et al., 2009) Chapter 8, Section 3 (Qasim, 1999) Chapter 5 (Vesilind [Ed.], 2003)
Step type	Fine	Stainless steel with step-shaped laminate	Step-shaped laminates are connected to a fixed end and a moveable end, allowing screenings to climb to top of the screen.	Chapter 5, Section 1 (Metcalf and Eddy, 2003) Chapter 11, Section 2.5.3 (WEF et al., 2009) Chapter 8, Section 3 (Qasim, 1999) Chapter 5 (Vesilind [Ed.], 2003)

Figure 3.1 illustrates the different types of grit removal chambers.

Collected grit must be removed, is often cleaned or washed, and then disposed. There are several ways to accomplish this and the reader is referred to the reference section for more information.

TABLE 3.2   Headloss equations for screens.

Size	Headloss equation	References
Coarse	$h_L = \dfrac{1}{C}\left(\dfrac{V^2 - v^2}{2g}\right)$	Chapter 5, Section 1 (Metcalf and Eddy, 2003) Chapter 11, Section 2.7.4.1 (WEF et al., 2009) Chapter 8, Section 3.2 (Qasim, 1999)
Fine	$h_L = \dfrac{1}{2g}\left(\dfrac{Q}{CA}\right)^2$	Chapter 5, Section 1 (Metcalf and Eddy, 2003) Chapter 11, Section 2.7.4.2 (WEF et al., 2009) Chapter 8, Section 3.2 (Qasim, 1999)

4.0   SEPTAGE ACCEPTANCE AND PRETREATMENT

Septage can come from a variety of sources including cesspools, privies, septic tanks, grease collection programs, and holding tanks. Sources of septage include residential, commercial, and industrial activities. As a result, its composition is not uniform, requiring specific considerations for each case for a wastewater

TABLE 3.3   Types of grit chambers.

Chamber type	Description	Minimum grit size designed to remove	References
Horizontal flow	Rectangular or square, rely on heavier particles to settle.	65 mesh (0.21 mm diameter) or 100 mesh (0.15 mm diameter)	Chapter 5, Section 6 (Metcalf and Eddy, 2003) Chapter 4 (Vesilind [Ed.], 2003)
Aerated	Air is introduced and creates a spiral flow pattern perpendicular to wastewater flow.	65 mesh (0.21 mm diameter) or larger	Chapter 5, Section 6 (Metcalf and Eddy, 2003) Chapter 11, Section 4.3.1 (WEF et al., 2009) Chapter 11, Section 3 (Qasim, 1999) Chapter 4 (Vesilind [Ed.], 2003)
Vortex	A rotating propeller maintains vortex flow of wastewater. Available with and without this central propeller.	50 mesh (0.30 mm) or larger	Chapter 5, Section 6 (Metcalf and Eddy, 2003) Chapter 11, Section 4.3.2 (WEF et al., 2009) Chapter 11, Section 3 (Qasim, 1999) Chapter 4 (Vesilind [Ed.], 2003)

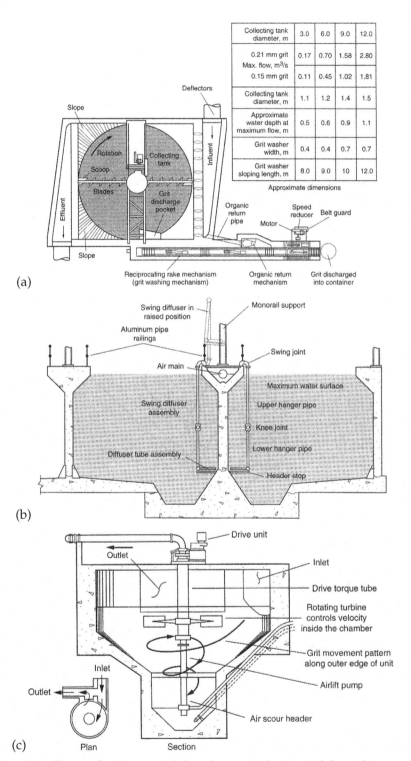

Collecting tank diameter, m	3.0	6.0	9.0	12.0
0.21 mm grit Max. flow, m³/s	0.17	0.70	1.58	2.80
0.15 mm grit	0.11	0.45	1.02	1.81
Collecting tank diameter, m	1.1	1.2	1.4	1.5
Approximate water depth at maximum flow, m	0.5	0.6	0.9	1.1
Grit washer width, m	0.4	0.4	0.7	0.7
Grit washer sloping length, m	8.0	9.0	10	12.0

Approximate dimensions

FIGURE 3.1 Types of grit removal chambers—(a) horizontal flow, (b) aerated, and (c) vortex (Metcalf and Eddy, 2003).

TABLE 3.4   Typical domestic septage characteristics (WEF, 1994).

Constituent	Concentration [mg/L]	
	Range	Typical
Total solids	5000 to 100 000	40 000
Suspended solids	4000 to 100 000	15 000
Volatile suspended solids	1200 to 14 000	7000
5-day biochemical oxygen demand	2000 to 30 000	6000
Chemical oxygen demand	5000 to 80 000	30 000
Ammonia	100 to 800	400
Total Kjeldahl nitrogen	100 to 1600	700
Total phosphorus	50 to 800	250
Heavy metals*	100 to 1000	300

*Primarily iron, zinc, and aluminum.

treatment plant (WWTP) that accepts septage including volume, effects of septage on plant processes, and odor control.

Table 3.4 describes typical septage characteristics.

Pretreatment for septage includes storage and equalization (see Section 5.0) and screening and grit removal. Septage may also be aerated to facilitate odor control and to help avoid a shock load when introduced to the WWTP. The addition of septage to the treatment processes (liquids and/or solids) has downstream effects (hydraulic and performance) that need to be considered. More discussion is contained in Section 6.3.2 of Chapter 11 in *Design of Municipal Wastewater Treatment Plants* (WEF et al., 2009).

5.0   EQUALIZATION

Equalization is needed to accommodate wide variations in flowrates and organic mass loadings to WWTPs. Equalization also can be used to minimize sizing of downstream processes in wastewater facilities and is considered either in-line or off-line as shown in Figure 3.2.

The design methodology involves determining the necessary storage volume, mixing, and aeration requirements. Consideration for infiltration and storm-related inflow that influence the variability of the influent flow should be taken into account.

6.0   REFERENCES

Davis, M. L. (2010) *Water and Wastewater Engineering: Design Principles and Practices*; William C. Brown Publishing Company: Dubuque, Iowa.

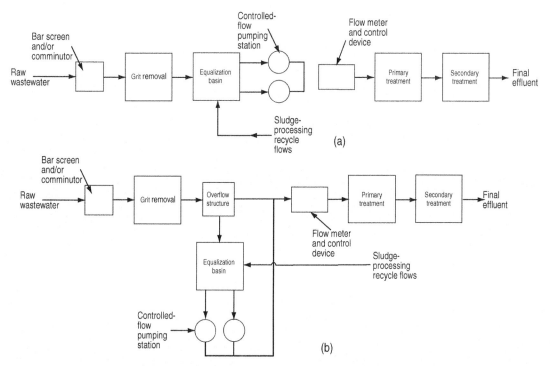

FIGURE 3.2   Two equalization schemes—(a) in-line equalization and (b) side-line equalization (taken from Metcalf and Eddy [2003] and Vesilind [Ed., 2003]).

Metcalf and Eddy, Inc. (2003) *Wastewater Engineering: Treatment and Reuse*, 4th ed.; McGraw-Hill: New York.

Qasim, S. (1999) *Wastewater Treatment Plants: Planning, Design and Operation*, 2nd ed.; CRC Press: Boca Raton, Florida.

Vesilind, P. A., Ed. (2003) *Wastewater Treatment Plant Design*; Water Environment Federation: Alexandria, Virginia.

Water Environment Federation; American Society of Civil Engineers; Environmental & Water Resources Institute (2009) *Design of Municipal Wastewater Treatment Plants,* 5th ed.; WEF Manual of Practice No. 8; ASCE Manuals and Reports on Engineering Practice No. 76; McGraw-Hill: New York.

Water Environment Federation (1994) *Preliminary Treatment for Wastewater Facilities*; WEF Manual of Practice No. OM-2; Water Environment Federation: Alexandria, Virginia.

Chapter 4

Primary Treatment

1.0 INTRODUCTION

Primary treatment involves the separation and removal of suspended solids and floatables (scum) including grease, oils, plastics, and soap from wastewater by physical–chemical methods. These methods involve settling of suspended solids or other processes in which the total suspended solids (TSS) and chemical oxygen demand (COD) or biochemical oxygen demand (BOD) loading of the incoming wastewater are reduced. *Sedimentation* is the term applied to settling of suspended particles that are heavier than water.

The most common form of primary treatment is quiescent sedimentation (conventional sedimentation) with skimming; collection; and removal of settled primary sludge, floating debris, and grease. Fine screens and/or sieves sometimes are used for primary treatment where discharge requirements or downstream processes (such as membrane biological reactors) do not require greater removals. Enhanced sedimentation methods such as chemically enhanced primary treatment and high-rate clarification (HRC) are used in large-scale treatment in which high seasonal hydraulic loading variations, limited land availability, and treatment levels higher than primary but not quite as stringent as secondary are required. Chemically enhanced primary treatment has been used to increase existing treatment capacities and to reduce influent loads to biological treatment. High-rate clarification has been used to treat wet-weather and combined sewer overflows and return flows such as filter backwash. Table 4.1

21

TABLE 4.1   Primary sludge characteristics (U.S. EPA, 1979).

Characteristic*	Range of values	Typical value	Comments
pH	5–8	6	—
Volatile acids, mg/L as ascetic acid	200 2 000	500	—
Heating value, kJ/kg	16 000–23 000	—	Depends on volatile content and primary sludge composition; reported values are on a dry basis
Btu/lb	6 800–10 000		
		10 285	Primary sludge 74% volatile
		7 600	Primary sludge 65% volatile
Specific gravity of individual solid particles	—	1.4	Increases with increased grit and silt
Bulk specific gravity (wet)	—	1.02	Increases with primary sludge thickness and with specific gravity of solids
		1.07	Strong wastewater from a combined system of storm and sanitary sewers
BOD_5 : VSS ratio	0.5–1.1	—	—
COD : VSS ratio	1.2–1.6	—	—
Organic nitrogen : VSS ratio	0.5–1.1	—	—
Volatile content, percent by weight of dry solids	64–93	77	Value obtained with no primary sludge recycle, good gritting; 42 samples, standard deviation 5
	60–80	65	
	—	40	Low value caused by severe storm
	—	40	Low value caused by industrial waste
Cellulose, percent by weight of dry solids	8–15	10	—
Hemicellulose, percent by weight of dry solids	—	3.2	—
Lignin, percent by weight of dry solids	—	5.8	—
Grease and fat, percent by weight of dry solids	6–30	—	Ether soluble
	7–35	—	Ether extract
Protein, percent by weight of dry solids	20–30	25	—
	22–28	—	—
Nitrogen, percent by weight of dry solids	1.5–4	2.5	Expressed as N
Phosphorus, percent by weight of dry solids	0.8–2.8	1.6	Expressed as P_2O_5; divide values as P_2O_5 by 2.29 to obtain values as P
Potash, percent by weight of dry solids	0–1	0.4	Expressed as K_2O, divide K_2O by 1.20 to obtain values as K

*BOD_5 = 5-day biochemical oxygen demand; COD = chemical oxygen demand; and VSS = volatile suspended solids.

provides typical removal rates for TSS, COD or BOD, phosphorus, and bacteria for some of the available primary treatment processes.

Suggested reading material for additional information includes the following:

- *Design of Municipal Wastewater Treatment Plants* (WEF et al., 2009) (Chapter 12, "Primary Treatment");

- *Wastewater Engineering: Treatment and Reuse* (Metcalf and Eddy, 2003) (Chapter 5, "Physical Unit Operations");

- *Wastewater Treatment Plants: Planning, Design and Operation* (Qasim, 1999) (Chapter 8, "Screening", and Chapter 11, "Grit Removal");

- *Wastewater Treatment Plant Design* (Vesilind [Ed.], 2003) (Chapter 5, "Primary Treatment"); and

- *Water and Wastewater Engineering: Design Principles and Practices* (Davis, 2010) (Chapter 21, "Preliminary Treatment").

2.0   SEDIMENTATION

Sedimenation is the gravity separation of wastewater solids from liquids. The types of sedimentation vary depending on whether the treatment focus is clarified liquid or thickened solids. The objective of primary sedimentation is clarified liquid. Chapter 5, Section 5.0 of Metcalf and Eddy (2003) and Chapter 5 of Vesilind ([Ed.], 2003) contain gravity separation theory including formulas. Different types of sedimentation are described in Table 4.2 and illustrated in Figure 4.1 of this handbook.

Table 4.3 summarizes design considerations for sedimentation systems.

The reference documents also provide information about primary sludge characteristics, collection, and disposal.

3.0   HIGH-RATE CLARIFICATION

High-rate clarification combines techniques of chemically enhanced particle settling and solids contact and recirculation with lamella plate and tube settlers to achieve rapid settling. High settling velocities combined with rapid flocculation kinetics can reduce required process footprints to less than 10% of conventional primary treatment (Jolis and Ahmad, 2001). High-rate clarification units are compact, have short startup times, and produce high-quality effluent. High-

TABLE 4.2   Types of sedimentation.

Type of sedimentation	Typical dimensions	Advantages	Disadvantages	References
Rectangular	15 to 90 m (50 to 300 ft) in length, 3 to 24 m (10 to 80 ft) in width, 3 to 4.9 m (10 to 16 ft) in depth	Good for sites with space constraint. Can use common walls for multiple units. Easier to cover for odor control.	Sludge removal equipment greater maintenance requirements than similarly sized circular tanks because drive bearings in rectangular tanks are submerged.	WEF et al. (2009), Chapter 12, Section 2 Metcalf and Eddy (2003), Table 5.21 Qasim (1999), Chapter 12, Section 3.1 Vesilind ([Ed.], 2003), Chapter 5
Circular	Diameter of 3 m (10 ft) to more than 60 m (200 ft). Depths typically range between 3 and 4.9 m (10 and 16 ft)	Can use relatively trouble-free, circular, primary sludge removal equipment (drive bearings are not under water).	Typically require more yard piping than rectangular tanks and require separate structures for flow distribution and sludge pumping.	WEF et al. (2009), Chapter 12, Section 2 Metcalf & Eddy (2003), Table 5.21 Qasim (1999), Chapter 12, Section 3.1 Vesilind ([Ed.], 2003), Chapter 5
Stacked (multilevel)	Design criteria are similar to conventional primary clarifiers.	Can be double-decked or even triple-decked to increase the available clarifier area without increasing the clarifier footprint.	Higher construction cost than conventional and more complex structural design.	WEF et al. (2009), Chapter 12, Section 2 Metcalf and Eddy (2003), Chapter 5, Section 7 Vesilind ([Ed.], 2003), Chapter 5
Plate-and-tube	Installed below effluent launders to a vertical depth of approximately 2 m (7 ft), increase effective surface area of the tank by a factor of 6 to 12 times. Spacing between plates is typically 40 to 120 mm (1 to 4 in.)	Offer more surface area in smaller footprint.	Inlet-and-outlet design is considered a weakness of stacked tanks because wastewater flow patterns might intersect with those of primary sludge.	WEF et al. (2009), Chapter 12, Section 2 Metcalf and Eddy (2003), Chapter 5, Section 5 Qasim (1999), Chapter 12, Section 3.3

rate clarification facilities can be located at the treatment plant or at remote satellite facilities that accept peak-flow diversions from the main plant; however, the operator attention required at startup may be a disadvantage for satellite facilities that typically are unstaffed. Four types of HRC methods are described in Table 4.4.

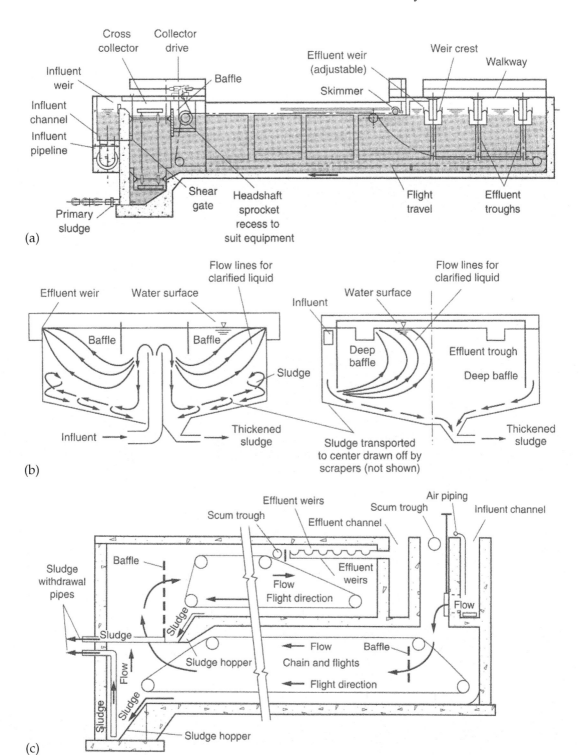

FIGURE 4.1 Types of clarifiers—(a) rectangular with chain and flight-type collector (Figure 5.40 [Metcalf and Eddy, 2003]), (b) circular (Figure 5.41 [Metcalf and Eddy, 2003]), (c) stacked (Figure 5.45 [Metcalf and Eddy, 2003]), and (d) plate and tube (Figure 5.27 [Metcalf and Eddy, 2003]).

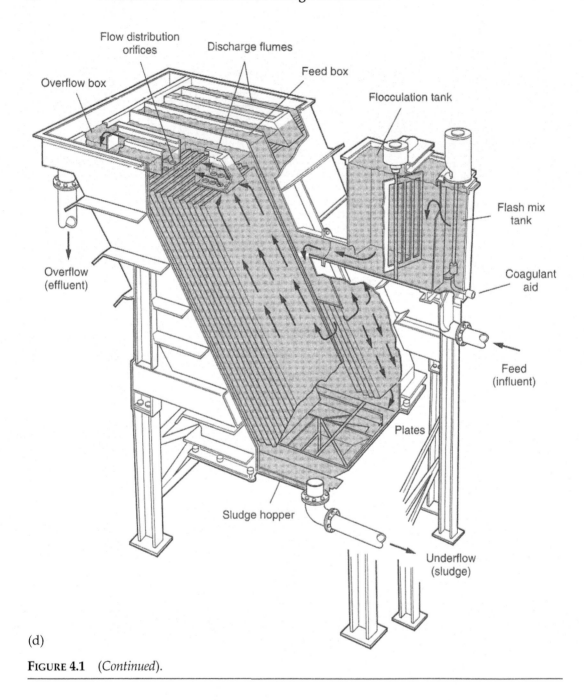

(d)

FIGURE 4.1   (*Continued*).

4.0   FINE SCREENS

Fine screens or sieves can be used in lieu of sedimentation for primary treatment, but may not achieve removal efficiencies of sedimentation. The use of screens instead of primary clarifiers can significantly reduce space requirements and investment costs. Chapter 2 describes fine screens in more detail.

TABLE 4.3 Design considerations for sedimentation systems.

Type of sedimentation	Description and purpose	Design equations*	Typical values*	References
Conventional (primary clarifiers)	Particles settle by gravity under quiescent conditions as grease and scum float to the top. Clarifiers can be rectangular, circular, stacked, and plate-and-tube settlers, among others.	$SOR = Q/A$ $HDT = Q/(A*d)$ HDT multiplier: $M = 1.82\ e^{0.03T}$ where M is a detention time multiplier, T is temperature of wastewater in °C. Critical scour (horizontal) velocity, V_H (m/s, ft/s) = $$\sqrt{\frac{(8k(s-1)gd)}{f}}$$ Where k is unitless constant, s is specific gravity (SG) of scoured particles, $g = 9.81\ m/s^2$ $(32.2\ ft/s^2)$, $d =$ scoured particle diameter, and $f =$ Darcy-Weisbach friction factor (unitless)	Removal efficiency: 50 to 70% TSS 25 to 50% COD or BOD demand $SOR = 30$ and 50 m^3/m^2-d (800 and 1200 gpd/sq ft) at average and peak flows, respectively $HDT = 1.5$ to 2.5 hours average flow conditions at $T = 20$ °C Scour velocity = 1.2 to 1.5 m/min (4 to 5 ft/min)	WEF et al. (2009), Chapter 12, Section 2 Metcalf and Eddy (2003), Table 5.20 and Chapter 5, Section 7 Qasim (1999), Chapter 12, Section 1 Vesilind ([Ed.], 2003), Chapter 5
Enhanced (preaeration)	Increase settling by preaerating raw wastewater.	Same as above	$HDT = 20$ to 30 min Min air rate = 0.82 m^3/m^3 (0.11 ft^3/gal)	WEF et al. (2009), Chapter 12, Section 3.1 Vesilind ([Ed., 2003), Chapter 5
Enhanced (chemically)	Allows a higher SOR than conventional, reduces footprint of clarifiers and aeration basins. However, primary sludge mass may increase.	Same as above	Removal efficiencies: 60 to 90% TSS 40 to 70% COD or BOD 70 to 90% phosphorus 80 to 90% bacteria loadings Rapid mix velocity gradient, $G =$ 300 m/m/s (300 ft/sec/ft) Flocculation $G = 50$ to 80 m/m/s (50 to 80 ft/sec/ft) 20 mg/L of ferric chloride and 0.2 mg/L of polymer to the headworks increased primary sludge production by approximately 45%	WEF et al. (2009), Chapter 12, Section 3 Vesilind ([Ed.], 2003), Chapter 5

*SOR = solids overflow rate, HDT = hydraulic detention time, TSS = total suspended solids, COD = checmical oxygen demand, and BOD_5 = 5-day biochemical oxygen demand.

TABLE 4.4   High-rate clarification methods.

Type of high-rate clarification	Description and purpose	Design equations	Typical values*	References
Plate and tube settler	Can be used with or without chemical addition; settlers increase capacity of existing clarifiers by increasing available settling area.	See 12.13–12.16 of WEF et al. (2009)		WEF et al. (2009), Chapter 12, Section 4.1 Metcalf and Eddy (2003), Chapter 5 Section 8
Ballasted flocculation	A ballasting agent is added along with coagulants to wastewater in a flash mixing zone.	See Example 5.11 and Table 5.24 in Metcalf and Eddy (2003) for equations and typical values, respectively.	SOR = 720 to 1200 m^3/m^2·d (12 to 20 gpm/sq ft) average flows and 2400 to 3100 m^3/m^2·d (40 to 60 gpm/sq ft) peak	WEF et al. (2009), Chapter 12, Section 4.2 Metcalf and Eddy (2003), Chapter 5, Section 8
Solids contact/sludge recirculation	Sludge is thickened and recirculated to influent end of process where it is combined with a coagulant before the rapid mix zone. Polymer is added in the flocculation zone.	See Example 5.11 and Table 5.24 in Metcalf and Eddy (2003) for equations and typical values, respectively.	Velocity gradient, G, = 200 to 400 s^{-1}	WEF et al. (2009), Chapter 12, Section 4.3 Metcalf and Eddy (2003), Chapter 5, Section 8
Swirl and vortex separators	Compact solids-separation units with no moving parts, use tangential inlet and surface overflows to help separate particles from wastewater.			WEF et al. (2009), Chapter 12, Section 4.4 Metcalf and Eddy (2003), Chapter 5, Section 9

*SOR = solids overflow rate.

5.0   PRIMARY SLUDGE AND SCUM COLLECTION AND REMOVAL

Settled primary sludge typically is scraped into a hopper where it is removed by gravity or pumping. Several types of mechanisms are presented in Table 4.5.

Primary sludge production can be estimated from the following equation:

$$S_M = \frac{Q \times \text{TSS} \times E}{1000} \text{ (metric)} \qquad (4.1)$$

$$S_M = Q \times \text{TSS} \times E \times 8.34 \text{ lb/gal (U.S.)} \qquad (4.2)$$

TABLE 4.5   Sludge and scum collection.

Collection mechanism	Description and purpose	Typical design values	References
Chain and flights	Two endless loops of chains with cross scrapers (flights) attached at 3-m (10-ft) intervals	6.1 to 9.1 m (20 to 30 ft) wide Travels approximately 0.6 m/min (2 ft/min)	WEF et al. (2009), Chapter 12, Section 5.2
Traveling bridge	Scraper-blade mechanism mounted on a bridge or carriage	Tank widths up to 30 m (100 ft) Travels approximately 1.8 m/min (6 ft/min) toward hopper and 3.7 m/min (12 ft/min) away from hopper	WEF et al. (2009), Chapter 12
Segmented rake, or plow-type	Scrapers drag the tank floor, plows located at an angle to the radial axis to force sludge towards the hopper at the center of the tank as the device rotates	Tip speed of 1.8 to 3.7 m/min (6 to 12 ft/min)	WEF et al. (2009), Chapter 12
Spiral-type scrapers	Continuously tapered spiral-shaped scraper blades allows faster operating tip speeds		WEF et al. (2009), Chapter 12

Where

S_M = mass of primary sludge, kg/d (lb/d);

Q = primary influent flow, m^3/d (mgd);

TSS = primary influent total suspended solids, mg/L; and

E = removal efficiency, fraction.

Composition of primary sludge and scum is variable and depends on the nature and degree of industrial development in the collection area. Typical sludge characteristics are listed in Table 4.6.

Primary sludge and scum is thickened in primary sedimentation tanks, stabilization facilities, or separate thickening units. Primary sedimentation tanks can be operated to consistently produce a thickened solids concentration of 3 to 6% solids by allowing a 0.6- to 0.9-m (2- to 3-ft) blanket of solids to build up and compact the primary sludge. The primary sludge draw-off system should be designed with capacity to allow either continuous withdrawal or intermittent withdrawal at a rate that will control the primary sludge blanket depth. If sedimentation tanks are to be operated to achieve additional primary sludge thickening, draw-off piping and pumps must be designed to handle the more con-

TABLE 4.6   Sludge characteristics (Metcalf and Eddy, 2003).

Type of solids (sludge)	Specific gravity	Solids concentration, % dry solids	
		Range	Typical
Primary only:			
Medium-strength wastewater	1.03	4 to 12	6
From combined sewer system	1.05	4 to 12	6.5
Primary and waste activated sludge	1.03	2 to 6	3
Primary and trickling filter humus sludge	1.03	4 to 10	5
Scum	0.95	Highly variable	

centrated sludge. Withdrawal lines should be at least 100 mm (4 in.) in diameter. As the solids concentration increases to more than 6%, risk of plugging increases because of the greater viscosity of the thickened primary sludge and its tendency to clog the piping. For this reason, suction piping should be as straight as possible and accessible for rodding, pigging, or flushing to clear obstructions.

6.0   REFERENCES

Davis, M. L. (2010) *Water and Wastewater Engineering: Design Principles and Practices*; William C. Brown Publishing Company: Dubuque, Iowa.

Jolis, D.; Ahmad, M. (2001) Pilot Testing of High Rate Clarification Technology in San Francisco. *Proceedings of the 74th Annual Water Environment Federation Technical Exposition and Conference* [CD-ROM]; Atlanta, Georgia, Oct 13–17; Water Environment Federation: Alexandria, Virginia.

Metcalf and Eddy, Inc. (2003) *Wastewater Engineering: Treatment and Reuse*, 4th ed.; McGraw-Hill: New York.

Qasim, S. (1999) *Wastewater Treatment Plants: Planning, Design and Operation*, 2nd ed.; CRC Press: Boca Raton, Florida.

U.S. Environmental Protection Agency (1979) *Process Design Manual for Sludge Treatment and Disposal*; EPA-625/1-79-011; U.S. Environmental Protection Agency: Washington, D.C.

Vesilind, P. A., Ed. (2003) *Wastewater Treatment Plant Design*; Water Environment Federation: Alexandria, Virginia.

Water Environment Federation; American Society of Civil Engineers; Environmental & Water Resources Institute (2009) *Design of Municipal Wastewater Treatment Plants*, 5th ed.; WEF Manual of Practice No. 8; ASCE Manuals and Reports on Engineering Practice No. 76; McGraw-Hill: New York.

Chapter 5

Biofilm Reactor Technology and Design

1.0 INTRODUCTION

Biological systems treating municipal wastewater require (1) the accumulation of active microorganisms in a bioreactor and (2) the separation of microorganisms from treated effluent. Biofilm reactors retain bacterial cells in a biofilm attached to fixed or movable carriers. These bacteria are protected from washout as long as they do not detach from the biofilm and can grow in locations where their food supply remains abundant. Detached biofilm fragments exit the system with the effluent stream.

The biofilm matrix consists of water and a variety of soluble and particulate components that include soluble microbial products, inert material, and extracellular polymeric substances. Biofilm and suspended growth reactors can meet similar treatment objectives for carbon oxidation, nitrification, denitrification, and desulphurization. Biofilm reactors have five primary compartments: (1) influent wastewater (distribution) system; (2) containment structure; (3) carrier with biofilm; (4) effluent water collection system; (5) and an aeration system (for aerobic processes and scour) or mixing system (for anoxic processes that require bulk-liquid agitation and biofilm carrier distribution).

31

Designing a successful biofilm system requires an understanding of the biological processes that occur and the various modeling approaches. Chapter 13 of *Design of Municipal Wastewater Treatment Plants* (WEF et al., 2009) provides detailed theory behind the processes summarized in this handbook and a discussion about modeling the processes.

Two processes, mass transfer and biochemical conversion, are characteristic of all biofilm reactors and influence biofilm structure and function. Mass transport inside the biofilm is controlled by molecular diffusion. If mass transfer to the biofilm is slow compared to biochemical conversion, the result is strong concentration gradients for substrates within the mass-transfer boundary layer and inside the biofilm.

Biofilms in wastewater treatment applications typically are mass-transfer limited. Therefore, biofilm reactor performance is surface-area dependent and not dependent on the total amount of biomass in the system.

Suggested reading material for additional information includes the following:

- *Design of Municipal Wastewater Treatment Plants* (WEF et al., 2009) (Chapter 13, "Biofilm Reactor Technology and Design");

- *Biofilm Reactors* (WEF, 2011);

- *Wastewater Engineering: Treatment and Reuse* (Metcalf and Eddy, 2003) (Chapter 9, "Attached Growth and Combined Biological Treatment Processes");

- *Wastewater Treatment Plants: Planning, Design and Operation* (Qasim, 1999); and

- *Wastewater Treatment Plant Design* (Vesilind [Ed.], 2003).

2.0   MOVING BED BIOFILM REACTORS

The moving bed biofilm reactor (MBBR) is a two- (anoxic) or three- (aerobic) phase system with a buoyant free-moving plastic biofilm carrier that requires energy (i.e., mechanical mixing or aeration) to ensure uniform distribution throughout the tank. Benefits of MBBR include the following:

- It can meet similar treatment objectives as activated sludge systems for carbon oxidation, nitrification, and denitrification, but requires a smaller tank volume than a clarifier-coupled activated sludge system;

- Biomass retention is clarifier independent. Therefore, solids loading to the liquid–solids separation unit is reduced significantly compared to activated sludge systems;

- Because it is a continuous flow process, it does not require a special operational cycle for biofilm thickness control. Hydraulic headloss and operational complexity is minimized;

- It offers much of the same flexibility to manipulate system flow sheet (to meet a specific treatment objective) as the activated sludge process. Multiple reactors can be configured in series without the need for intermediate pumping or return activated sludge pumping (to accumulate mixed liquor);

- It can be coupled with a variety of different liquid–solids separation processes including sedimentation basins, dissolved air flotation, ballasted flocculation, and membranes; and

- It is well-suited for retrofit installation into existing municipal wastewater treatment plants (WWTPs).

An MBBR may be a single reactor or several reactors in a series. Typically, each MBBR has a length-to-width ratio (L:W) in the range of 0.5:1 to 1.5:1. Plans with a L:W greater than 1.5:1 can result in non-uniform distribution of free-moving plastic biofilm carriers.

Moving bed biofilm reactors contain a plastic biofilm carrier volume ranging from 25 to 67% of the liquid volume. This parameter is referred to as the *carrier fill*. Sieves typically are installed with one MBBR wall and allow treated effluent to flow through to the next treatment step while retaining the free-moving plastic biofilm carriers. Carbon oxidation, nitrification, or combined carbon oxidation and nitrification MBBRs use a diffused aeration system to uniformly distribute plastic biofilm carriers and meet process oxygen requirements. Plastic biofilm carriers in denitrification MBBRs are homogenized by mechanical mixers. Each component is submerged. Plastic biofilm carriers must be removed before draining and servicing or repairing air diffusers.

Biofilms primarily develop on the protected surface inside of the plastic biofilm carrier. Plastic biofilm carriers have a bulk specific surface area, net specific surface area, bulk liquid volume displacement, and net liquid volume displacement.

The rate of soluble substrate transformation in biofilm systems is defined in terms of mass flux in grams per square meters per day. Therefore, it is convenient to quantify the loading rate in similar terms. The net specific surface area of a plastic biofilm carrier is directly related to the calculation of MBBR pollutant loading. The volumetric load can be multiplied by the net specific surface area to calculate a surface loading rate.

Plastic biofilm carriers are retained in an MBBR by horizontally configured cylindrical sieves or vertically configured flat sieves. Aerobic zones typically contain cylindrical sieves; anoxic zones contain flat-wall sieves.

Low-pressure diffused air is applied to aerobic MBBRs. The airflow enters the reactor through a network of air piping and diffusers that are attached to the tank bottom. Airflow has the dual purpose of meeting process oxygen requirements and uniformly distributing plastic biofilm carriers throughout the aerobic

MBBR. To promote uniform distribution of the plastic biofilm carriers, the diffuser grid layout and drop pipe arrangement provides a rolling water circulation pattern. Fine- and coarse-bubble diffusers have been used in free-floating plastic biofilm carrier reactors.

Denitrification MBBRs use mechanical mixers to agitate the bulk of the liquid and to uniformly distribute plastic biofilm carriers. The mechanical mixers may be platform-mounted hyperbolic (dry motor) or rail-mounted submersible (wet motor) units.

Relevant considerations when selecting an MBBR configuration include site-specific treatment objectives, wastewater characteristics, site layout, existing basin configuration (if a retrofit), system hydraulics, existing treatment scheme (if applicable), and the potential to retrofit existing tanks. Although the process mechanical features of an MBBR are typically consistent, biofilms grown in carbon oxidation, nitrification, denitrification, and combined carbon oxidation and nitrification MBBRs are variable and depend on local environmental conditions.

Biodegradable soluble organic carbon is quickly consumed in an MBBR. Carbon-oxidizing MBBRs are classified as low-rate, normal-rate, or high-rate bioreactors. Low-rate carbon-oxidizing MBBRs promote conditions for nitrification in downstream reactors. High- and normal-rate MBBRs are strictly carbon-oxidizing bioreactors. High-rate MBBRs typically are designed to receive total 5-day biochemical oxygen demand (BOD_5) loads as high as 45 to 60 $g/m^2 \cdot d$ at 15 °C. Such high surface area loadings, however, result in short hydraulic residence time (HRT). At least two reactors in series should be used, even at high loads.

Like all biofilm reactors, the rate of ammonia-nitrogen oxidation in an MBBR is influenced by organic load, bulk-liquid dissolved oxygen concentration, bulk-liquid ammonia-nitrogen concentration, temperature, pH, and alkalinity. While studying a pilot-scale combined carbon oxidation and nitrification MBBR receiving primary effluent, a (tertiary) nitrification MBBR receiving secondary effluent, and maintaining a 4- to 6-g/m^3 bulk-liquid dissolved oxygen concentration in both units, the following was observed:

- Total BOD_5 load of 1 to 2 $g/m^2 \cdot d$ resulted in nitrification rates from 0.7 to 1.2 $g/m^2 \cdot d$,
- Total BOD_5 load of 2 to 3 $g/m^2 \cdot d$ resulted in nitrification rates from 0.3 to 0.8 $g/m^2 \cdot d$, and
- Total BOD_5 load greater than 5 $g/m^2 \cdot d$ resulted in virtually no nitrification.

Operating at higher dissolved oxygen concentrations increases ammonia nitrogen flux in the oxygen-limited region, but provides little benefit once ammonia becomes rate-limiting at approximately 2.5 g/m^3.

The rate of denitrification in an MBBR is influenced by the external carbon source, bulk-phase carbon-to-nitrogen ratio (C:N), wastewater temperature, bulk-liquid dissolved oxygen concentration, and bulk-liquid macronutrient concentration (primarily phosphorus).

Predenitrification typically is used in the activated sludge process. Predenitrification MBBRs are situated upstream of combined carbon oxidation and nitrification MBBRs. The electron acceptor nitrate and nitrite-nitrogen is supplied by an internal recirculation stream that directs nitrified MBBR effluent to the predenitrification MBBR. When internal recirculation of nitrified effluent is included, the MBBR retention screens must be sized to handle total flow, including recycle streams, rather than just the forward flow. Predenitrification MBBR performance is primarily dependent on the availability of soluble BOD_5 in the influent wastewater stream. When ample soluble BOD_5 concentration exists, predenitrification MBBRs can achieve 50 to 70% nitrogen removal. Nitrate and nitrite-nitrogen transformation rates in a predenitrification MBBR are typically in the range 0.3 to 0.6 g NO_3-N_{eq}/m^2·d (at 10 °C).

Postdenitrification MBBRs require the addition of a supplemental electron donor (i.e., an external carbon source), but do not require recirculation of a nitrified effluent stream to receive the electron acceptor nitrate and nitrite-nitrogen. Where possible, combined predenitrification and postdenitrification MBBRs should be considered when high levels of nitrogen removal are required. This helps to optimize performance, efficiency, and operational flexibility.

Biofilm reactors, including the MBBR, require proper preliminary treatment. Robust screening and grit removal is recommended to prevent sieve blinding and long-term accumulation of inert material such as rags, plastics, and sand in the tank. Manufacturers typically recommend no larger than 6- to 12-mm screen spacing if primary treatment is also provided. Fine screens (3 mm) are recommended for secondary installations without primary treatment. Other design considerations for MBBRs include

- Installation of plastic biofilm carriers,
- Proper aeration system,
- Material compatibility,
- Headloss through media retention sieves,
- Solids separation process, and
- Tank geometry and bulk flow velocity.

3.0   BIOLOGICALLY ACTIVE FILTERS

Biological wastewater treatment and suspended solids removal are carried out in biologically active filters (BAFs) under either aerobic or anoxic conditions. In a BAF, the media acts simultaneously to support the growth of biomass and as a filtration medium to retain filtered solids. Accumulated solids are removed from the BAF through backwashing. There is a direct interaction between the media characteristics and the process because the configuration (sunken media or floating media) and flow and backwash regimes depend on media density. Media may be natural mineral, structured plastic, or random plastic.

The BAF reactor can be used for carbon oxidation or biochemical oxygen demand (BOD) removal only, combined BOD removal and nitrification, combined nitrification and dentrification, tertiary nitrification, and tertiary denitrification. Once the raw wastewater has undergone screening, grit removal, and primary treatment, the BAF process can include full secondary treatment for a facility or can be constructed for operation in parallel to an existing secondary treatment process. Using BAF as a tertiary treatment process for nitrification and/or denitrification as an upgrade to existing secondary processes is common.

The acronym, "BAF," is being expanded herein to cover all "biologically active filters," including those that operate under anoxic conditions for denitrification, which have been referred to as *denitrification filters.* The BAF reactors can be characterized into the following groups according to their media configurations and flow regime:

- Downflow BAF with media heavier than water. These BAFs are backwashed using an intermittent countercurrent flow regime;

- Upflow BAF with media heavier than water. These BAFs are backwashed using an intermittent concurrent flow regime;

- Biologically active filter with floating media. These BAFs are backwashed using an intermittent countercurrent flow regime;

- Continuous backwashing filters. These filters operate in an upflow mode and consist of media heavier than water that continuously moves downward, countercurrent to the wastewater flow. Media is directed continuously to a center airlift where it is scoured, rinsed, and returned to the top of the media bed; and

- Nonbackwashing, submerged filters. These processes consist of submerged, static media and are often referred to as *submerged aerated filters* (SAFs). Solids are intended to be carried through the reactor and removed through a dedicated solids separation process.

Several media types are available for use in BAF reactors. Media selection is integral to treatment objectives, flow and backwashing regimes, and specific process equipment manufacturers. Media typically can be categorized as mineral media and plastic media.

Backwashing filters maximizes capture and run times and guarantees proper effluent quality. Proper backwashing requires filter bed expansion and rigorous scouring, followed by efficient rinsing. Poor filter cleaning will result in shortened filter runs, accumulation of solids, and deteriorating performance. Accumulation of solids and media (mudballing) produces short-circuiting of water flow and can result in excessive media loss.

Several physical conditions within BAF systems significantly affect performance, including oxygen availability and airflow velocity, filtration velocity, media packing density, and backwash efficiency. These factors all affect external mass transfer and, indirectly, penetration into the biofilm. Because of the importance of these parameters and, perhaps, because of uncertainty of actual media-specific surface area, BAF performance results typically are expressed as a function of substrate volumetric loading rates rather than surface area.

Parameters governing treatment capacity of BAF are as follows:

- Substrate loading (volumetric loading rates in terms of kilograms BOD per cubic meters per day or kilograms nitrogen per cubic meters per day), which will determine media volume;

- Filtration rate, or total volume of wastewater applied per area of media per unit time (in cubic meters per square meters per day), also is used to determine filter surface area; and

- Solids holding capacity, which will determine backwash frequency.

Tables 13.13 through 13.17 of *Design of Municipal Wastewater Treatment Plants* (WEF et al., 2009) provide chemical oxygen demand (COD)- and BOD-applied loading rates and removal efficiencies based on the type of BAF and functional purpose (nitrification, denitrification, etc.). Temperature, effluent requirements, fluid velocities (air and water), and loading influence nitrification capacity. Several issues must be considered in the design of BAF reactors, supporting facilities, and upstream and downstream processes, including

- Preliminary and primary treatment,
- Backwash handling facilities,
- Process aeration, and
- Supplemental carbon feed facilities.

4.0 EXPANDED AND FLUIDIZED BED BIOFILM REACTORS

Expanded bed biofilm reactors and fluidized bed biofilm reactors (FBBRs) are attached-growth systems with a range of applications in aerobic, anoxic, and anaerobic biological treatment. They use small media particles that are suspended in vertically flowing wastewater so that the media becomes fluidized and the bed expands. Individual particles become suspended once the drag force of the flowing wastewater overcomes gravity and they are separated from each other. The particles are in continual relative motion but are not transported by the wastewater, which passes through the bed at a relatively fast rate (30 to 50 m/h). Ideally, the wastewater passes through in plug-flow mode with minimal backmixing, although most systems have some degree of recycle to maintain vertical velocity. This technology has been used for anaerobic digestion, carbon oxidation, nitrification, and denitrification of both industrial and municipal wastewaters. In municipal applications, it typically has been used for tertiary denitrification in plants that have low total nitrogen effluent goals.

The degree of bed expansion determines whether a bed is deemed expanded or fluidized. Beds less than double static bed height (100% expanded) are considered expanded; those that are more than double the static bed height (100% expanded) are fluidized. A lower degree of bed expansion is advantageous because it requires a lower flow velocity, less energy, and increases effective biomass concentration, which reduces the footprint. In aerobic processes, however, it increases volumetric oxygen demand because of increased biomass concentration.

Starting with a static bed that partially fills the column, the vertical flow velocity is chosen to expand the bed to its initial design height, which is typically 50% of available height. Microorganisms attach to the media particles and grow to form a biofilm. This results in an increase in particle size but a decrease in composite particle (bioparticle) density. Thus, despite their initial differences, all media tend toward a similar specific gravity (approximately 1.1) as the biofilm thickness increases. Because of the size increase and density decrease, the bed continues to expand until it reaches full design height, at which point biofilm thickness must be controlled.

Whether this generic technology is used for aerobic, anoxic, or anaerobic processes, all are based on a similar basic design. This design consists of a column in which the particles are fluidized and the bed expanded and a recycle line that is used to maintain a fixed, vertical hydraulic flow. In this way, bed expansion is kept constant and bioparticles are retained irrespective of influent flowrate. Anoxic and anaerobic designs are the simplest; aerobic designs require a system to supply oxygen. Aeration typically is achieved during recycle, during which influent wastewater mixes with recycled effluent from the top of the bed.

A summary of advantages and disadvantages of the FBBR compared to the BAF or MBBR process is provided in Table 13.20 of *Design of Municipal Wastewater Treatment Plants* (WEF et al., 2009). In general, however, the key advantage of the FBBR configuration is the large specific surface area for biofilm growth. This area results in a high concentration of active biomass, a high rate of reaction, and a small footprint. However, aerobic processes can be oxygen-limited. A disadvantage can be the degree of recycle required to maintain upward velocity for bed expansion and bioparticle fluidization, which can increase pumping costs.

One key design consideration is upward velocity. This velocity is chosen according to the size and specific gravity of the support media particles and includes an upward velocity range for 0.5-mm silica sand of 36 to 60 m/h; other designers recommend a range of 30 to 36 m/h. A key factor that can affect upward flow velocity is the amount of entrained gas because of its effect on fluid density. Most plants will have a control system for varying gas flow according to the dissolved oxygen concentration, which inevitably affects the degree of bed expansion.

Another consideration is recirculation. To maintain a constant degree of bed expansion, the vertical flow velocity if fixed and differences in influent flowrates are addressed by recycling a fraction of process effluent. For tertiary nitrification, the basic design rule is to size the reactor so that it can take the full influent flowrate without recirculation during extreme wet weather when wastewater is at its most dilute.

The influent distribution manifold is a critical design feature in the FBBR. This distribution system must be balanced to

- Achieve uniform distribution of flow across the entire reactor cross section,

- Support media and prevent it from falling through the manifold,

- Avoid plugging,

- Minimize biofilm shearing, and

- Minimize headloss.

The media should allow colonization by a variety of microorganisms that can develop into a firmly attached biofilm. Small particles provide a large surface area, and the material should be available in a narrow size to minimize classification (stratification) upon fluidization. Mineral particles of about 1 mm nominal diameter typically are used.

Continued growth of biofilm causes an increase in bioparticle volume and degree of bed expansion, resulting in the bed exceeding its design volume. Therefore, it is necessary to have a system to control biofilm thickness and prevent bioparticles from leaving with the treated effluent. Any control system should maintain the initial particle inventory. A variety of systems have been developed to control biofilm thickness using either internal control or external control.

There are two approaches to supplying oxygen, either in the bed or in the recirculation loop. Oxygen typically is supplied using air, nitrogen-depleted air, oxygen-rich air, or pure oxygen. An alternative is to add oxygen to air from a cryogenic source. Key factors affecting the rate of oxygen transfer from the gas phase to wastewater include the surface area of gas bubbles and the relative velocity between the gas and liquid phases.

Table 5.1 presents typical design criteria for denitrifying FBBRs that use silica sand media. Section 5.6 in Chapter 13 of *Design of Municipal Wastewater Treatment Plants* (WEF et al., 2009) provides additional design criteria for nitrifying and tertiary denitrification FBBRs and Section 5.7 contains a design example for a denitrifying FBBR.

5.0   ROTATING BIOLOGICAL CONTACTORS

Rotating biological contactor (RBC) design criteria presented in this chapter are limited to carbon oxidation and nitrification. The RBC uses a cylindrical, synthetic media bundle that is mounted on a horizontal shaft. The media is partially submerged (typically 40%) and slowly (1 to 1.6 rpm) rotates to expose the biofilm to substrate in the bulk of the liquid (when submerged) and to air (when not submerged). As a secondary treatment process, RBC has been applied where

TABLE 5.1   Design criteria for denitrifying fluidized bed biofilm reactors (Metcalf and Eddy, 2003; Sadick et al., 1996; U.S. EPA, 1993) (WEF et al., 2009; Table 13.22).

Parameter	Unit	Value range	Typical
Packing			
Type		Sand	Sand
Effective size	mm	0.3 to 0.5	0.4
Sphericity	Unitless	0.8 to 0.9	0.8 to 0.85
Uniformity coefficient	Unitless	1.25 to 1.50	≤ 1.4
Specific gravity	Unitless	2.4 to 2.6	2.6
Initial depth	m	1.5 to 2.0	2.0
Bed expansion	%	75 to 150	100
Empty-bed upflow velocity	m/h	36 to 42	36
Hydraulic loading rate	$m^3_{effluent}/m^2_{bioreactor\ area}\cdot d$	400 to 600	500
Recirculation ratio	Unitless	2:1 to 5:1	2:1 to 5:1
NO_3^--N loading			
13 °C	kg/m^3-d	2.0 to 4.0	3.0
20 °C	kg/m^3-d	3.0 to 6.0	5.0
Empty-bed contact time	Min	10 to 20	15
Methanol − NO_3^--N ratio	Unitless	3.0 to 3.5	3.2
Specific surface area*	(m^2/m^3)	1 000 to 3 000	2 000 to 3 000
Biomass concentration	mg/L	15 000 to 40 000	30 000 to 40 000

*Grady et al. (1999).

average effluent water quality standards are less than or equal to 30 mg/L BOD_5 and total suspended solids (TSS). When the RBC is used in conjunction with effluent filtration, the process is capable of meeting more stringent effluent water quality limits of 10 mg/L BOD_5 and TSS. Nitrification RBCs can produce effluent having less than 1 mg/L ammonia-nitrogen remaining in the effluent stream.

Media-supporting shafts typically are rotated by mechanical drives. Diffused air-drive systems and an array of air-entraining cups that are fixed to the periphery of the media (to capture diffused air) have been used to rotate the shafts. The RBC process has the following advantages: operational simplicity, low energy costs, and rapid recovery from shock loadings. The literature has documented several examples of RBC failure resulting from shaft, media, or media support system structural failure; poor treatment performance; accumulation of nuisance macro fauna; poor biofilm thickness control; and inadequate performance of air-drive systems for shaft rotation. Table 5.2 contains design criteria for RBCs.

6.0   TRICKLING FILTERS

The trickling filter is a three-phase system with fixed biofilm carriers. Wastewater enters the bioreactor through a distribution system and trickles down over the biofilm surface and air moves upward or downward in the third phase. Biofilm develops on biofilm carriers. Trickling filter components typically

TABLE 5.2   Design criteria for rotating biological contactors ($g/m^2{\cdot}d \times 0.204 = lb/10^3$ sq ft·d and $m^3/m^2{\cdot}d \times 24.5424 = gal/sq\ ft{\cdot}d$) (Metcalf and Eddy, 2003; Table 9.8).

Parameter	Unit	Treatment level*		
		BOD removal	BOD removal and nitrification	Separate nitrification
Hydraulic loading	$m^3/m^2{\cdot}d$	0.08 to 0.16	0.03 to 0.08	0.04 to 0.10
Organic loading	g soluble $BOD/m^2{\cdot}d$	4 to 10	2.5 to 8	0.5 to 1.0
		8 to 20	5 to 16	1 to 2
	g soluble $BOD/m^2{\cdot}d$			
Maximum first-stage organic loading	g soluble $BOD/m^2{\cdot}d$	12 to 15	12 to 15	
		24 to 20	24 to 30	
	g soluble $BOD/m^2{\cdot}d$			
NH_3 loading	g $N/m^2{\cdot}d$		0.75 to 1.5	
Hydraulic retention time	h	0.7 to 1.5	1.5 to 4	1.2 to 3
Effluent BOD	mg/L	15 to 30	7 to 15	7 to 15
Effluent NH_4-N	mg/L		<2	1 to 2

*Wastewater temperature above 13 °C (55 °F).

include a distribution system, containment structure, rock or plastic biofilm carrier, underdrain, and ventilation system.

Primary effluent is either pumped or flows by gravity to the distribution system that uniformly distributes wastewater over the trickling filter biofilm carriers in intermittent doses. The distributors may be hydraulically or electrically driven.

Trickling filter biofilm carriers include rock, random (synthetic), vertical flow (synthetic), and 60-deg crossflow (synthetic) media. Both vertical flow and crossflow media are constructed with corrugated plastic sheets. Modular plastic trickling filter media (i.e., self-supporting vertical flow or crossflow modules) are used almost exclusively for new trickling filter-based WWTPs.

Rock and random plastic media are not self-supporting when stacked and require structural support to contain the media within the bioreactor. Containment structures typically are precast or panel-type concrete tanks. When self-supporting media such as plastic modules are used, other materials such as wood, fiberglass, and coated steel are used as containment structures.

The trickling filter underdrain system is designed to meet two objectives: collect treated wastewater for conveyance to downstream unit processes and create a plenum that allows for the transfer of air throughout the media. Clay or concrete underdrain blocks typically are used for rock media because of the required structural support. A variety of support systems, including concrete piers and reinforced fiberglass grating, are used for other media types.

If site conditions do not allow gravity flow, a pumping station is needed to lift primary effluent and recirculate unsettled trickling filter effluent (also known as *underflow*) to the influent stream. Typically, trickling filter underflow is recirculated to the distribution system to achieve the hydraulic load required for proper media wetting and biofilm thickness control.

Trickling filters can be categorized by four modes of operation or application: (1) roughing, (2) carbon oxidation, (3) carbon oxidation and nitrification, and (4) nitrification. These operating criteria are summarized in Table 5.3.

Trickling filters require oxygen to sustain aerobic biochemical reactions. Ventilation is essential to maintain aerobic conditions. Current design practice requires adequate sizing of underdrains and effluent channels to permit free airflow and can be achieved through natural draft or forced ventilation.

Numerous investigators have attempted to delineate the fundamentals of the trickling filter process by developing relationships among variables that affect operation. Analyses of operating data have established equations or curves and have led to the development of various empirical formulas. Chapter 13, Section 7.4, of *Design of Municipal Wastewater Treatment Plants* (WEF et al., 2009) contains detailed design assistance for using any of the following formulas: National Research Council, Galler and Gotaas, Kincannon and Stover, Velz equation, Schulze equation, Germain equation, Eckenfelder formula, Institution of Water and Environmental Management formula, and Logan model. More details about

TABLE 5.3   Typical operating criteria for various trickling filters (WEF et al., 2009; Table 13.26).[a]

Design parameter	Roughing	Carbon oxidizing (carbonaceous BOD)	Carbonaceous BOD and nitrification	Nitrifying
Media used[b]	VF	RA, RO, XF or VF	RA, RO, or XF	RA or XF
Wastewater source	Primary effluent	Primary effluent	Primary effluent	Secondary effluent
Hydraulic loading, $m^3/m^2 \cdot d$ (gpm/sq ft)	52.8 to 178.2 (0.9 to 2.9)	13.7 to 88.0 (0.25[c] to 1.5)	13.7 to 88.0 (0.25[d] to 1.5)	35.2 to 88.0 (0.6 to 1.5)
Contaminant loading, $kg/m^3 \cdot d$ (lb BOD_5/d/ 1000 cu ft)	1.6 to 3.52 (100 to 220)	0.32 to 0.96 (20 to 60)	0.08 to 0.24 (5 to 15)	N/A
$g/m^2 \cdot d$ (lb NH_3-N/d/ 1000 sq ft)	N/A	N/A	0.2 to 1.0 (0.04 to 0.2)	0.5 to 2.4 (0.1 to 0.5)
Effluent quality, mg/L (unless noted)	40 to 70% BOD_5 conversion	15 to 30% BOD_5 and TSS	<10 BOD_5 <3 NH_3-N	0.5 to 3 NH_3-N
Predation	No appreciable growth	Beneficial	Detrimental (nitrifying biofilm)	Detrimental
Filter flies	No appreciable growth	No appreciable growth	No appreciable growth	No appreciable growth
Depth, m (ft)	0.91 to 6.10 (3 to 20)	≤12.2 (40)	≤12.2 (40)	≤12.2 (40)

BOD = biochemical oxygen demand, BOD_5 = 5-day biochemical oxygen demand, TSS = total suspended solids, and N/A = not applicable.

[b]Media: VF = vertical flow, RA = random pack, XF = crossflow, and RO = rock.

[c,d]Applicable shallow trickling filters; gpm/sq ft = gallons per minute per square foot of trickling filter plan area (gpm/sq ft × 58.674 = $m^3/m^2 \cdot d$) (cubic meter per day per square meter of trickling filter plan area; lb BOD_5/d/ 1000 cu ft × 0.0160 = $kg/m^3 \cdot d$ (kilograms per day per cubic meter of media); and lb NH_3-N/d/1000 sq ft × 4.88 = $g/m^2 \cdot d$ (grams per day per square meter of media).

the applicability of the various models are described in the same section of *Design of Municipal Wastewater Treatment Plants* (WEF et al., 2009).

7.0   EMERGING BIOFILM REACTORS

This section highlights biofilm processes that are new, emerging, or existing, but not widely used in the United States. The discussion is divided into two topics: (1) membrane biofilm reactors, a type of fixed-bed biofilm reactor, and (2) suspended biofilm reactors.

During the late 1980s, researchers found that gas transfer membranes could be used to deliver a gaseous substrate, such as oxygen, hydrogen, or methane, to a biofilm naturally forming on the outer surface of the membrane. When used to deliver oxygen, some researchers call them *membrane-aerated bioreactors*; more commonly, however, they have been called *membrane biofilm reactors* (MBfR).

Hollow-fiber membranes typically are used in MBfRs because, with outside diameters as low as 100 mm, they can provide specific surface areas as high as 5000 m^2/m^3, although membrane sheets also have been used. Unlike membrane bioreactors, in which membranes act as water filters, the pores of MBfRs are filled with gas and, therefore, are unlikely to foul with solids or bacteria. Under certain conditions, however, pores may become wetted, greatly reducing gas transfer rates. The fibers are collected into a gas-supplying manifold at one end and are sealed at the opposite end. Pressurized gas in the lumen (interior) of the fiber diffuses through the dry pores and into the biofilm coating the fiber. When used in this "dead-end" mode, all of the gas supplied to the MBfR passes into the biofilm, allowing high gas-use efficiencies. Membrane biofilm reactors can be hydrogen-based or oxygen-based. Hydrogen-based MBfRs initially were developed for drinking water treatment, where addition of an electron donor was needed for the reduction of nitrate or other oxidized contaminants. Early pilot-scale tests demonstrated that MBfRs could effectively remove nitrate and perchlorate from groundwater. Oxygen-based MBfRs can be used to provide "passive aeration" and have been studied in bench- and pilot-scale tests since the late 1980s. Bench-scale tests showed that these MBfRs can achieve concurrent COD removal, nitrification, and denitrification. Nitrification typically occurs in the inner portions of the biofilm, close to the air- or oxygen-filled membrane, and denitrification and BOD removal occur in the outer portions, when the bulk-liquid dissolved oxygen concentrations are low.

Bench- and pilot-scale tests also have been carried out on hybrid suspended and attached growth MBfRs for removal of BOD and nitrogen from wastewater. This process is similar to a cord-type integrated fixed-film activated sludge process, where, instead of cords, hollow-fiber membranes are retrofitted into an activated sludge tank.

Several emerging suspended biofilm reactors include reactors based on aerobic granules, anammox biofilm reactors, biofilm airlift reactors, and internal circulation reactors.

Granules are large and dense microbial aggregates, with diameters typically ranging from 1 to 3 mm. Although granules are not classic biofilms, because they are not grown on an inert substratum they behave like them, forming stable aggregates with gradients in their microbial community structure. Granules have much higher settling velocities than activated sludge flocs, and processes based on granular sludge have excellent solid–liquid separation, high biomass retention, and high volumetric treatment capacity.

Granules in anaerobic systems were first used in upflow anaerobic sludge blanket (UASB) reactors and the anaerobic sequencing batch reactor (SBR). More recently, granules have been found in aerobic reactors, mainly SBRs. An important advantage is that granular sludge systems have a much smaller footprint than conventional activated sludge systems. Granular sludge systems typically do not meet effluent requirements for suspended solids without post-treatment. Aerobic granule processes can simultaneously convert organic substrates, nitrogen compounds, and phosphorus.

The Anammox process is a novel technology that removes nitrogen from wastewaters using the unique metabolism of anammox bacteria. The Anammox process can be performed using either flocs or biofilms. The process was developed by the Technical University of Delft (Delft, the Netherlands) and Paques BV (Balk, the Netherlands). Anammox bacteria use ammonium as an electron donor and nitrite as an acceptor, producing dinitrogen gas without the need for a carbon source or electron donor. This process typically is run in tandem with nitrite-producing processes such as the single reactor high activity ammonia removed over nitrite process, or SHARON process.

Anammox bacteria are slow-growing, with a doubling time of around 11 days, but high volumetric loadings can be obtained using fixed-film Anammox processes. The Anammox process has been studied with MBBRs, RBCs, anaerobic biological filters, and granular sludge bioreactors. A key aspect of the Anammox process is the formation of granular biomass, which greatly increases biomass concentration. Loading rates of up to 10 kg $N/m^2 \cdot d$ have been achieved.

Biofilm airlift reactors were developed in the Netherlands in the late 1980s for aerobic wastewater treatment, including the oxidation of BOD, sulfide, and ammonia. Biofilm airlift reactors are typically in a tower configuration, which is divided vertically into riser and downcomer sections. Air is introduced at the bottom of the riser section, traverses the length of the reactor, and exits at the top. The upward bubble movement provides mixing and sludge granules in response to the high upflow velocities, which wash out smaller particles. Nitrification is easily achieved with this process. Commercial versions of this process include CIRCOX, which has a high loading capacity (4 to 10 kg $COD/m^3 \cdot d$), short HRTs (0.5 to 4 hours), high biomass settling velocities (50 m/h), and high biomass concentrations (15 to 30 g/L). Nitrification is easily achieved with this process. A modified CIRCOX that was developed to include an anoxic compartment for denitrification was tested at pilot and full scale. Anaerobic versions of biofilm airlift reactors, called *gas-lift reactors,* use gases such as methane, hydrogen, or nitrogen gas instead of air to provide the circulation. These gases can be degradation byproducts formed in the reactor (e.g., methane).

The internal circulation reactor consists of two sequential UASB processes, one high-rate and the second low-rate. The reactor is in a tower configuration, where the lower part contains the high-rate reactor and the upper part the low-rate reactor. The low-rate reactor polishes the effluent from the high-rate reactor. In the lower tower, an expanded bed of granular sludge converts organic matter to biogas. The gas is collected in a separator and lifts water and sludge to the upper compartment, where the gas is separated and the sludge is returned via a down pipe.

8.0   REFERENCES

Grady, L. E.; Daigger, G. T.; Lim, H. (1999) *Biological Wastewater Treatment*, 2nd ed.; Marcel Dekker: New York.

Metcalf and Eddy, Inc. (2003) *Wastewater Engineering: Treatment and Reuse*, 4th ed.; McGraw-Hill: New York.

Qasim, S. (1999) *Wastewater Treatment Plants: Planning, Design and Operation*, 2nd ed.; CRC Press: Boca Raton, Florida.

Sadick, T.; Semon, J.; Palumbo, D.; Keenan, P.; Daigger, G. (1996) Fluidized-Bed Denitrification. *Water Environ. Technol.*, **8** (8), 81–85.

U.S. Environmental Protection Agency (1993) *Nitrogen Control Manual*; EPA-625/R-93-010; U.S. Environmental Protection Agency, Office of Wastewater Management: Washington, D.C.

Vesilind, P. A., Ed. (2003) *Wastewater Treatment Plant Design*; Water Environment Federation: Alexandria, Virginia.

Water Environment Federation (2011) *Biofilm Reactors*; WEF Manual of Practice No. 35; McGraw-Hill: New York.

Water Environment Federation; American Society of Civil Engineers; Environmental & Water Resources Institute (2009) *Design of Municipal Wastewater Treatment Plants*, 5th ed.; WEF Manual of Practice No. 8; ASCE Manuals and Reports on Engineering Practice No. 76; McGraw-Hill: New York.

Chapter 6

Suspended Growth Biological Treatment

1.0 INTRODUCTION

Suspended growth systems for wastewater treatment are predominantly aerobic processes, typically referred to as *activated sludge,* with a variety of reactor configurations and flow patterns. Anaerobic suspended growth processes for liquid-phase treatment are also in use.

An activated sludge process uses a suspension of diverse microorganisms to treat wastewater. The dry weight of these microorganisms is 95% or more organic in composition. Suspension of microorganisms in an activated sludge process is typically 70 to 90% organic substances and 10 to 30% inorganic substances because of inert materials in the wastewater. When metal salts are used for phosphorus removal and precipitation, the organic fraction can be lower. Composition of the organic fraction of biomass is approximated by the following empirical formula:

$$C_5H_7O_2NP_{0.2} \qquad\qquad (6.1)$$

Suggested reading material for additional information includes the following:

- *Design of Municipal Wastewater Treatment Plants* (WEF et al., 2009) (Chapter 14, "Suspended Growth Biological Treatment");

- *Wastewater Engineering: Treatment and Reuse* (Metcalf and Eddy, 2003) (Chapter 5, "Physical Unit Operations", Chapter 8, "Suspended Growth Biological Treatment Processes", and Chapter 10, "Anaerobic Suspended and Attached Growth Biological Treatment Processes");

- *Wastewater Treatment Plants Planning Design and Operation* (Qasim, 1999) (Chapter 13, "Biological Waste Treatment");

- *Wastewater Treatment Plant Design* (Vesilind [Ed.], 2003) (Chapter 6, "Suspended Growth Biological Treatment", and Chapter 8, "Biological Nutrient Removal");

- *Nutrient Removal* (WEF, 2011); and

- *Biological Wastewater Treatment* (Grady et al., 2011).

2.0 PROCESS CONFIGURATIONS AND TYPES

Basic activated sludge configurations include

- Complete mix,
- Plug flow,
- Oxidation ditch, and
- Combination (capable of being operated in more than one configuration).

Activated sludge processes can be classified by loading or organic feed rate. Common terms are *conventional*, *low rate*, and *high rate*. Table 6.1 provides a summary of general characteristics for various processes.

Types of feeding and aeration schemes include conventional, contact stabilization, step-feed or step-aeration process, and tapered aeration, all of which are described further in Chapter 14, Section 2.3, of *Design of Municipal Wastewater Treatment Plants* (WEF et al., 2009). Other variations of suspended growth biological treatment that are discussed in Chapter 14, Section 2.5, of *Design of Municipal Wastewater Treatment Plants* (WEF et al., 2009) include pure oxygen, sequencing batch reactors (SBRs), and activated carbon addition.

TABLE 6.1 Operational characteristics of activated sludge processes (BOD = biochemical oxygen demand) (from Metcalf & Eddy, Inc., *Wastewater Engineering: Treatment and Reuse*, 4th ed. Copyright © 2003, The McGraw-Hill Companies, New York, N.Y., with permission).

Process modification	Flow model	Aeration system	BOD removal efficiency, %	Remarks
Conventional	Plug flow	Diffused-air, mechanical aerators	85–95	Use for low-strength domestic wastes; process is susceptible to shock loads
Complete-mix	Continuous-flow stirred-tank reactor	Diffused-air, mechanical aerators	85–95	Use for general application, process is resistant to shock loads but is susceptible to filamentous growths
Step feed	Plug flow	Diffused-air	85–95	Use for general application for a wide range of wastes
Modified aeration	Plug flow	Diffused-air	60–75	Use for intermediate degree of treatment where cell tissue in the effluent is not objectionable
Contact stabilization	Plug flow	Diffused-air, mechanical aerators	80–90	Use for expansion of existing systems and package plants
Extended aeration	Plug flow	Diffused-air, mechanical aerators	75–95	Use for small communities, package plants, and where nitrified element is required; process is flexible
High-rate aeration	Continuous-flow stirred-tank reactor	Mechanical aerators	75–90	Use for general applications with turbine aerators to transfer oxygen and control floc size
Kraus process	Plug flow	Diffused-air	85–95	Use for low-nitrogen, high-strength waste
High purity oxygen	Continuous-flow stirred-tank reactors in series	Mechanical aerators (sparger turbines)	85–95	Use for general application with high-strength waste and where limited space is available at site; process is resistant to slug loads area of land is available; process is flexible
Oxidation ditch	Plug flow	Mechanical aerators (horizontal axis type)	75–95	Use for small communities or where large area of land is available; process is flexible
Sequencing batch reactor	Intermittent-flow stirred-tank series reactor	Diffused-air	85–95	Use for small communities where land area is limited; process is flexible and can remove nitrogen and phosphorus
Deep shaft reactor	Plug flow	Diffused-air	85–95	Use for general application with high-strength waste, process is resistant to slug loads
Single-stage nitrification	Continuous-flow stirred-tank reactors or plug flow	Mechanical aerators, diffused-air	85–95	Use for general application for nitrogen control where inhibitory industrial waste is not present
Separate stage nitrification	Continuous-flow stirred-tank reactors or plug flow	Mechanical aerators, diffused-air	85–95	Use for upgrading existing systems, where nitrogen standards are stringent, or where inhibitory industrial waste is present and can be removed in earlier stages

3.0 PROCESS DESIGN FOR CARBON OXIDATION AND NITRIFICATION

3.1 Carbon Oxidation

Figure 6.1 illustrates a typical suspended growth system flow diagram with nomenclature for the design parameters.

Design equations for the sizing of a single completely mixed reactor based on completely mixed reactors is presented in Table 6.2. For details, qualifications, and explanations of the design equations, the reader is referred to Chapter 14, Section 3.1, of *Design of Municipal Wastewater Treatment Plants* (WEF et al., 2009).

Table 14.5 of *Design of Municipal Wastewater Treatment Plants* (WEF et al., 2009) presents ranges and typical values for the kinetic coefficients in Table 6.2.

3.2 Nitrification

During nitrification, ammonia-nitrogen is oxidized to nitrate by the staged activities of autotrophic species represented by nitrosomonas and nitrobacter. Each

Influent
Q = Flow
S_o = Soluble, Biodegradable Substrate
X_o = Cells, Active Biomass
Z_{io} = Nonvolatile Solids
Z_{no} = Volatile, Nonbiodegradable Solids
Z_{bo} = Biodegradable Solids
M_o = Total Suspended Solids

Effluent
Q_e = Flow
X_e = Total Cells, Active Biomass
Z_{ie} = Inert Solids, Inorganic
S_e = Soluble, Biodegradable Substrate
M_e = Total Suspended Solids

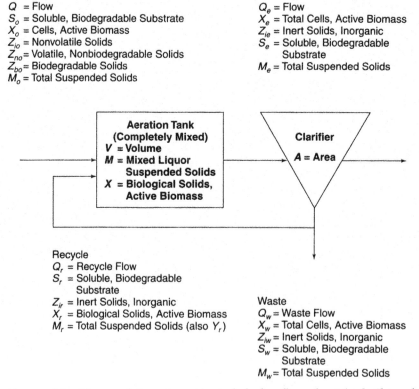

Recycle
Q_r = Recycle Flow
S_r = Soluble, Biodegradable Substrate
Z_{ir} = Inert Solids, Inorganic
X_r = Biological Solids, Active Biomass
M_r = Total Suspended Solids (also Y_r)

Waste
Q_w = Waste Flow
X_w = Total Cells, Active Biomass
Z_{iw} = Inert Solids, Inorganic
S_w = Soluble, Biodegradable Substrate
M_w = Total Suspended Solids

FIGURE 6.1   Nomenclature for activated sludge flow sheet (volatile and non-volatile represent organic and inorganic solids, respectively) (WEF et al., 2009).

TABLE 6.2 Design equations for carbon oxidation.

Parameter	Equations	References
Hydraulic residence time	$\mathrm{HRT} = \dfrac{V}{Q}$	Equation 14.1 (WEF et al., 2009)
	$\dfrac{1}{\mathrm{SRT}} = \dfrac{\mu_{\max} S_e}{K_s + S_e} - b$	Equation 14.2 (WEF et al., 2009)
Reactor biosolids	$X = \dfrac{\mathrm{SRT}}{\mathrm{HRT}} Y_{net}(S_o - S_e)$	Equation 14.3 (WEF et al., 2009)
Net cell yield	$Y_{net} \dfrac{Y}{1 + b\,\mathrm{SRT}}$	Equation 14.4 (WEF et al., 2009)
Quantity of sludge to be wasted	$M_{wTSS} = Q\left\{ \dfrac{Y_{net}(S_o - S_e)}{fv} + \left[fd\,b\,\mathrm{SRT}\dfrac{Y_{net}(S_o - S_e)}{fv} \right] + Z_{io} + Z_{no} \right.$	Equation 14.5 (WEF et al., 2009)
Waste sludge generation	$X_{MLSS} = \dfrac{\mathrm{SRT}}{\mathrm{HRT}}\left\{ \dfrac{Y_{net}(S_o - S_e)}{fv} + \left[fd\,b\,\mathrm{SRT}\dfrac{Y_{net}(S_o - S_e)}{fv} \right] + Z_{io} + Z_{no} \right.$	Equation 14.6 (WEF et al., 2009)
Aeration tank volume	$\mathrm{SRT} = VX_{TSS}/M_{wTSS} = VX_{TSS}/X_{wTSS}Q_w$	Equation 14.7 (WEF et al., 2009)
Return activated sludge pumping requirements	$\alpha r = \dfrac{Q_r}{Q} = \dfrac{X}{X_r - X} = \dfrac{X_{TSS}}{X_{rTSS} - X_{TSS}}$	Equation 14.8 (WEF et al., 2009)
Total oxygen demand	$R_c = Q(S_o - S_e) - B[Q\,Y_{net}(S_o - S_e)(1 + fd\,b\,\mathrm{SRT})]$	Equation 14.9 (WEF et al., 2009)

Where
   V = aeration tank volume, length^3;
   Q = wastewater inflow, length^3/time;
   Q_r = sludge recycle flow, length^3/time;
   X = reactor biological solids, mass/length^3;
   X_r = sludge recycle flow biological solids, mass/length^3
   Y = true cell yield, mass/mass;
   S_o = influent biodegradable substrate, mass/length^3;
   S_e = effluent soluble biodegradable substrate, mass/length^3;
   SRT = solids retention time;
   Q_w = sludge waste flow, length^3/time;

(continues on next page)

TABLE 6.2   Design equations for carbon oxidation (*Continued*).

K_s = half-velocity coefficient, mass/length^3;
μ_{max} = maximum specific growth rate, 1/time;
b = endogenous decay coefficient, 1/time;
fd = cell debris coefficient, mass/mass;
fv = biomass volatile solids content, typically 0.85, mass/mass;
Y_{net} = net cell yield accounting for decay, mass/mass;
X_{TSS} = mixed liquor total suspended solids, mass/length^3;
X_{rTSS} = sludge recycle flow total suspended solids, mass/length^3;
X_{wTSS} = waste sludge flow total suspended solids, mass/length^3;
Z_{io} = influent nonvolatile suspended solids, mass/length^3;
Z_{no} = influent volatile nonbiodegradable solids, mass/length^3;
αr = return sludge recycle ratio, dimensionless, typically 20 to 100% and up to 150%
R_c = mass of oxygen required per unit time to satisfy carbonaceous oxidation, mass/time;
M_{wTSS} = mass of total solids generated or removed as effluent suspended solids and waste activated sludge per day, mass/time; and
B = oxygen equivalent of cell mass, often calculated as 1.42 mass O_2/mass volatile suspended solids, mass/mass.

gram of ammonia oxidized to nitrate (both expressed as N) will result in 4.57 g of oxygen consumed, 7.14 g of alkalinity (as calcium carbonate) destroyed, and 0.15 g of new cells (nitrifiers) produced.

Design equations for nitrification in complete-mixed, suspended growth systems are presented in Table 6.3. For details, qualifications, and explanations of the design equations, the reader is referred to Chapter 14, Section 3.2, of *Design of Municipal Wastewater Treatment Plants* (WEF et al., 2009).

Table 14.6 of *Design of Municipal Wastewater Treatment Plants* (WEF et al., 2009) presents ranges and typical values for the kinetic coefficients presented in Table 6.3.

For a description of activated sludge processes for biochemical oxygen demand (BOD) removal and nitrification, the reader is referred to Table 8.15 of *Wastewater Engineering: Treatment and Reuse* (Metcalf and Eddy, 2003). Table 8.17 of the same publication provides advantages and limitations of activated sludge processes for BOD removal and nitrification.

For typical design parameters for commonly used activated sludge processes for BOD removal and nitrification, the reader is referred to Table 6.4.

4.0   PROCESS DESIGN FOR NUTRIENT CONTROL

4.1   Enhanced Biological Phosphorus Removal Processes

Phosphorus removal can be achieved by using enhanced biological phosphorus removal (EBPR) or chemical addition. Figure 6.2 shows phosphorus concentrations through the biological reactors.

TABLE 6.3   Design equations for nitrification.

Parameter	Equations	References
Minimum solids retention time for nitrification	$SRT_{Nmin} = \dfrac{1}{\mu_N - b_N}$	Equation 14.10 (WEF et al., 2009)
Nitrifier specific growth rate	$\mu_N = \mu_{N,max} \dfrac{N_e}{K_N + N_o} \dfrac{DO}{K_o + DO}$	Equation 14.11 (WEF et al., 2009)
Design solids retention time	$SRT_{design} = SRT_{Nmin}(SF)$	Equation 14.12 (WEF et al., 2009)
Net nitrification yield	$Y_{Nnet} = \dfrac{Y_N}{1 + b_N \, SRT_{design}}$	Equation 14.13 (WEF et al., 2009)
Solids wasted	$M_{NTSS} = Q \left\{ \dfrac{Y_{Nnet}(N_o - N_e)}{fv} + \left[fd\, b_N\, SRT_{design} \dfrac{Y_{Nnet}(N_o - N_e)}{fv} \right] \right\}$	Equation 14.14 (WEF et al., 2009)
Oxygen required	$R_N = 4.57\,(N_o - N_e) - 2.86(N_o - N_e - N_{3e}) - B\,fv\,M_{NTSS}$	Equation 14.15 (WEF et al., 2009)

Where

SRT_{Nmin} = minimum solids retention time for nitrification, time;

μ_N = nitrifier specific growth rate, 1/time;

$\mu_{N,max}$ = maximum nitrifier specific growth rate, 1/time;

N_o, N_e = influent and effluent oxidizable nitrogen concentrations, respectively, mass/length^3;

K_N, K_o = half-velocity constants for ammonia and oxygen, respectively, mass/length^3;

Y_N = nitrification yield coefficient, mass/mass;

Y_{Nnet} = net nitrification yield coefficient, mass/mass;

DO = reactor dissolved oxygen concentration, mass/length^3;

SRT_{design} = design solids retention time, time;

SF = safety or design factor, dimensionless;

b_N = endogenous decay coefficient for autotrophs based on biomass in aerated zone, 1/time;

fd = cell debris coefficient, mass/mass;

fv = biomass volatile solids content, typically 0.85, mass/mass;

M_{NTSS} = mass of total autotrophic solids generated or removed as effluent suspended solids or wasted, per day, mass/time;

R_N = mass of oxygen required per unit time to satisfy nitrification oxygen demand, mass/time; and

NO_{3e} = effluent nitrate-nitrogen, mass/length^3.

A specialized heterotrophic microbial population, collectively called phosphate-accumulating organisms (PAOs), is capable of storing soluble phosphorus in excess of their minimum growth requirements and can sequester up to 0.38 mg P/mg volatile suspended solids (VSS) (Henze et al., 2008). As a result, mixed liquor from an EBPR system can contain 0.06 to 0.15 mg P/mg VSS (Henze et al.,

TABLE 6.4 Design parameters for activated sludge processes (BOD_5 = 5-day biochemical oxygen demand; MLSS = mixed liquor suspended solids) (from Metcalf & Eddy, Inc., *Wastewater Engineering: Treatment and Reuse*, 4th ed. Copyright © 2003, The McGraw-Hill Companies, New York, N.Y., with permission).

Process modification	θ_c, d	F:M, lb BOD_5 applied/d/lb MLVSS[a]	Volumetric loading, lb BOD_5/d/10³ cu ft	MLSS, mg/L	V/Q·h	Q_r/Q
Conventional	5–15	0.2–0.4	20–40	1 500–3 000	4–8	0.25–0.75
Complete-mix	5–15	0.2–0.6	50–120	2 500–4 000	3–5	0.25–1.0
Step feed	5–15	0.2–0.4	40–60	2 000–3 500	3–5	0.25–0.75
Modified aeration	0.2–0.5	1.5–5.0	75–150	200–1 000	1.5–3	0.05–0.25
Contact stabilization	5–15	0.2–0.6	60–75	(1 000–3 000)[b] (4 000–10 000)[c]	(0.5–1.0)[b] (3–6)[e]	0.5–1.50
Extended aeration	20–30	0.05–0.15	10–25	3 000–6 000	18–36	0.5–1.50
High-rate aeration	5–10	0.4–1.5	100–1 000	4 000–10 000	2–4	1.0–5.0
Kraus process	5–15	0.3–0.8	40–100	2 000–3 000	4–8	0.5–1.0
High-purity oxygen	3–10	0.25–1.0	100–200	2 000–5 000	1–3	0.25–0.5
Oxidation ditch	10–30	0.05–0.30	5–30	3 000–6 000	8–36	0.75–1.50
Sequencing batch reactor	NA	0.05–0.30	5–15	1 500–5 000[d]	12–50	NA
Deep shaft reactor	NI	0.5–5.0	NI	NI	0.5–5	NI
Single-stage nitrification	8–20	0.10–0.25 (0.02–0.15)[d]	5–20	2 000–3 500	6–15	0.50–1.50
Separate stage nitrification	15–100	0.050–0.20 (0.04–0.15)[d]	3–9	2 000–3 500	3–6	0.50–2.00

[a] MLVSS = mixed liquor volatile suspended solids.
[b] Contact unit.
[c] Solids stabilization unit.
[d] Total Kjeldahl nitrogen/MLVSS.
[e] MLSS varies depending on the portion of the operating cycle.
Note: lb/10³ cu ft × 0.016 0 = kg/m³·d.
lb/d/lb = kg/kg·d.
NA = not applicable.
NI = no information.

54

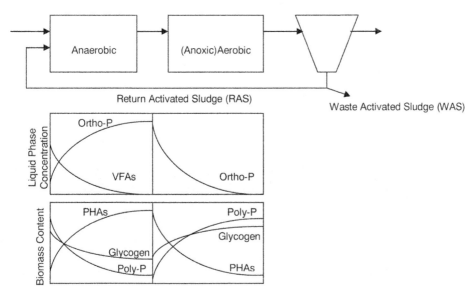

FIGURE 6.2   Typical concentration patterns observed in a generic enhanced biological phosphorus removal system (VFA = volatile fatty acids and PHAs =
polyhydroxyalkanoates) (WEF et al., 2005).

2008). The higher the mixed liquor PAO fraction, the greater the phosphorus content of the waste sludge and the larger amount of phosphorus removed; therefore, the intent of EBPR system design and operation is to maximize PAO
growth. For a full discussion of the process principles, the reader is referred to
Chapter 14, Section 4.1.1, of *Design of Municipal Wastewater Treatment Plants* (WEF
et al., 2009).

   The advantages and limitations of some EBPR processes are summarized in
Table 6.5, and typical design criteria are provided in Table 6.6. For a description
of these suspended growth processes for phosphorus removal, the reader is
referred to Table 8.25 of *Wastewater Engineering: Treatment and Reuse* (Metcalf and
Eddy, 2003).

   The reader is referred to Table 8.27 of *Wastewater Engineering: Treatment and
Reuse* (Metcalf and Eddy, 2003) for advantages and limitations of additional
EBPR processes.

   Factors that affect performance of the EBPR process include influent characteristics, especially the ratio of volatile fatty acids (VFAs) to total phosphorus,
the absence of dissolved oxygen, nitrites, and nitrates in the anaerobic zone, dissolved oxygen limitations in the aerobic zone, pH, solids retention time (SRT),
hydraulic residence time (HRT), wastewater temperature, secondary phosphorus release, recycle rate, and available carbon sources, all of which are discussed
in detail in Chapter 14, Section 4.1.3, of *Design of Municipal Wastewater Treatment
Plants* (WEF et al., 2009).

TABLE 6.5 Advantages and limitations of EBPR processes (A/O = anaerobic/oxic; BOD = biochemical oxygen demand; HRT = hydraulic residence time; SBR = sequencing batch reactor; TSS = total suspended solids; and RAS = return activated sludge) (from Metcalf & Eddy, Inc., *Wastewater Engineering: Treatment and Reuse*, 4th ed. Copyright © 2003, The McGraw-Hill Companies, New York, N.Y., with permission).

Process	Advantages	Limitations
A/O (Phoredox)	• Relatively simple operation • Low BOD:P ratio possible • Relatively short HRT • Produces good settling sludge • Good phosphorus removal	• Impacted by nitrate in RAS • Limited process control flexibility
SBR	• Automated operation solids washout unlikely during hydraulic surges • Quiescent conditions could produce lower effluent TSS • Flexible operation	• Larger tank volume to incorporate anaerobic condition • Design is more complex • More suitable for smaller flows
PhoStrip	• Can be incorporated easily into existing systems	

TABLE 6.6 Typical design parameters for commonly used biological phosphorus removal processes (UCT = University of Cape Town and VIP-Virginia Initiative Plant) (WEF et al., 2009).[a]

Design parameter/ process	SRT, d	MLSS, mg/L	τ, h Anaerobic zone	τ, h Anoxic zone	τ, h Aerobic zone	RAS, % of influent	Internal recycle % of influent
A/O	2–5	3 000–4 000	0.5–1.5	—	1–3	25–100	
A²/O	5–25	3 000–4 000	0.5–1.5	0.5–1	4–8	25–100	100–400
UCT	10–25	3 000–4 000	1–2	2–4	4–12	80–100	200–400 (anoxic) 100–300 (aerobic)
VIP	5–10	2 000–4 000	1–2	1–2	4–6	80–100	100–200 (anoxic) 100–300 (aerobic)
Bardenpho (5-stage)	10–20	3 000–4 000	0.5–1.5	1–3 (1st stage) 2–4 (2nd stage)	4–12 (1st stage) 0.5–1 (2nd stage)	50–100	200–400
PhoStrip	5–20	1 000–3 000	8–12		4–10	50–100	10–20
SBR[b]	20–40	3 000–4 000	1.5–3	1–3	2–4		

[a]Adapted from WEF (1998).
[b]SBR = sequencing batch reactor.

4.2   Nitrogen Removal Processes

Biological nitrogen removal is a two-step process that typically requires nitrification in an aerobic environment followed by denitrification in an anoxic environment. These reactions are affected by the specific environmental conditions in the reactor, including pH, wastewater temperature, dissolved oxygen concentration, substrate type and concentration, and the presence or absence of toxic substances. Nitrification is the sequential oxidation of ammonium nitrogen to nitrite-nitrogen and then to nitrate-nitrogen. Biological denitrification reduces nitrate-nitrogen to nitrogen gas, as shown in the following sequence:

$$NO_3^- \rightarrow NO_2^- \rightarrow NO \rightarrow N_2O \rightarrow N_2 \qquad (6.2)$$

Unit process configurations for biological nitrogen removal can be simulated through use of process modeling techniques using International Water Association-type activated sludge models. Process modeling is described in detail in *An Introduction to Process Modeling for Designers* (WEF, 2009). Key design criteria for nitrogen removal common to biological treatment configurations include SRT, temperature, recycle rates, and dissolved oxygen concentrations throughout the process. These criteria should be established before use of a process simulator, but can be refined throughout the modeling task as design details are optimized.

A significant advantage of using a process simulator for the design of a treatment system is the efficiency with which optimization of the treatment configuration can be achieved. Multiple treatment scenarios and configuration alternatives can be evaluated in a reasonably short period of time. Completing a sensitivity analysis on a basin configuration is a common practice to help determine the final basin layout. Ideally, one parameter is adjusted at a time, allowing the designer to see the resulting effects. The sensitivity analysis, however, can be completed for any number of variables. An example would be to quantify performance based on a range of mixed liquor recycle flowrates. Most commercial process simulators can provide a dynamic simulation, which can aid in a sensitivity analysis. Table 6.7 lists suspended growth process configurations for nitrogen removal.

For a description of suspended growth processes for biological nitrogen removal, the reader is referred to Table 8.21 of *Wastewater Engineering: Treatment and Reuse* (Metcalf and Eddy, 2003). The advantages and limitations of nitrogen removal processes are summarized in Table 8.23, and typical design criteria are provided in Table 8.22 of the same publication.

4.3   Phosphorus and Nitrogen Removal Processes

Biological removal of both nitrogen and phosphorus in suspended growth processes requires a process that has anaerobic (no electron acceptors) zones, anoxic (low oxygen levels) zones, and aerobic zones. Combined phosphorus and nitrogen removal processes are presented in Table 6.8.

TABLE 6.7   Suspended growth processes for nitrogen removal.

Process	Description/performance	Reference
Ludzack-Ettinger and Modified Ludzack-Ettinger	Most common process. Effluent nitrate is 6 to 10 mg/L as NO_3.	Figure 14.40, Figure 14.41 (WEF et al., 2009)
Four-stage Bardenpho™	Effluent total nitrogen as low as 2 to 4 mg/L.	Figure 14.42 (WEF et al., 2009)
Step-feed	Improves capacity for an existing basin or reduces volume for a new basin.	Figure 14.43 (WEF et al., 2009)
Simultaneous nitrification and denitrification	May reduce sludge settleability caused by low dissolved oxygen levels.	Chapter 14, Section 4.2.2.1.4 (WEF et al., 2009)
Oxidation ditch	Effluent nitrate is typically 5 to 10 mg/L as NO_3.	Figure 14.44 (WEF et al., 2009)
Sequencing batch reactor (SBR)	Best suited for relatively small systems with highly variable wastewater flow and strength.	Chapter 14, Section 4.2.2.2.1 (WEF et al., 2009)
Continuous-feed intermittent decant systems	Improved carbon use efficiency compared to SBRs.	Chapter 14, Section 4.2.2.2.2 (WEF et al., 2009)
Biofilm processes (integrated fixed-film activated sludge systems, moving bed biofilm reactors, etc.)	Increased biomass improves net denitrification rates.	Chapters 13 and 15 (WEF et al., 2009)
Nitritation and denitritation	Limited full-scale applications. Typically used for sidestream treatment. Reduced operation (aeration) costs.	Chapter 14, Section 4.2.3 (WEF et al., 2009)

These combined phosphorus and nitrogen removal processes are described in Table 8.25 of *Wastewater Engineering: Treatment and Reuse* (Metcalf and Eddy, 2003). Process advantages and limitations are summarized in Table 6.5 and typical design criteria are provided in Table 6.6.

4.4   External Carbon Addition

Denitrification requires the presence of both a degradable carbon source and nitrate. The external carbon source can either be a separate stream imported into the treatment facility, such as methanol, or a stream created within the plant, such as fermentate of primary sludge. Table 14.21 of *Design of Municipal Wastewater Treatment Plants* (WEF et al., 2009) shows typical characteristics of a range of selected carbon sources and Table 14.22 presents selected denitrification kinetic and stoichiometric coefficients for carbon alternatives. Options for fermentation configurations are described in Chapter 14, Section 4.4.2, of the same publication.

TABLE 6.8   Combined phosphorus and nitrogen removal processes.

Process	Description/performance	Reference
Five-stage Bardenpho™	Provides anaerobic, anoxic, and aerobic stages for removal of phosphorus, nitrogen, and carbon.	Figure 14.46 (WEF et al., 2009)
A²/O™	Secondary effluent total phosphorus concentrations as low as 1 to 2 mg/L P and total nitrogen concentrations as low as 8.0 mg/L.	Figure 14.50 and Table 14.20 (WEF et al., 2009)
University of Cape Town (UCT) and modified UCT	Can achieve both phosphorus removal and partial nitrogen removal to 6 to 8 mg/L.	Figures 14.53 and 14.54 (WEF et al., 2009)
Virginia Initiative Plant	Modification of the UCT process.	Figure 14.55 (WEF et al., 2009)
Johannesburg	Benefits when compared to other combined removal systems: (1) anaerobic zone mixed liquor is at full concentration; (2) using endogenous respiration for nitrogen removal does not require carbon from the feed, thus resulting in efficient carbon usage; and (3) denitrified mixed liquor recycle stream is eliminated.	Figure 14.56 (WEF et al., 2009)
PhoStrip II™	Combined removal to less than 1.0 mg/L of total phosphorus and 10.0 mg/L of total nitrogen.	Figure 14.57 (WEF et al., 2009)
Sequencing batch reactor	Can be operated to achieve combined carbon and nitrogen oxidation, nitrogen removal, and phosphorus removal by controlling the sequence and duration of cycles.	Figure 14.58 (WEF et al., 2009)

Adding external carbon benefits nutrient removal when there is inadequate carbon in the process influent to either serve as an electron donor for nitrogen removal or as a source for VFAs to drive biological release, and subsequent uptake, of soluble phosphorus.

There are three significant locations in a suspended growth process that external carbon can be beneficially added (see Figure 14.59 of *Design of Municipal Wastewater Treatment Plants* [WEF et al., 2009]): directly to the wastewater feeding the process; directly to anoxic zones; or to the anaerobic zones, should the process influent not contain adequate VFAs to support biological phosphorus removal.

The reader is referred to Chapter 14, Section 4.5, of *Design of Municipal Wastewater Treatment Plants* (WEF et al., 2009) for other nutrient removal activated sludge process design considerations, including baffles, mixing, aeration, degasification, and scum and foam control.

5.0   ANAEROBIC TREATMENT OF WASTEWATER

Anaerobic treatment eliminates three of the biggest constraints on process loading that occur in aerobic processes: (1) oxygen-transfer rates, (2) solids flux limitations, and (3) high energy inputs for aeration that hinder floc formation.

Table 6.9 provides advantages and disadvantages of anaerobic treatment. For additional advantages and disadvantages of anaerobic processes compared to aerobic processes, the reader is referred to Table 10.1 of *Wastewater Engineering: Treatment and Reuse* (Metcalf and Eddy, 2003).

A wide range of reactor types exist for anaerobic treatment, and some of these are illustrated in Figure 6.3.

For municipal applications, most installations are based on the upflow anaerobic sludge blanket (UASB) reactor. Information on other anaerobic reactor types is available in Sections 10.5 and 10.6 of *Wastewater Engineering: Treatment and Reuse* (Metcalf and Eddy, 2003), in *Anaerobic Reactors* (Chernicharo, 2007), and in *Review Anaerobic Reactor Design Concepts for the Treatment of Domestic Wastewater* (van Haandel et al., 2006).

Hydraulic residence time for UASB reactors are provided in Table 6.10. Table 6.11 presents summary guidelines for the main hydraulic criteria and Table 6.12 provides other design criteria for UASB reactors treating domestic wastewater. For recommended design considerations for the UASB gas solids separator, the

TABLE 6.9   Advantages and disadvantages of anaerobic treatment.

Advantages	Disadvantages
Lower energy consumption	Lower removal efficiencies for organics, suspended solids, and pathogens.
Potential for energy recovery	Requires aerobic post-treatment to meet standard effluent criteria for secondary and advanced treatment.
Low sludge production	May require supplemental alkalinity.
Design simplicity	Pathogens and colloidal solids are not adequately removed.
Low land area requirements	Do not provide any significant nutrient removal.
Improved sludge dewatering	Extended startup periods (approximately 12 to 20 weeks) are required.
Ability to store sludge for long periods	Odors and corrosive and dangerous gases are a potential problem.

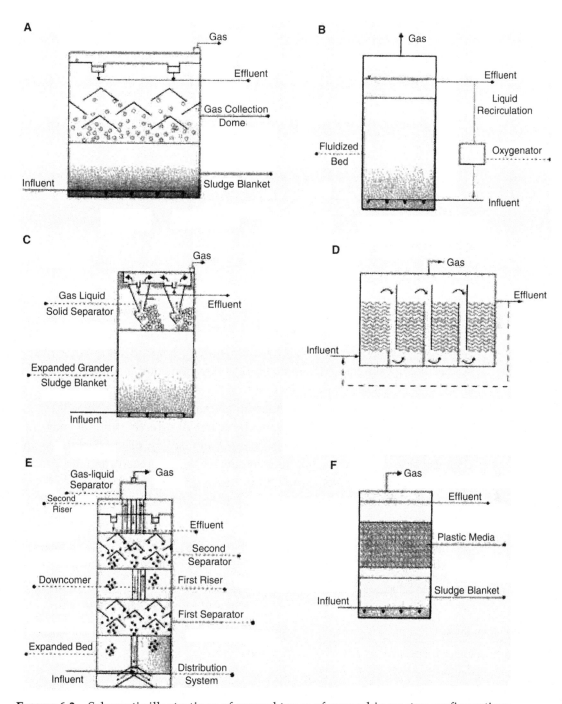

FIGURE 6.3 Schematic illustrations of several types of anaerobic reactor configurations—
(a) upflow sludge blanket, (b) biofilm fluidized bed, (c) expanded granular sludge bed,
(d) anaerobic baffled reactor, (e) internal circulation, and (f) anaerobic hybrid reactor
(Nicolella et al., 2000).

TABLE 6.10   Recommended hydraulic detention times for UASB reactors treating domestic wastewater (Lettinga and Hulshoff Pol, 1991; reprinted from *Water Science and Technology*, with permission from the copyright holders, IWA).

Sewage temperature (°C)	Hydraulic detention time (hour)	
	Daily average	Minimum (during 4 to 6 hours)
16 to 19	>10 to 14	>7 to 9
20 to 26	>6 to 9	>4 to 6
>26	>6	>4

reader is referred to Chapter 5, Section 4.3.2, of *Design of Municipal Wastewater Treatment Plants* (WEF et al., 2009) and Table 10.6 of *Wastewater Engineering: Treatment and Reuse* (Metcalf and Eddy, 2003).

6.0   MEMBRANE BIOREACTORS

A membrane bioreactor (MBR) is a combination of suspended growth activated sludge biological treatment and membrane filtration equipment performing the solids and liquid separation function that is traditionally accomplished using secondary clarifiers. Low-pressure membranes are typically used in MBRs.

Details on specific products must be obtained directly from the manufacturer. Membrane tank dimensions, nature and design of the backpulse and chemical cleaning systems, building layouts for the equipment, and the size and operation of the blowers that provide air to scour the membranes are all affected by the particular type of membrane equipment that is selected.

TABLE 6.11   Summary of the main hydraulic criteria for the design of UASB reactors treating domestic wastewater (Chemicharo, 2007; reprinted with permission from IWA Publishing).

Criterion/parameter	Range of values, as a function of flow		
	For Q_{ave}	For Q_{max}	For Q_{peak}[a]
Hydraulic volumetric load (m³/m³/d)	<4.0	<6.0	<7.0
Hydraulic detention time (h)[b]	6 to 9	4 to 6	>3.5 to 4
Upflow velocity (m/h)	0.5 to 0.7	<0.9 to 1.1	<1.5
Velocity in apertures to the settler (m/h)	<2.0 to 2.3	<4.0 to 4.2	<5.5 to 6.0
Surface loading rate in the settler (m/h)	0.3 to 0.8	<1.2	<1.6
Hydraulic detention time in the settler (h)	1.5 to 2.0	>1.0	>0.6

[a]Flow peaks with duration between 2 and 4 hours.

[b]Sewage temperature in the range of 20 to 26 °C.

TABLE 6.12   Other design criteria for UASB reactors treating domestic wastewater (TSS = total suspended solids; COD = chemical oxygen demand) (Chemicharo [2007]; reprinted with permission from IWA Publishing).

Criterion/parameter	Range of values
Influent distribution	
Diameter of the influent distribution tube (mm)	75 to 100
Diameter of the tube exit mouth (mm)	40 to 50
Distance between the top of the distribution tube and the water level in the settler (m)	0.20 to 0.30
Distance between the exit mouth and the bottom of the reactor (m)	0.10 to 0.15
Influence area of each distribution tube (m^2)	2.0 to 3.0
Biogas collector	
Minimum biogas release rate ($m^3/m^2/h$)	1.0
Maximum biogas release rate ($m^3/m^2/h$)	3.0 to 5.0
Methane concentration in the biogas (%)	70 to 80
Settler compartment	
Overlap of the gas deflectors in relation to the opening of the settler	0.10 to 0.15
Minimum slope for settler walls (°)	45
Optimum slope of the settler walls (°)	50 to 60
Depth of the settler compartment (m)	1.5 to 2.0
Effluent collector	
Submergence of the scum baffle or the perforated collection tube (m)	0.20 to 0.30
Number of triangular weirs (units/m^2 of the reactor)	1 to 2
Production and sampling of the sludge	
Solids production yield (kg TSS/kg $COD_{applied}$)	0.10 to 0.20
Solids production yield, in terms of COD (kg COD_{sludge}/kg $COD_{applied}$)	0.11 to 0.23
Expected solids concetration in the excess sludge (%)	2 to 5
Sludge density (kg/m^3)	1 020 to 1 040
Diameter of the sludge discharge pipes (mm)	100 to 150
Diameter of the sludge sampling pipes (mm)	25 to 50

The reader is referred to Chapter 14, Section 6.3.1, of *Design of Municipal Wastewater Treatment Plants* (WEF et al., 2009) for MBR process configurations. Table 6.13 presents some advantages and disadvantages of MBR systems; Table 6.14 provides typical design and operational data.

Table 6.15 summarizes typical effluent quality produced from a municipal MBR facility that is designed to achieve nutrient removal.

The reader is referred to Table 8.30 of *Wastewater Engineering: Treatment and Reuse* (Metcalf and Eddy, 2003) for additional operations and performance data for an MBR.

7.0   OXYGEN-TRANSFER SYSTEMS

Table 6.16 summarizes the general characteristics of primary types of oxygen-transfer equipment. More detailed information is contained in Chapter 25, Sections 8.2 through 8.5, of *Design of Municipal Wastewater Treatment Plants* (WEF

TABLE 6.13   Advantages and disadvantages of MBR systems compared to conventional activated sludge systems.

Advantages	Disadvantages
Effluent quality is less dependent on the mixed liquor concentration and sludge properties	Limited peaking ability to handle peak flow conditions. Upstream equalization tank may be required.
High-quality final effluent, low total suspended solids, turbidity	High energy consumption
Smaller plant footprint (reduced aeration volume, secondary clarifiers and effluent filters can be eliminated)	Increased foam formation
High SRT, reduced sludge production	Chemical costs for cleaning
Modular, easily expandable, and retrofitable	Membrane replacement costs
Flexible operations, can operate within a wide range of mixed liquor suspended solids concentrations and SRTs	Prepurchase/preselection required
Comparable capital costs to new conventional tertiary filtration	Limited available data to determine long-term performance

et al., 2009); Section 5.12 of *Wastewater Engineering: Treatment and Reuse* (Metcalf and Eddy, 2003); and *Design Manual: Fine Pore Aeration Systems* (U.S. EPA, 1989).

Transfer rates for diffused air systems are reported as oxygen-transfer efficiency, expressed as a percentage; oxygen-transfer rate (OTR), expressed in units of mass/time; or aeration efficiency, expressed in units of mass/time/unit of power. Mechanical devices are typically rated on the basis of OTR or aeration efficiency. Aeration devices also furnish sufficient energy for mixing. Mixing energy should be sufficient to thoroughly disperse dissolved substrate and oxygen throughout a given segment of an aeration tank and keep mixed liquor suspended solids (MLSS) suspended.

An air supply system consists of three basic components: air filters and other conditioning equipment (including diffuser cleaning systems), blowers, and air piping. Table 6.17 provides typical design criteria for these components.

Aerator design and testing, based on transforming the clean water test data to process water conditions, is critical to a successful aeration system and is discussed in Chapter 14, Sections 8.7 and 8.8, of *Design of Municipal Wastewater Treatment Plants* (WEF et al., 2009).

Clean water test data, based on protocols outlined in *ASCE Standard for Measurement of Oxygen Transfer in Clean Water* (ASCE, 1992), provide the primary basis for specification of aeration equipment. The design process for aeration equipment for diffused air systems is detailed in *Design Manual: Fine Pore Aeration Sys-*

TABLE 6.14 Typical design and operational data for MBR systems.

Parameter	Range	References
Design criteria		
Fine screening (following 6-mm screens at headworks or primary clarifiers)	6 mm at headworks 1- to 2-mm openings	Chapter 14, Sections 6.4.1 and 6.4.2 (WEF et al., 2009)
Mixed liquor recycle pumping	200 to 400% plant flow (for solids circulation) 300 to 800% plant flow (when part of denitrification systems)	Chapter 14, Section 6.5.1 (WEF et al., 2009)
Air scour	0.2 to 0.6 Nm^3/h per square meter of membrane area (0.01 to 0.03 scfm/sq ft)	Chapter 14, Sections 6.5.3 and 6.6.1.2 (WEF et al., 2009)
Maintenance cleaning	Once per day to once per week Duration: <2 hours	Chapter 14, Section 6.6.3 (WEF et al., 2009)
Recovery cleaning	Every 2 to 6 months Duration: 6 to 24 hours	Chapter 14, Section 6.6.3, (WEF et al., 2009)
Operational data		
Solids retention time	≥8 days	Chapter 14, Section 6.3.1.1 (WEF et al., 2009)
Mixed liquor suspended solids	8000 to 18 000 mg/L	Chapter 14, Section 6.3.1.2 (WEF et al., 2009)
Dissolved oxygen (in various zones)	Anaerobic: 0.0 to 0.1 mg/L Anoxic: 0.0 to 0.5 mg/L Aerobic: 1.5 to 3.0 mg/L Membranes: 2.0 to 6.0 mg/L	Chapter 14, Section 6.3.1.3 (WEF et al., 2009)

TABLE 6.15 Typical municipal MBR effluent quality ($cBOD_5$ = 5-day carbonaceous BOD; TSS = total suspended solids; and NTU = nephelometric turbidity unit) (WEF et al., 2009).

Parameter	Units	Values
$cBOD_5$	mg/L	<5
TSS	mg/L	<1
Ammonia	mg/L as N	<1
Total nitrogen (with pre-anoxic zone)	mg/L	<10
Total nitrogen (with pre- and post-anoxic zones)	mg/L	<3
Total phosphorus (with chemical addition)	mg/L	<0.2 (typical) <0.05 (achievable)
Total phosphorus (with Bio-P removal)	mg/L	<0.5
Turbidity	NTU	<0.2
Bacteria	Log removal	Up to 6 log (99.9999%)
Viruses	Log removal	Up to 3 log (99.9%)

TABLE 6.16 Characteristics of aeration equipment (Arora et al., 1985; Boyle, 1996; Goronszy, 1979; Groves et al., 1992; Wilford and Conlon, 1957).

Equipment type	Equipment characteristics	Processes where used	Advantages	Disadvantages	Reported clean water performance[a]	
					SOTE, %	SAE, kg/kW·h[b]
Diffused air						
Porous diffusers	Ceramic, plastic, flexible membranes, dome, disk, panel tube, plate configurations, total floor grids, single or dual roll, fine bubble	High-rate; conventional, extended, step, contact stabilization, activated sludge systems	High-efficiency: good operational flexibility; turndown approximately 5:1	Potential for air- or water-side clogging; typically require air filtration; high initial cost; low alpha	15–45	1.9–6.6
Nonporous diffusers	Fixed orifice; perforated pipe, sparger, slotted tube, valved orifice, static tube; coarse bubble; typically single or dual roll; some total floor grids	Same as for porous diffusers	Do not typically clog easy maintenance; high alpha	Low oxygen transfer efficiency; high initial cost	9–13	1.3–1.9
Others						
jets	Compressed air and pumped liquid mixed in nozzle and discharged fine bubble	Same as for porous diffusers	Good mixing properties high SOTE	Limited geometry clogging of nozzles; requires blowers and pumps; primary treatment required; low SAE	15–24	2.2–3.5
U-tube	30- to 300 ft shaft was blown into inlet of down leg	Activated sludge with limited geometry	High efficiency because driving force is increased	Limited geometry; typically effective for strong waste	NA	NA

Mechanical surface Radial flow, low speed (20–100 r/min)	Low output speed: large diameter turbine; floating, fixed-bridge, or platform mounted; used with gear reducer	Same as for porous diffuser	Tank design flexibility; high pumping capacity	Aerosols some icing in cold climates; initial cost higher than axial flow aerators; gear reducer may cause maintenance problems	15–21
Axial flow, high speed (900–1800 r/min)	High output speed; small diameter propeller, direct, motor-driven units mounted on floating structure	Aerated lagoons and reaeration	Low initial cost; may adjust to varying water level; flexible operation	Some icing in cold climates; poor maintenance accessibility; mixing capacity may be inadequate	—
Horizontal rotor	Low output speed; used with gear reducer; steel or plastic bars, plastic discs	Oxidation ditch, applied either as an aerated lagoon or as an activated sludge	Moderate initial cost; good maintenance accessibility	Subject to operational variable, which may affect efficiency; tank geometry is limited	1.5–2.1
Submerged turbine	Units contain a low-speed turbine and provide compressed air to diffuser rings, open pipe, or air draft; fixed-bridge application; may employ draft tube	Same as for porous diffusers, oxidation ditches	Good mixing; high capacity input per unit volume; deep tank application; operational flexibility; no icing or splash	Require both gear reducer and blower; high total power requirements; high cost	1.1–2.1 (Typical) 2.0–3.0 (Drain tube turbine)
Asparating	Same as axial flow; high speed	Aerated lagoons; temporary installations	Low cost flexible operation	Same as axial flow, high speed	0.5–0.8

[a] Manufacturer's data in clean water at standard conditions; diffused air units expressed as SOTE and SAE mechanical devices as SAE. Range of values accounts for different equipment, geometry, gas flow, power input, and other factors (SAE—wire-to-water).
[b] Wire-to-water SAE for diffused air calculated from ??? compression relationship where ambient temperature = 30°C, submergence = 4.3, barometric pressure = 100 ha (1 atm), and blower/motor efficiency = 70%.

TABLE 6.17   Air supply and aeration system design criteria (SBR = sequencing batch reactor).

Device	Criteria	Reference
Inlet air filtration (viscous, impingement, dry barrier, and electrostatic precipitation)	95% removal of particles with diameters 10 μm and larger	Chapter 14, Section 8.5.1 (WEF et al., 2009)
Blowers		
Positive displacement (constant volume, varying pressure operations [i.e., SBR] filters)	0.14 to 1400 m³/min (5 to 50 000 acfm) at discharge pressures ranging from 7 to 100 kPa (1 to 15 psig)	Chapter 14, Section 8.5.2, Figure 14.95 (WEF et al., 2009)
Centrifugal (constant pressure, varying volume operations [i.e., aeration tanks])	14 to 4200 m³/min (500 to 150 000 acfm)	Chapter 14, Section 8.5.2, Figure 14.95 (WEF et al., 2009)
Single-stage, high-efficiency integral gearbox compressor or high-speed direct-drive compressor (turbo compressor)	11 to 2000 m³/min (400 to 70 000 acfm), medium pressure (27 to 210 kPa [4 to 30 psig])	Chapter 14, Section 8.5.2 and Figure 14.95 (WEF et al., 2009)
Mixing requirements to maintain 0.15 m/s (0.5 ft/sec) mixed liquor velocity		
Diffused aeration system		
Spiral roll systems (minimum airflows)	0.28 to 0.65 m³/m·min of header length (3 to 7 scfm/ft) or 0.25 to 0.42 L/m³·s (15 to 25 scfm/1000 cu ft)	Chapter 14, Section 8.6 (WEF et al., 2009)
Full floor grid configuration	0.61 L/m²·s (0.12 scfm/sq ft)	Chapter 14, Section 8.6 (WEF et al., 2009)
Mechanical aerators	16 to 30 W/m³ (0.6 to 1.15 hp/1000 cu ft)	

tems (U.S. EPA, 1989). The same process may be used for mechanical or other aeration systems up to the point of calculating standard OTRs for appropriate basin configurations and design loads. At that point, the designer may use standard aeration efficiencies to estimate numbers of units and standard power requirements. Aerator spacing may be determined from the characteristics of the selected transfer device. Finally, mixing may be evaluated based on equipment placement.

8.0   SECONDARY CLARIFICATION

Gravity clarification traditionally has been used to separate MLSS from effluent in suspended growth systems. Table 6.18 lists many of the factors that affect clarifier performance.

TABLE 6.18   Factors that affect clarifier performance (adapted from Ekama et al. [1997]; reprinted with permission from IWA Publishing).

Category	Factors
Hydraulic and load factors	Wastewater (ADWF, PDWF, PWWF)*
	Surface overflow rate
	Weir loading rate
	Solids loading rate
	Hydraulic retention time
	Underflow recycle ratio
External physical features	Tank configuration
	Surface area
	Depth
	Flow distribution
	Turbulence in conveyance structure
Internal physical features	Presence of flocculation zone
	Sludge collection mechanism
	Inlet arrangement
	Weir type, length and position
	Baffling
	Hydraulic flow patterns and turbulence
	Density and connection currents
Site conditions	Wind and wave action
	Water temperature variation
Sludge characteristics	MLSS concentration
	Sludge age
	Flocculation, settling and thickening characteristics
	Type of biological process

*ADWF = average dry weather flow, PDWF = peak dry weather flow, and PWWF = peak wet weather flow.

Key design parameters for secondary clarifiers are summarized in Table 6.19.

For more typical design information for secondary clarifiers, the reader is referred to Table 8.7 of *Wastewater Engineering: Treatment and Reuse* (Metcalf and Eddy, 2003). A step-by-step summary for sizing clarifiers is provided in Chapter 14, Section 9.3.7, of *Design of Municipal Wastewater Treatment Plants* (WEF et al., 2009).

Further details and more in-depth analysis of the design of secondary clarifiers can be found in *Clarifier Design* (WEF, 2005). For a design example of suspended growth biological treatment, the reader is referred to Chapter 14, Section 10.0, of *Design of Municipal Wastewater Treatment Plants* (WEF et al., 2009).

TABLE 6.19 Design considerations for secondary clarifiers (SOR = surface overflow rate and SLR = surface loading rate).

Parameter	Typical values	References
Average SOR	16 to 28 m^3/m^2·d (200 to 700 gpd/sq ft)	Chapter 14, Section 9.3.1, Table 14.37 (WEF et al., 2009)
Peak SOR	24 to 64 m^3/m^2·d (600 to 1600 gpd/sq ft)	
Average SLR	4 to 8 kg/m^2·h (0.8 to 1.5 lb/sq ft·hr)	Chapter 14, Section 9.3.2, Table 14.37 (WEF et al., 2009)
Peak SLR	9 kg/m^2·h (1.6 lb/sq ft·hr)	
Sidewater depth	3.5 to 6 m	Table 8.7 (Metcalf and Eddy, 2003)
Rectangular clarifiers		
Length	30 to 60 m (100 to 200 ft)	Chapter 14, Section 9.4.2 (WEF et al., 2009)
Width	6 to 10 m (20 to 33 ft)	Chapter 14, Section 9.4.2 (WEF et al., 2009)
Depth	4 to 5 m (12 to 16 ft)	Chapter 14, Section 9.4.2 (WEF et al., 2009)
Weir loading rates	250 to 375 m^3/m·d (20 000 to 30 000 gpd/ft)	Chapter 14, Section 9.4.2 (WEF et al., 2009)
Sludge collection	Midtank or effluent end Chain and flight	Chapter 14, Section 9.4.2 (WEF et al., 2009)
Circular clarifiers		
Diameter	50 m (150 ft)	Chapter 14, Section 9.5.2 (WEF et al., 2009)
Depth	3 to 4.6 m (10 to 15 ft)	Table 14.40 (WEF et al., 2009)
Inlet	Energy-dissipating inlet	Chapter 14, Section 9.5.4 (WEF et al., 2009) Figures 14.138 and 14.141 to 14.144 (WEF et al., 2009)
Weir loading rates	250 to 375 m^3/m·d (20 000 to 30 000 gpd/ft)	Chapter 14, Section 9.5.7 (WEF et al., 2009)
Floor slope	Scrapers (plows): 1 on 12. Hydraulic suction: 1 or 2% slope acceptable; 1-on-12 slope can also be used.	Chapter 14, Section 9.5.8.6 (WEF et al., 2009)
Sludge withdrawal	Scrapers (plows) Hydraulic suction (organ/riser pipe or Tow-Bro® design [Siemens, Munich, Germany])	Figure 14.154, (WEF et al., 2009) Chapter 14, Section 9.5.8.2, Figures 14.156 and 14.157 (WEF et al., 2009)
Return activated sludge pumping	One centrifugal pump per clarifier directly connected to sludge removal hoppers or hydraulic suction mechanisms	Chapter 14, Section 9.5.8.6 (WEF et al., 2009)

9.0   REFERENCES

American Society of Civil Engineers (1992) *ASCE Standard Measurement of Oxygen Transfer in Clean Water*, 2nd ed.; ANSI/ASCE 2-91; American Society of Civil Engineers: Reston, Virginia.

Arora, M. L.; Barth, E. F.; Umphres, M. B. (1985) Technology Evaluation of Sequencing Batch Reactors. *J. Water Pollut. Control Fed.*, **57,** 867–875.

Boyle, W. C. (1996) Fine Pore Aeration: An Update on Its Status. In *Enhancing Design and Operation of Activated Sludge Plants*. Proceedings of the Central States Water Environment Association Seminar; Madison, Wisconsin.

Chemicharo, C. A. L. (2007) *Anaerobic Reactors*; IWA Publishing: London, England.

Ekama, G. A.; Barnard, J. L.; Gunthert, F. W.; Krebs, P.; McCorquodale, J. A.; Parker, D. S.; Wahlberg, E. J. (1997) *Secondary Settling Tanks: Theory, Modeling, Design, and Operation*; Scientific Technical Report No. 6; IWA Publishing: London, England.

Goronszy, M. (1979) Intermittent Operation of the Extended Aeration Process for Small Systems. *J. Water Pollut. Control Fed.*, **51,** 274–287.

Grady, C. P. L., Jr.; Daigger, G. T.; Love, N. G.; Filipe, C. D. M. (2011) *Biological Wastewater Treatment*, 3rd ed.; IWA Publishing: Boca Raton, Florida.

Groves, K. P.; Daigger, G. T.; Simpkin, T. J.; Redmon, D. T.; Ewing, L. (1992) Evaluation of Oxygen Transfer Efficiency and Alpha Factor on a Variety of Diffused Aeration Systems. *Water Environ. Res.*, **64,** 691–698.

Henze, M; val Loosdrecht, M. C. M.; Ekama, G.A.; Brdjanovic, D. (2008) *Biological Wastewater Treatment Principles, Modeling and Design*; IWA Publishing: London, England.

Lettinga, G.; Hulshoff Pol, L. W. (1991) UASB-Process Design for Various Types of Wastewaters. *Water Sci. Technol.*, **24** (8), 87–107.

Metcalf and Eddy, Inc. (2003) *Wastewater Engineering: Treatment and Reuse*, 4th ed.; McGraw-Hill: New York.

Nicolella, C.; van Loosdrecht, M. C. M.; Heijnen, J. J. (2000) Wastewater Treatment with Particulate Biofilm Reactors. *J. Biotechnol.*, **80,** 1–33.

Qasim, S. R. (1999) *Wastewater Treatment Plants: Planning, Design and Operation*; CRC Press: Boca Raton, Florida.

U.S. Environmental Protection Agency (1989) *Design Manual: Fine Pore Aeration Systems*; EPA-625/1-89-023; U.S. Environmental Protection Agency, Center for Environmental Research Information: Cincinnati, Ohio.

van Haandel, A. C.; Kato, M. T.; Cavalcanti, P. F. F.; Florencio, L. (2006) Review Anaerobic Reactor Design Concepts for the Treatment of Domestic Wastewater. *Rev. Environ. Sci. Bio/Technol.*, **5,** 21–38.

Vesilind, A. P., Ed. (2003) *Wastewater Treatment Plant Design*; Water Environment Federation: Alexandria, Virginia.

Water Environment Federation (2005) *Clarifier Design*; Manual of Practice FD–8; McGraw-Hill: New York.

Water Environment Federation (2009) *An Introduction to Process Modeling for Designers*; Manual of Practice No. 31; Water Environment Federation: Alexandria, Virginia.

Water Environment Federation (2011) *Nutrient Removal*; WEF Manual of Practice No. 34; McGraw-Hill: New York.

Water Environment Federation; American Society of Civil Engineers; Environmental and Water Resources Institute (2005) *Biological Nutrient Removal (BNR) Operation in Wastewater Treatment Plants*; WEF Manual of Practice No. 29/ASCE/EWRI Manuals and Reports on Engineering Practice No. 109; McGraw-Hill: New York.

Water Environment Federation; American Society of Civil Engineers; Environmental & Water Resources Institute (2009) *Design of Municipal Wastewater Treatment Plants,* 5th ed.; WEF Manual of Practice No. 8; ASCE Manuals and Reports on Engineering Practice No. 76; McGraw-Hill: New York.

Wilford, J.; Conlon, T. P. (1957) Contact Aeration Sewage Treatment Plants in New Jersey. *Sew. Ind. Wastes*, **29,** 845–855.

10.0 SUGGESTED READINGS

U.S. Environmental Protection Agency (1993) *Nitrogen Control*; EPA-625/R-93-010; U.S. Environmental Protection Agency: Washington, D.C.

Water Environment Federation; U.S. Environmental Protection Agency; Water Environment Research Foundation (2012) *Solids Process Design and Management*; McGraw-Hill: New York.

Chapter 7

Integrated Biological Treatment

1.0 INTRODUCTION TO INTEGRATED BIOLOGICAL TREATMENT

Integrated biological treatment processes are called *two-stage, series, dual,* or *coupled processes.* In *Design of Municipal Wastewater Treatment Plants* (WEF et al., 2009), however, the term integrated biological treatment is used to denote (1) conventional coupling in series of two different reactors of which at least one is a fixed biofilm reactor and (2) integrated fixed-film activated sludge (IFAS).

Conventional integrated biological treatment (IBT) systems use a fixed biofilm reactor (first stage) in series with a suspended growth biological reactor (second stage). The fixed biofilm reactor typically consists of a biological tower, and the suspended growth reactor is typically an aeration basin or small contact channel. This combination results in a two-stage coupled unit process that has unique design parameters with treatment efficiency capabilities that often exceed those of the individual parent systems. The IFAS system combines both fixed film and suspended growth in the same reactor tank.

Designers have used integrated processes widely, especially to compensate for system weaknesses. For example, fixed biofilm processes are known for their shockload resistance, volumetric efficiency, low energy requirements, and low maintenance requirements. On the other hand, suspended growth biological treatment process is known for producing high-quality effluent and operating under various treatment modes to achieve different effluent quality objectives. Another advantage is the role of fixed biofilm as a biological selector to improve activated sludge settling characteristics.

By combining these two processes, designers have taken advantage of the individual parent (single-stage) processes. Plant upgrades in which a trickling filter or an activated sludge process was added typically result in an IBT system, although many new plants have used combined systems (Parker and Richards, 1994).

The fixed biofilm primarily removes soluble 5-day biochemical oxygen demand (BOD_5). The activated sludge (suspended growth) process can provide a variety of functions, including flocculation to improve clarification, removal of residual soluble BOD_5, nitrification, denitrification, and phosphorus removal to meet advanced wastewater treatment requirements.

Although each process can be designed individually, they must be viewed as a combined system and developed accordingly. Removal of biodegradable organic matter drives design of the fixed biofilm. Suspended growth, however, is designed according to the amount of biodegradable organic matter removed in the fixed biofilm process and establishment of conditions necessary for flocculation. A certain degree of flocculation will take place in the fixed biofilm; the suspended growth process must be sized to achieve the remaining flocculation.

Typically, higher organic loads on the fixed biofilm mean that higher organic stabilization and flocculation will need to take place.

Chapter 15 of *Design of Municipal Wastewater Treatment Plants* (WEF et al., 2009) does not repeat design guidance for individual treatment processes already described, that is, attached-growth (biofilm) treatment and suspended growth biological treatment. Highlighted in this section are special descriptions, sizes, or design considerations that depart from the individual or parent processes described elsewhere in *Design of Municipal Wastewater Treatment Plants* (WEF et al., 2009).

Suggested reading material for additional information includes the following:

- *Design of Municipal Wastewater Treatment Plants* (WEF et al., 2009) (Chapter 15, "Integrated Biological Treatment");

- *Nutrient Removal* (WEF, 2010b) (Chapter 6);

- *Biofilm Reactors* (WEF, 2010a) (Chapters 6 and 11);

- *Wastewater Engineering: Treatment and Reuse* (Metcalf and Eddy, 2003) (Chapter 9, "Attached Growth and Combined Biological Treatment Processes"); and

- *Wastewater Treatment Plant Design* (Vesilind [Ed.], 2003) (Chapters 7 and 18).

2.0 OVERVIEW OF INTEGRATED BIOLOGICAL TREATMENT SYSTEMS

Many combinations of treatment process trains are possible, depending on the type of parent process used, loading to the treatment units, and the point at which biological or recycle solids are reintroduced to the main flow stream. Figure 7.1 outlines the process of four conventional IBT systems.

2.1 Trickling Filter Solids Contact

The trickling filter solids contact (TF/SC) process uses a trickling filter that has low to moderate organic loads followed by a small, aerated solids-contact tank or channel with secondary clarifiers that polish the trickling filter effluent through flocculation and additional organics removal. By combining the trickling filter with a solids-contact tank or channel, the trickling filter reactor size is smaller than required when used alone. The magnitude of the size reduction will depend on specific application and effluent requirements.

Conventional TF/SC does not include return solids reaeration before the solids contact tank or channel, although reaerating the return sludge before the

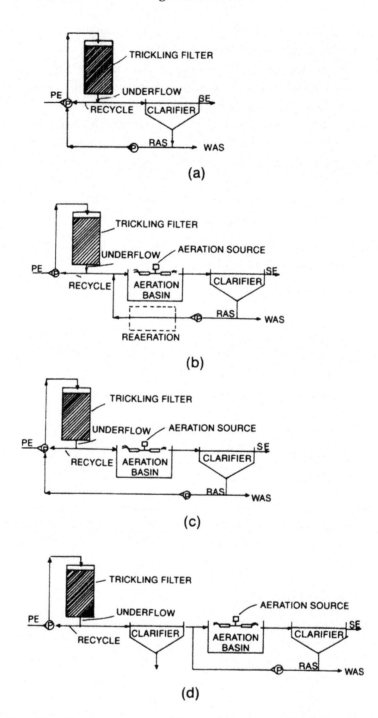

FIGURE 7.1   Combined process operations—(a) activated biofilter, (b) trickling filter–solids contact and roughing filter–activated sludge, (c) biofilter–activated sludge, and (d) trickling filter–activated sludge (PE = primary effluent, SE = secondary effluent, RAS = return activated sludge, and WAS = waste activated sludge) (WEF et al., 2009).

solids-contact tank can enhance bioflocculation and may allow for a smaller tank or channel to be used. When both solids reaeration and solids contact are used, the acronym "TF/SCR" is used.

2.2   Roughing Filter Activated Sludge

A common method of upgrading existing activated sludge plants is to install a roughing filter ahead of the activated sludge process. As shown in Figure 7.1, both the TF/SC and roughing filter activated sludge (RF/AS) processes have the same process flow schematic. However, with RF/AS, a much smaller trickling filter is used so that the suspended growth biological reactor must be larger to provide a significant amount of oxygen for soluble BOD_5 removal and biomass stabilization. This differs from the TF/SC process in which the trickling filter is larger and provides almost all of the soluble BOD_5 removal, thus allowing the solids contact channel or tank to be smaller and provide enhanced solids floccu-lation and effluent clarity. Because some of the soluble BOD_5 is left to be metab-olized in the activated sludge tank, filament growth is typically sufficient with the RF/AS process and results in a more stable floc.

2.3   Activated Biofilter

Figure 7.1 illustrates the activated biofilter (ABF) process schematic. The ABF uses a biofilm reactor to treat low to moderate organic loads; a final clarifier immediately follows, with no suspended growth biological reactor in between.

Unlike conventional trickling filter operation, return sludge is incorporated with the primary effluent and recycled over the biofilm media. Thus, suspended growth contact is achieved as return sludge, and primary effluent is mixed and passed through the biofilm reactor. Improved solids settleability typically occurs with the ABF process.

2.4   Biofilter Activated Sludge

The biofilter activated sludge (BF/AS) process is similar to that of the RF/AS except that the return activated sludge (RAS) is recycled over the biofilm reactor as it is in the ABF process. Also, similar to RF/AS, the BF/AS process is designed for high organic loads. With the BF/AS process, incorporating RAS recycle over the biofilm reactor has sometimes reduced bulking from filamentous bacteria, especially with food processing wastes.

2.5   Trickling Filter Activated Sludge

The trickling filter activated sludge (TF/AS) process is designed for high organic loads similar to those of RF/AS or BF/AS. A unique feature of TF/AS, however, is that an intermediate clarifier is provided between the biofilm and suspended growth biological reactor. The intermediate clarifier removes sloughed solids from the fixed-film reactor underflow before the fixed-film effluent enters the suspended growth reactor, reducing the effects these solids may have on the suspended growth dynamics. Because an intermediate clarifier is used, the TF/AS process is not a directly coupled system. The TF/AS schematic is illustrated in Figure 7.1.

A benefit of the TF/AS integrated process is that solids generated from carbonaceous BOD_5 removal in the trickling filter can be removed before second-stage activated sludge treatment. This is often a preferred mode where ammonia removal is required. The second stage of the process is designed to be dominated by nitrifying microorganisms. The clarification step can reduce required nitrifying aeration volume, which is a significant advantage for larger plants or plants processing higher strength wastewater.

2.6   Integrated Fixed-Film Activated Sludge

The IFAS process takes the integrated processes further by combining attached and suspended growth environments into one bioreactor system. Because of the uniqueness of the IFAS configuration and design, it is discussed in greater detail in Chapter 15, Section 4.0 of *Design of Municipal Wastewater Treatment Plants* (WEF et al., 2009).

3.0   DESIGN OF CONVENTIONAL INTEGRATED BIOLOGICAL TREATMENT SYSTEMS

Design considerations for conventional integrated processes are similar to those for the parent processes. The designer should review appropriate parent processes and special design considerations for integration.

The design of integrated biological processes is a balance between two biological treatment reactors; neither the biofilm nor the suspended growth process can be sized separately. Good design includes consideration of the total integrated facility, including interactions among all units, especially the secondary clarifier. Table 7.1 details some of the appropriate design criteria for these conventional IBT systems.

4.0   DESIGN OF INTEGRATED FIXED-FILM ACTIVATED SLUDGE SYSTEMS

4.1   Introduction

Integrated fixed-film activated sludge plants can be designed by adding biofilm support media (biofilm carrier particles) to activated sludge basins. The IFAS plant can use three categories of biofilm: fixed bed, plastic carrier moving media, and sponge-type media.

TABLE 7.1   General design criteria for IBT processes (IBT = integrated biological treatment) (WEF et al., 2009).

System	Appropriate design criteria	
	Range	Commonly used
Activated biofilter		
Media type	High rate	High rate
Five-day biochemical oxygen demand loading, kg/m^3·d (lb/d/1000 cu ft)	0.2–1.2 (12–75)	0.5 (30)
Hydraulic loading, L/m^2·s (gpm/sq ft)	0.5–3.4 (0.8–5.0)	1.4 (2.0)
Filter mixed liquor suspended solids, mg/L	1 500–3 000	2 000
Trickling filter/solids contact		
Media type	Rock or high rate	High rate
Five-day biochemical oxygen demand loading, kg/m^3·d (lb/d/1000 cu ft)	0.3–1.6 (20–100)	0.8 (50)
Hydraulic loading, L/m^3·s (gpm/sq ft)	0.1–1.4 (0.1–2.0)	0.7 (1.0)
Channel mixed-liquor suspended solids, mg/L	1 500–3 000	2 000
Hydraulic retention time, hour	0.2–1.0	0.75
Solids retention time, day	0–2	1.0
Return activated sludge, mg/L	6 000–12 000	8 000
Diffused air, L/m^3·s (scfm/1000 gal)	250–500 (2 000–4 000)	370 (3 000)
Mechanical, W/m^3 (hp/mil. gal)	12–26 (60–130)	20 (100)
Roughing filter, trickling filter, or biofilter with activated sludge		
Media type	High rate	High rate
Five-day biochemical oxygen demand loading, kg/m^3·d (lb/d/1000 cu ft)	1.2–4.8 (75–300)	2.4 (150)
Hydraulic loading, L/m^2·s (gpm/sq ft)	0.5–3.4 (0.8–5.0)	0.7 (1.0)
Basin mixed liquor suspended solids, mg/L	1 500–4 000	2 500
Hydraulic retention time, hour	0.5–4.0	2.0
Solids retention time, days	1.0–7.0	3.0
Food/mass, mg/kg·s (lb/d/lb)	5.8–13.9 (0.5–1.2)	10.4 (0.9)
Total available oxygen, g/kg (lb/lb)	600–1 200 (0.6–1.2)	900 (0.9)
Oxygen typically used, g/kg (lb/lb)	300–900 (0.3–0.9)	600 (0.6)

The principle of the IFAS system is to enhance biochemical oxygen demand (BOD) and nitrogen removal above the removal that could have been achieved using mixed liquor suspended solids (MLSS) in a suspended growth-only reactor of like volume. The interaction and exchange between the biofilm and the mixed liquor increases the design complexity relative to activated sludge and moving bed biofilm reactors (MBBRs).

4.2   Parameters Influencing Organics Removal in the Biofilm of Integrated Fixed-Film Activated Sludge Systems

Biofilm flux rate is the rate of transport of a particular substrate or electron acceptor across the liquid-biofilm interface. Typical units of flux are in grams of substrate removed per square meter of biofilm surface per day or kilograms per 1000 square meters per day. Table 7.2 shows the biofilm specific surface areas and typical fill fractions applied in IFAS systems for secondary treatment.

4.3   Parameters Influencing Removals in the Mixed Liquor Suspended Solids

As with activated sludge systems, removal of chemical oxygen demand (COD) per unit of tank volume in the IFAS system increases with increases in mixed liquor volatile suspended solids (MLVSS), concentrations of substrate (biodegradable soluble COD), and dissolved oxygen (or oxidized-nitrogen) in the mixed liquor. For the same tank volume, an increase in the mixed liquor solids retention time (SRT) increases the concentration of MLVSS. This, in turn, increases the COD uptake rate, expressed in kilograms per cubic meters per day, in the MLVSS, which reduces the quantity of COD that has to be removed by the biofilm. The result is a decrease in the biofilm surface area required.

4.4   Empirical Design Methods

There are three methods for designing IFAS systems that are based on empirical data. These are (1) the equivalent sludge age approach, (2) the measured rate per quantity of media approach, and (3) using kinetic rates from a pilot study. The

TABLE 7.2   Biofilm specific surface area for various types of media (HRT = hydraulic residence time) (WEF et al., 2009).

Type of system	Media	Media fill volume percentage*	Biofilm specific surface area (m^2/m^3)	Recommended MLSS (mg/L)	Minimum aerobic HRT (h) at 12 °C
Activated sludge	None	0	0	3000	7
IFAS, fixed bed	Bioweb, Accuweb	70–80	50–100	3000	5
IFAS, sponge MBBR	Linpor, Captor	20–40	100–150	2500	4
IFAS, plastic carrier MBBR	K1 (Kaldnes), Entex, ActiveCell (Hydroxy)	20–65	150–300[2]	3500	4

*External volume of frame for cord-type fixed-bed media; external volume of cuboids or cylinders with biofilm for moving bed media. Note that fill volume fraction is not the fraction of liquid volume in the activated sludge tank displaced by the media.

equivalent sludge age method calculates the quantity of biomass fixed to the media, which is then added to the quantity in the mixed liquor. An equivalent SRT is calculated by dividing the total biomass (in the biofilm and mixed liquor) by the daily wasting rate. In the second approach, suppliers use kinetic rates per quantity of media they have measured from other plants and pilot studies that used the same media.

4.5   Process Kinetics Design Method (Biofilm Rate Model)

The following approach may be used for preliminary sizing. It is based on rates observed in full-scale and pilot studies and in calibrated process models.

4.5.1   Define Range of Flux Rates

Primary effluent (reactor influent) with a COD/total Kjehldahl nitrogen (TKN) ratio of 7.5:1 to 15:1 can use the following rates at a mixed liquor temperature of 15 °C and an aerobic zone dissolved oxygen of 3 mg/L:

- Aerobic COD uptake—0.5 to 5 kg/1000 m^2·d and
- Nitrification—0.05 to 0.5 kg/1000 m^2·d.

To adjust rates for temperature, an Arrhenius adjustment coefficient of 5% for each 1 °C change in temperature can be used. The breadth of these ranges is indicative of the applicability of this system to accommodate a wide range of conditions.

The actual value of flux rate for the media location and application is discussed in the following section.

4.5.2   Quantify Removal

Recommended fraction of removals in mixed liquor and biofilm to quantify the biofilm surface area required in IFAS systems are based on analysis performed with process kinetics models. These removals are at 15 °C. The recommended fraction of removals is as follows:

- At 2-day MLSS SRT, 50% of COD and 80% of nitrification is on the biofilm; the rest is in the MLVSS;
- At 4-day MLSS SRT, 25% of COD and 50% of nitrification is on the biofilm; and
- At 8-day MLSS SRT, 20% of nitrification is on the biofilm.

The aforementioned MLSS SRTs may be increased by 3% for a 1 °C increase in temperature.

The surface area of biofilm required is the higher of the two needed for COD removal and nitrification. The rates based on BOD typically would be half the rates based on COD.

4.5.3   Select Flux Rates Based on Location along Aerobic Zone

It is recommended that the aerobic zone be divided into thirds as follows:

- Apply rates of 75, 50, and 25% of the maximum rate for COD uptake for the first third, second third, and third third of the aerobic zone, respectively, and

- Apply rates of 25, 50, and 75% of the maximum rates for ammonium-nitrogen uptake for the first third, second third, and third third of the aerobic zone, respectively, when targeting and effluent ammonium-nitrogen of 1 mg/L.

Nitrification rates in the middle and last third of the aerobic zone should be decreased in proportion to ammonium-nitrogen concentration in the mixed liquor when the effluent quality required is less than 1 mg/L. For example, at an effluent ammonium-nitrogen of 0.5 mg/L, the rate applied in the last third should be $0.75 \times 0.5/1.0 = 0.375$ of the rate above 1 mg/L.

4.5.4   Additional Analysis To Finalize a Design

It is recommended that designers use one of the software models discussed in Chapter 10 of *Nutrient Removal* (WEF, 2010b) or Chapter 11 of *Biofilm Reactors* (WEF, 2010a).

5.0   REFERENCES

Metcalf and Eddy, Inc. (2003) *Wastewater Engineering: Treatment and Reuse,* 4th ed.; McGraw-Hill: New York.

Parker, D. S.; Richards, J. T. (1994) Discussion of: Process and Kinetic Analysis of Nitrification in Coupled Trickling Filter/Activated Sludge Processes. *Water Environ. Res.,* **65,** 750.

Vesilind, P. A., Ed. (2003) *Wastewater Treatment Plant Design*; Water Environment Federation: Alexandria, Virginia.

Water Environment Federation (2010a) *Biofilm Reactors*; WEF Manual of Practice No. 35; McGraw-Hill: New York.

Water Environment Federation (2010b) *Nutrient Removal*; WEF Manual of Practice No. 34; McGraw-Hill: New York.

Water Environment Federation; American Society of Civil Engineers; Environmental & Water Resources Institute (2009) *Design of Municipal Wastewater Treatment Plants,* 5th ed.; WEF Manual of Practice No. 8; ASCE Manuals and Reports on Engineering Practice No. 76; McGraw-Hill: New York.

Chapter 8

Physical and Chemical Processes for Advanced Wastewater Treatment

1.0 INTRODUCTION

This chapter describes technologies and processes that can be applied to treat secondary effluent from biological treatment to achieve certain quality requirements for water discharge, reuse, recycle, or other advanced treatment purposes.

This chapter presents design information for unit processes that provide effluent polishing, nutrient removal, or removal of toxic constituents. The six unit processes discussed are filtration, adsorption, chemical treatment, membrane processes, air stripping, and breakpoint chlorination. Effluent reoxygenation is briefly discussed.

Table 16.1 of *Design of Municipal Wastewater Treatment Plants* (WEF et al., 2009) summarizes comments for each of the aforementioned criteria relevant to each add-on process. Treatability studies to screen candidate processes typically are necessary; pilot studies to verify performance of proprietary systems are advisable.

Suggested reading material for additional information includes the following:

- *Design of Municipal Wastewater Treatment Plants* (WEF et al., 2009) (Chapter 16, "Physical and Chemical Processes for Advanced Wastewater Treatment");

- *Wastewater Engineering: Treatment and Reuse* (Metcalf and Eddy, 2003) (Chapter 6, "Chemical Unit Processes", and Chapter 11, "Advanced Wastewater Treatment");

- *Wastewater Treatment Plants: Planning, Design and Operation* (Qasim, 1999) (Chapter 12, Section 5 "Enhanced Sedimentation", and Chapter 24, Section 3, "Overview of Advanced Wastewater Treatment Technology");

- *Wastewater Treatment Plant Design* (Vesilind [Ed.], 2003) (Chapter 10, "Physical–Chemical Processes");

- *Water and Wastewater Engineering: Design Principles and Practice* (Davis, 2010) (Chapters 6 through 13, 21, 25, and 26);

- *Nutrient Control Design Manual* (U.S. EPA, 2009); and

- *Biological Nutrient Removal (BNR) Operation in Wastewater Treatment Plants* (WEF et al., 2005).

2.0   SECONDARY EFFLUENT FILTRATION

In advanced wastewater treatment, filtration is used to remove the residual total suspended solids (TSS) in secondary effluent. In addition to TSS removal, filtration is used to remove particulate carbonaceous 5-day biochemical oxygen demand and deposits produced by alum, iron, or lime precipitation of phosphates in secondary effluent. The main secondary effluent filtration technologies are depth filtration (involving use of granular or synthetic compressible medium), disk filtration, and membrane filtration. Membrane filtration will be described in a subsequent section. The reader is referred to Section 11.4 of *Wastewater Engineering Treatment and Reuse* (Metcalf and Eddy, 2003) for a detailed discussion of available filtration technologies.

2.1   Depth Filtration

Granular media filters may be classified according to direction of flow, type, and number of media composing the bed, driving force, and method of flow control.

Downflow systems are the most common filtration processes for municipal applications. Dual-media and multimedia bed filters may be a combination of garnet, sand, and anthracite, each of which has different characteristics that may be desirable for certain influent loadings. Table 16.3 in *Design of Municipal Wastewater Treatment Plants* (WEF et al., 2009) presents typical characteristics of some granular filter media. The driving force for filtration may be either gravity or applied pressure though pumping. Constant pressure, constant rate, and variable declining rate are three basic methods of flow control.

Filtration rates vary significantly between different types of filtration technologies. Table 8.1 highlights peak-hour filtration rates, adapted from *Design of Municipal Wastewater Treatment Plants* (WEF et al., 2009) and *Wastewater Engineering Treatment and Reuse* (Metcalf and Eddy, 2003). The range of values indicated spans from average day to peak hour flows. It is important to note state code may govern the maximum filtration rate.

The filter media is backwashed with filter effluent water and, depending on the influent characteristics, the system may incorporate an air scour feature. Backwashing requirements will vary based on the filtration method and solids loading rate. Care should be taken to ensure the backwash flow does not affect other unit processes. Table 16.4 of *Design of Municipal Wastewater Treatment Plants* (WEF et al., 2009) presents a design example for a depth filter involving the use of granular medium. Table 8.2 illustrates design velocities and flow volumes.

2.2 Compressible Medium Filtration

The compressible medium filtration (CMF), also known as the *Fuzzy Filter,* is a semicontinuous operation depth filter. It is unique because it uses a synthetic compressible medium instead of granular medium. As the name implies, the unit can operate at variable compression ratios to adjust filtration performance.

The CMF is able to operate at high filtration rates (e.g., 800 to 1600 L/m²·min [20 to 40 gpm/sq ft]) because of reduced headloss development resulting from

TABLE 8.1 Typical filtration rates for various depth filtration technologies.

Type of filter	Filtration rate	
	L/m²·min	gpm/sq ft
Slow sand	1 to 2	0.02 to 0.05
Rapid sand (shallow bed)	80 to 240	2 to 6
High-rate granular	200 to 250	5 to 6
High-rate granular with chemical	300	7.5
Dual media or multimedia	240 to 320	6 to 8
Pressure	410	10

TABLE 8.2   Design velocities and flow volumes (WEF et al., 2009).

Flow description	Velocity		Maximum flow per unit of filter area	
	m/s	ft/s	m/h	gpm/sq ft
Influent	0.3 to 1.2	1 to 4	7.3 to 19.6	3 to 8
Effluent	0.9 to 1.8	3 to 6	7.3 to 19.6	3 to 8
Wash water supply	1.5 to 3.0	5 to 10	36.7 to 61.1	15 to 25
Wash water drain	0.9 to 2.4	3 to 8	36.7 to 61.1	15 to 25
Filter to waste	1.8 to 3.7	6 to 12	2.4 to 14.7	1 to 6

high porosity of the medium. This higher rate of filtration drastically reduces the process footprint. Removal performance can be increased approximately 50 to 70% with chemical addition. Chemical type, dose, and addition duration should be selected carefully to prevent medium blinding. The typical terminal headloss value for the CMF is between 1 and 3 m (3 and 10 ft).

2.3   Disc Filtration

The disc filter involves use of surface mechanisms in which filtration occurs primarily on the surface of the media compared to depth filtration mechanisms discussed previously. Several proprietary disc filters now exist for secondary effluent filtration with different configurations and media. The typical technologies have either inside-out or outside-in flow patterns and offer various media types such as metal mesh, cloth mesh, and thick-pile cloth. The design engineer should review the available technologies because design and operational and filtration characteristics vary between techniques. The main advantage of disc filtration is the reduced space requirement. Headloss may be less for disc filtration; however, it is dependent on the nominal pore size of the media.

The fully submerged disc filter is a continuous operation filter and is one of the most common configurations for secondary effluent filtration. The media are typically made of a woven nylon, which may act similar to depth filtration. For submerged disc applications, accumulated particles are removed from the cloth membrane surface by the liquid suction applied to each side of the disc.

Like fully submerged discs, filtration is continuous in partially submerged disc filters. The main differences between the two are medium type, flow direction, and submergence. Some common partially submerged disc filter technologies involve use of a cloth medium made from woven polyester cloth with insignificant thickness. Commonly, a mesh material with a pore size of 10 μm is used.

Most disc filters can be operated up to 240 to 280 L/m²·min (6 to 7 gpm/sq ft), with typical maximum design filtration rates between 240 to 260 L/m²·min

(6 and 6.5 gpm/sq ft). The disc filters backwash more frequently because of the low head operational characteristics and low terminal headloss design values.

Several recent variations of disc filters have emerged in the wastewater treatment industry. One emerging disc filter uses woven stainless steel as the filtering medium instead of cloth material. The steel medium disc filter is a continuous operation filter like other disc filters. Secondary effluent is introduced in the middle of the discs. Filter discs retain the solids while the filtered water flows to the outside of the discs into the collection well. As filtration continues, particulates accumulate on the surface of the stainless steel medium, increasing headloss. Typical maximum design filtration rates can reach 500 $L/m^2{\cdot}min$ (12.0 gpm/sq ft).

3.0   ACTIVATED CARBON ADSORPTION

Use of activated carbon in wastewater treatment systems is a proven process for removal of soluble refractory organic compounds. Activated carbon can be used in two forms: granular activated carbon (GAC) and powdered activated carbon. The most common method currently used is GAC in column vessels.

There are three types of activated carbon available for treatment; these are coconut shell, coal, and lignite. Table 16.7 of *Design of Municipal Wastewater Treatment Plants* (WEF et al., 2009) lists characteristics of commercially available carbon media. The treated wastewater is percolated through the column until the entire depth of the media is saturated with organic material. The spent carbon media may be replaced or regenerated. Table 8.3 lists typical carbon dosages for various column wastewater influents. Common design parameters include average and design flow, influent characteristics, effluent quality, contact time, and adsorption capacity of carbon.

TABLE 8.3   Typical carbon dosages for various column wastewater influents (WEF et al., 2009).

Prior treatment	Typical carbon dosage required/mil. gal column throughput*	
	g/m^3	lb/mil gal
Coagulated, settled, and filtered activated sludge effluent	24 to 48	200 to 400
Filtered secondary effluent	48 to 72	400 to 600
Coagulated, settled, and filtered raw wastewater (physical–chemical)	72 to 216	600 to 1800

*Loss of carbon during each regeneration cycle is typically 5 to 10%. Makeup carbon is based on carbon dosage and the quality of the regenerated carbon.

4.0 CHEMICAL TREATMENT

Chemicals are used for a variety of municipal treatment applications, including enhancing flocculation and sedimentation; conditioning solids; adding nutrients; neutralizing acid base; precipitating phosphorus; and disinfecting or controlling odors, algae, or activated sludge bulking. This section describes chemicals used for advanced treatment processes. For chemicals used for conventional processes and biological treatment, the reader is referred to Chapter 9 of *Design of Municipal Wastewater Treatment Plants* (WEF et al., 2009). Discussion of chemical treatment in this chapter will, therefore, be limited to phosphorus precipitation and neutralization.

4.1 Phosphorus Precipitation

When considering removal of phosphorus from wastewater, the form and solubility of phosphorus are important. Phosphorus enters a treatment plant in the following three forms: orthophosphate, polyphosphate, and organic phosphates. The coagulant (alum, ferric chloride, ferrous sulfate, ferric sulfate, lime, etc.), is mixed rapidly and flocculated prior to settling. These chemicals react with the soluble portion of phosphorus compounds to create a precipitate. These insoluble phosphorus compounds typically do not release phosphorus in other units of the treatment plant or in the receiving waterbody.

As illustrated in Figure 8.1, for aluminum and iron salts, phosphorus removal efficiency varies directly with chemical dosage up to the point where mole requirements (molecular weight in grams of any particular compound)

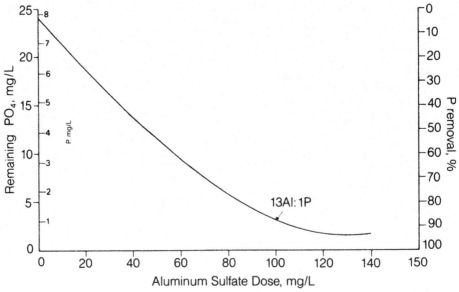

FIGURE 8.1 Typical phosphorus reduction with alum (WEF et al., 2009).

for phosphate precipitation and side reactions have been satisfied. These side reactions may significantly increase chemical requirements. Optimum dosages cannot be calculated readily because of ambiguity of the side reactions involved. As a result, laboratory jar tests may be used to determine actual chemical requirements. See the references at the end of this chapter for additional information on required dosages. Typically, a residual phosphorus concentration of 0.1 to 0.2 mg/L may be achieved with granular-medium filtration. However, as noted in Figure 8.1, significantly higher chemical dosages are required to achieve effluent phosphorus concentrations below 1.0 mg/L. The reader is referred to Example 6.2 in *Wastewater Engineering Treatment and Reuse* (Metcalf and Eddy, 2003) for a design example for determination of alum dosage for phosphorus removal.

Both ferric and ferrous iron compounds may be used in the chemical precipitation of phosphorus. Although both types of compounds produce equivalent results, ferric chloride is used more often. The stoichiometric reactions for alum and ferric chloride are shown in the following equations:

$$Al_2(SO_4)_3 (14 \, H_2O) + 2 \, H_2PO_4^2 + 4 \, HCO_3^2 \rightarrow 2 \, AlPO_4 + 4 \, CO_2 + 3 \, SO_4^2 + 18 \, H_2O \tag{8.1}$$

Equation 8.1 indicates that an alum-to-phosphorus mole ratio of 0.87:1 is required. This corresponds to an alum-to-phosphorus weight ratio of 9.6:1.

$$FeCl_3 (6 \, H_2O) + H_2PO_4^2 + 2 \, HCO_3^2 \rightarrow FePO_4 + 3 \, Cl^2 + 2 \, CO_2 + 8 \, H_2O \tag{8.2}$$

Equation 8.2 indicates that an iron-to-phosphorus mole ratio of 1:1 is required. This corresponds to an iron-to-phosphorus weight ratio of 1.8:1.

These reactions precipitate as a metal–phosphate; however, additional metal salt addition will precipitate as a metal–hydroxide. The metal–hydroxide floc also provides supplemental phosphorus removal mechanisms.

Metal salt addition uses alkalinity to form these reactions. Alkalinity reductions should be an important design consideration for low alkalinity waters or nitrified effluent.

Addition of chemicals to the process will increase solids production. Depending on the chemical dose, addition of metals upstream of the primary clarifier results in a primary sludge mass increase of 50 to 100% because of phosphate and hydroxide precipitates and improved suspended solids removal. However, because of a reduced loading to the biological system, a 60 to 70% increase is typical across the entire plant. For metal addition to secondary processes, waste mixed liquor solids mass may increase by 35 to 45% and the overall plant solids mass increase may be 5 to 25%. Alum addition may further increase solids volume because settled solids concentration in clarifiers may decrease by as much as 20%. The reader is referred to Example 6.1 in *Wastewater*

Engineering Treatment and Reuse (Metcalf and Eddy, 2003) for a design example for estimation of chemical sludge production. Tertiary phosphorus removal may also be performed using the ballasted flocculation process.

4.2   pH Adjustment

Removal of excess acidity or alkalinity by chemical addition to provide a final pH of approximately 7 is called *neutralization.* Most effluents must be neutralized to a pH of 6 to 9 before discharge. There are three critical components of any pH control system: (1) mixing intensity or turnover time in the reactor, (2) response time of the control system, and (3) the ability of the chemical metering system to match process requirements

Other factors that complicate the design of pH control systems include the amount of buffering capacity in wastewater, the change in mass flowrate of the hydrogen ion, and variations in wastewater flowrate or temperature. In processes where tight pH control is required, cascade control offers significant improvements in process control and reliability.

Adjusting the pH of or neutralizing an acidic process waste stream by adding an alkaline reagent requires development of a titration. From the titration curve, the acidity values as milligrams per liter of calcium carbonate may be determined for any desired pH level.

Many acceptable methods may be used to neutralize or adjust over-acidity in a raw waste or process waste stream. The most common method involves adding the proper amounts of concentrated caustic soda (NaOH), soda ash (Na_2CO_3), or magnesium hydroxide $Mg(OH)_2$ to low pH wastewater. Chemical characteristics are available from chemical distributors and are summarized in Table 6.15 of *Wastewater Engineering Treatment and Reuse* (Metcalf and Eddy, 2003). Calcium and magnesium oxides are considerably less expensive than sodium alkalies and are more widely used. Many of these neutralization chemicals require precautions in handling to avoid contact burns. Design of chemical handling and storage facilities should be chemical-specific to avoid corrosive and moisture-related concerns.

In some instances, downward adjustment of the pH of a wastewater stream is necessary. The pH may be decreased by adding carbon dioxide (recombination) or acid. Sulfuric acid is the most widely used. The hazardous and corrosive nature of concentrated acids demands special handling, maintenance, and safety considerations.

4.3   Rapid Mixing

Rapid mixing provides a brief contact area with high-intensity mixing to facilitate distribution of chemical amongst a flow stream. The most common type of mixing device for wastewater treatment is the rotating impeller mixer. Typically, only turbine and propeller mixers are used for rapid mixing applications. To avoid vortexing with impeller mixers, it is important to consider placing the mixer off-center, installing vertical baffles, or manipulating inlet and outlet locations.

Mixing may also be accomplished by several other devices, including pump discharge piping, baffled channels, hydraulic jump mixers, pneumatic mixing by the injection of compressed air, and inline static mixing devices.

The following formula has been developed for determining the power requirements of an impeller mixer to maintain turbulent hydraulic conditions:

$$P = r \, K_T \, n^3 D^5 / g_c \tag{8.3}$$

Where

P = power requirement, N/m·s or Watt (ft/lbf·sec);
r = mass density of the fluid, 1000 kg/m^3 (62.4 lb/cu ft) for water;
n = impeller revolutions per second, s^{-1};
D = diameter of the impeller, m (ft);
g_c = gravitational acceleration factor, $\dfrac{19.79 \, \text{m/kg}}{N \cdot s^2} \dfrac{32.17 \, \text{ft/lb}_m}{\text{sec}^2 \cdot \text{lb}_f}$; and
K_T = constant.

The mean temporal velocity gradient, G (s^{-1}), describes the degree of mixing of the system. As G increases, the degree of mixing increases. In domestic wastewater treatment, values of G typically range from 300 to 1500 s^{-1} for rapid mixing.

4.4   Chemical Feed Systems

Feeding systems are necessary for the addition of reagents in the form of solid, liquid, or gas to the waste stream at a controlled rate. Table 16.13 in *Design of Municipal Wastewater Treatment Plants* (WEF et al., 2009) provides generalized chemical feed system details. Chemical feeder control may be manual, automatically proportioned to flow, dependent on some form of process feedback, or a combination of any of these.

A dry feed installation consists essentially of a hopper, a feeder, and a dissolver tank. All three units are sized based on waste volume, treatment rate, and an optimum length of time for chemical feeding and dissolving. The best applications of dry feed systems have high treatment rates, more stable chemicals, and more fluid materials. Less fluid materials, such as powdered or granular material, may arch or bridge in a hopper; the hopper needs vibration for continuous flow.

Liquid feed systems are best applied for chemical treatment with lower treatment rates, less stable chemicals, chemicals that are better fed as liquids to avoid handling of dusty or more dangerous chemicals, or materials available only as liquids. Liquid feed units include piston, positive-displacement diaphragm, and balanced diaphragm pumps and liquid gravity feeders. The unit best suited for a particular application depends on feed pressure, chemical corrosiveness, treatment rate, accuracy desired, viscosity and specific gravity of the fluid, other liquid properties, and type of control.

Types of chemical feeders are described in Table 8.4.

TABLE 8.4   Types of chemical feeders (WEF et al., 2009).

		Equipment limitations		
Feeder type	Use	General	Capacity, m^3/h^a	Feed rate range[b]
Dry feeder				
Volumetric				
Oscillating plate	Any material, granules or powder		0.001–3.1	40–1
Oscillating throat	Any material, any particle size		0.002–9.0	40–1
(universal)	Most materials, including NaF,	Use disk	0.001–0.09	20–1
Rotating disk	granules or powder	unloader for arching		
Rotating cylinder (star)	Any material, granules or powder		0.7–180	10–1 or
			0.65–27.0	100–1
Screw	Dry, free-flowing material, powder or granular		0.005–1.7	20–1
Ribbon	Dry, free-flowing material, powder, granular, or lumps		0.000 2–0.015	10–1
Belt	Dry, free-flowing material up to 40 mm (1.5 in.) in diameter, powder or granular		0.009–270	10–1
Gravimetric				
Continuous-belt and scale	Dry, free-flowing, granular material or floodable material	Use hopper agitator to maintain constant density	0.002–0.18	100–1
Loss in weight	Most materials—powder, granular, or lumps		0.002–7.2	100–1
Solution feeder				
Nonpositive displacement				
Decanter (lowering pipe)	Most solutions, light slurries		0.009–0.9	100–1
Orifice	Most solutions	No slurries	0.015–0.45	10–1
Rotameter (calibrated valve)	Clear solutions	No slurries	0.000 5–0.015	
			0.000 2–0.018	10–1
Loss in weight (tank with control valve)	Most solutions	No slurries	0.000 2–0.018	30–1
Positive displacement				
Rotating dipper	Most solutions or slurries		0.009–2.7	100–1
Proportioning pump				
Diaphragm	Most solutions (special unit for 5% slurries)[c]		0.000 4–0.014	100–1
Piston	Most solutions, light slurries		0.000 1–15.3	20–1

[a]Volumetric feed capacities are given because chemical specific gravities must be known to specify mass feed capacity.
[b]Ranges apply to purchased equipment. Overall feed ranges can be extended more.
[c]Use special heads and valves for slurries.

5.0 MEMBRANE PROCESSES

Membrane processes can be pressure- or vacuum-driven or can depend on electrical potential gradients, concentration gradients, or other driving forces. Four main membrane categories, classified by the size of the separated particles or materials, are commercially used presently and can be expressed in microns and/or Daltons molecular weight cutoff, highlighted in Figure 8.2.

The first two membrane processes listed in Table 8.5, microfiltration and ultrafiltration membranes, are low-pressure membranes (LPM) and are commonly available as flat-sheet, tubular, or hollow-fiber modules; the last two, nanofiltration and reverse osmosis, are high-pressure membranes (HPM) and are provided as spiral-wound modules. While LPMs are designed to remove suspended and colloidal matter from water, HPM is designed to remove dissolved constituents. Table 8.5 compares the relative pressures required for typical installations of membrane processes. For reuse applications, systems may incorporate a LPM followed by a HPM to obtain high-quality effluent. Another membrane process, electrodialysis, uses electricity as opposed to hydraulic pressure to force water through the membrane. Full-scale use of electrodialysis for wastewater applications is limited and will not be covered in this handbook. This chapter does not describe the membrane bioreactor (MBR) process in-depth; Chapter 14 of *Design of Municipal Wastewater Treatment Plants* (WEF et al., 2009), however, provides more details on the MBR process.

Any membrane process is a separation process. Feedwater is separated into two streams: product water (permeate) and reject water (brine, concentrate). The

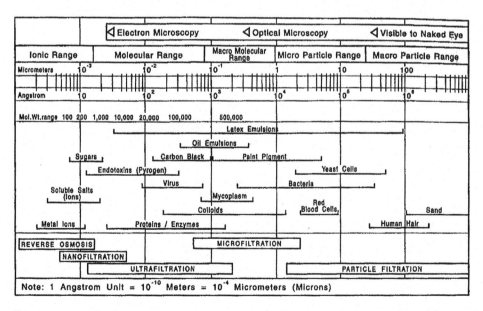

FIGURE 8.2   Membrane size comparison with wastewater constituents.

TABLE 8.5 Comparison of membrane processes (WEF et al., 2009).

Process	Materials removed	Applications	Transmembrane pressures kPa (psi)
Microfiltration	Suspended solids and large colloids	Removal of bacteria, flocculated materials, and TSS	69–173 (10–25)
Ultrafiltration	Colloids, proteins, microbiological contaminants, and large organic molecules	Virus removal, removal of colloids and some organic molecules	
Nanofiltration	Organic molecules with weights greater than 200 to 400, some TDS[a] reduction	Removal of color, TOC,[b] hardness, radon, and TDS reduction	345–1 550 (50–225)
Reverse osmosis	Dissolved salts, inorganic molecules, organic molecules with molecular weights greater than 100	Desalination, wastewater reuse, food and beverage processing, industrial process water	1 379–6 895 (200–1 000)

[a]TDS = total dissolved solids.
[b]TOC = total organic carbon.

permeate flow compared to the feed flow expressed as a percent reflects the system recovery. As an example, when a system fed by 22.7 m^3/h (100 gpm) permeate produces 17 m^3/h (75 gal) of permeate, the system recovery is 75%.

In addition to significant process differences, LPM may require minimal pretreatment or no pretreatment at all for several applications compared to HPM, which does not tolerate suspended and colloidal solids, and their properties are significantly degraded even when short spikes of suspended solids and/or colloids occur. To increase the efficiency and life of a membrane process, effective pretreatment of feedwater for nanofiltration and reverse osmosis is required. Selection of proper pretreatment minimizes fouling, scaling, and membrane degradation. This leads to optimization of product quality, salt rejection, product recovery, and operating costs.

The membrane industry has adopted the following four categories for membrane fouling:

(1) Inorganic scale—control with antiscalant, system recovery;
(2) Particulate fouling—minimize feedwater turbidity and silt density index;
(3) Organic fouling—minimize feedwater dissolved organics; and
(4) Biofouling—control with flux, shock chlorination.

Fouling refers to the entrapment of particulates such as iron floc or silt; *scaling* refers to the precipitation and deposition within the system of sparingly soluble salts such as calcium sulfate ($CaSO_4$) and barium sulfate ($BaSO_4$). Table 8.6 provides a matrix of pretreatment techniques for the various fouling compounds. The majority of membrane fouling is reversible, such as inorganic scale through the use of acid-cleaning cycles. However, some fouling is irreversible and, despite thorough cleaning cycles, the membranes may not exhibit declining flux rates over time. This declining capacity must be accounted for when sizing units for future flow conditions. Disposal of wastewater brine presents significant engineering and economic problems.

Table 16.16 of *Design of Municipal Wastewater Treatment Plants* (WEF et al., 2009) provides a design example for secondary effluent membrane filtration. A reverse osmosis design example can be found in Chapter 24, Section 3, of *Wastewater Treatment Plants: Planning, Design and Operation* (Qasim, 1999).

6.0   AIR STRIPPING FOR AMMONIA REMOVAL

Under properly controlled conditions, air stripping can remove ammonia-nitrogen (NH_4-N) from wastewater because ammonia (NH_3) exists predominantly in the un-ionized, gaseous form at high pH levels. No ammonia stripping facilities are known to be routinely in use in the United States. Critical elements to consider in designing an ammonia stripping tower include selection of tower packing, air-to-water flowrate, hydraulic loading rate, air and liquid temperatures, and process control measures.

7.0   AMMONIA REMOVAL BY BREAKPOINT CHLORINATION

Oxidation by chlorine can remove ammonia from wastewater. This process, known as *breakpoint chlorination,* is practical only as an effluent polishing technique, not for removing high levels of influent nitrogen. Discussed in detail in *Design of Municipal Wastewater Treatment Plants* (WEF et al., 2009), breakpoint occurs when the ammonia is reduced to zero and free chlorine residual is established. The reader is referred to Chapter 11 of this handbook for further information.

8.0   EFFLUENT REOXYGENATION

Reoxygenation of treated wastewater effluent is often necessary if permit limits dictate minimum dissolved oxygen concentrations. Two principal categories of reoxygenation systems are cascade reoxygenation and mechanical or diffused air reoxygenation. To ensure adequate dissolved oxygen is provided at the discharge, reoxygenation typically is the last step in the treatment process.

TABLE 8.6 Summary of pretreatment alternatives for reverse osmosis membrane process (WEF et al., 2009).

Pretreatment	CaCO$_3$	CaSO$_4$	BaSO$_4$	SrSO$_4$	CaF$_2$	SiO$_2$	SDI	Fe	Al	Bacteria	Oxid. agents	Org. matter
Acid addition	●[a]							○[b]				
Scale inhibitor	○	●	●	●	●							
Softening with IX[c]	●	●	●	●	●							
Dealkalization with IX	○	○	○	○	○	○						
Lime softening	○	○	○	○	○	○	○	○				○
Preventive cleaning	○	○	○	○	○	○	○	○	○	○		○
Adjustment of operation parameter						●						
Media filtration						○	○	○	○			
Oxidation–filtration								●				
In-line coagulation							○	○	○			
Coagulation–flocculation						○	●	○				●
Micro-/ultrafiltration						●	●	○	○	○		●
Cartridge filter						○	○	○	○	○		
Chlorination										●		
Dechlorination											●	
Shock treatment										○		
Preventive disinfection										○		
GAC[d] filtration										○	●	●

● = very effective.

[a]

[b]○ = possible.

[c]IX = ion exchange.

[d]GAC = granular activated carbon.

Cascade aerators are simple and are common where sufficient hydraulic head is available. Equations 16.9 through 16.15 of *Design of Municipal Wastewater Treatment Plants* (WEF et al., 2009) estimate aeration rates for cascade aerators. At locations where hydraulic head is not available or cascade systems are not applicable, mechanical reoxygenation systems may be required. These techniques encompass a wide range of mechanically assisted reoxygenation systems; those most commonly installed are mechanical surface aeration and diffused air systems.

The following two references offer useful descriptions of various reoxygenation systems that are available: *Process Design Manual for Upgrading Existing Wastewater Treatment Plants* (U.S. EPA, 1971) and *Design of Municipal Wastewater Treatment Plants* (WEF et al, 2009). Both references contain calculation methods for estimating operational variables for cascade reoxygenation systems.

9.0 REFERENCES

Davis, M. (2010) *Water and Wastewater Engineering: Design Principles and Practice*; McGraw-Hill: New York.

Metcalf and Eddy, Inc. (2003) *Wastewater Engineering: Treatment and Reuse*, 4th ed.; McGraw-Hill: New York.

Qasim, S. (1999) *Wastewater Treatment Plants: Planning, Design and Operation*, 2nd ed.; CRC Press: Boca Raton, Florida.

U.S. Environmental Protection Agency (2009) *Nutrient Control Design Manual*; EPA-600/R-09-12; U.S. Environmental Protection Agency: Washington, D.C.

U.S. Environmental Protection Agency (1971) *Process Design Manual for Upgrading Existing Wastewater Treatment Plants*; Technology Transfer, Program No. 17090 GNQ, Contract No. 14-12-933; U.S. Environmental Protection Agency: Washington, D.C.

Vesilind, P. A., Ed. (2003) *Wastewater Treatment Plant Design*; Water Environment Federation: Alexandria, Virginia.

Water Environment Federation; American Society of Civil Engineers; Environmental & Water Resources Institute (2009) *Design of Municipal Wastewater Treatment Plants*, 5th ed.; WEF Manual of Practice No. 8; ASCE Manuals and Reports on Engineering Practice No. 76; McGraw-Hill: New York.

Water Environment Federation; American Society of Civil Engineers; Environmental and Water Resources Institute (2005) *Biological Nutrient Removal (BNR) Operation in Wastewater Treatment Plants*; Manual of Practice No. 29; ASCE/EWRI Manuals and Reports on Engineering Practice No. 109; McGraw-Hill: New York.

Chapter 9

Sidestream Treatment

1.0 INTRODUCTION

Sidestreams are flows containing nutrients, solids, and organic or inorganic constituents that are generated within a wastewater treatment plant, typically during biosolids processing. Common sidestreams include overflow from gravity thickeners, filtrate from belt filter presses or gravity belt thickeners, centrate from centrifuges, or scrubber water from incinerators. This chapter focuses on nutrient-rich sidestreams that are generated during dewatering of digested biosolids. A conceptual schematic of a mainstream treatment plant, including its biosolids processing and sidestreams, is shown in Figure 9.1.

Sidestreams, particularly those returned intermittently, can have a large effect on all treatment processes. The biological nutrient removal process can be easily overloaded by centrate (or filtrate). The potential effects of sidestreams on nitrification, denitrification, and phosphorus removal are summarized in Table 9.1.

The sidestream resulting from anaerobic digestion and dewatering will contain higher concentrations of ammonia, total suspended solids (TSS), particulate biochemical oxygen demand (BOD), alkalinity, and phosphorus than typical wastewater, varying as a function of the type of digestion and upstream solids processing and liquid stream processes. Nutrient concentrations will be elevated under one or more of the following conditions: (1) the liquid stream uses biological phosphorus removal, (2) a waste activated sludge pretreatment method is

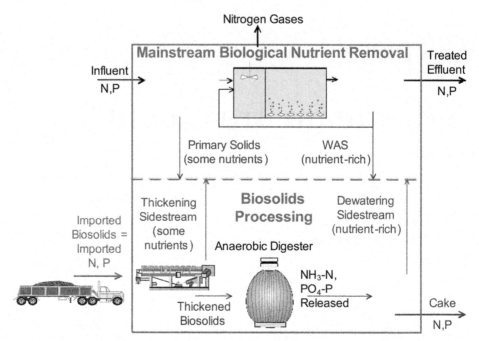

FIGURE 9.1   Conceptual mass balance and sidestream sources for a typical wastewater treatment plant (WAS = waste activated sludge) (WEF et al., 2009).

used to enhance digestion, and (3) advanced anaerobic digestion technology is used to enhance volatile solids destruction.

Sidestream characteristics that could be observed for various liquid and solids treatment scenarios are presented in Table 9.2.

Sidestream flow equalization is often the easiest and most cost-effective way to manage sidestreams. Although equalization does not necessarily break the nutrient cycle, it enables operators to manage the additional loads by returning sidestreams in a controlled manner. Equalization can be accomplished either operationally with a continuous dewatering schedule (24 hours per day, seven days per week), or through design by incorporating a flow equalization basin where the sidestream is stored and returned gradually for facilities with inter-mittent dewatering operations.

Suggested reading material for additional information includes

- *Design of Municipal Wastewater Treatment Plants* (WEF et al., 2009) (Chapter 17, "Sidestream Treatment");

- *Wastewater Engineering: Treatment and Reuse* (Metcalf and Eddy, 2003) (Tables 14.49 and 14.50); and

- *Solids Process Design and Management* (WEF et al., 2012) (Chapter 22, "Sidestreams from Solids Treatment Processes").

TABLE 9.1 Checklist for mainstream treatment of sidestreams (WEF et al., 2009).

Mainstream process	Sidestream affects on design and operation
Nitrification	☐ Ammonia loads (from anaerobic digestion) increases aeration requirements, which affects blower design and operation
	☐ Ammonia loads affect diffuser system design
	☐ Ammonia loads affect alkalinity requirements, though sidestreams from post-anaerobic digestion typically contain alkalinity concentrations that are 2 to 3 times the ammonia concentration
	☐ Effluent ammonia spikes may occur, which could adversely affect effluent quality
Denitrification	☐ Nitrate loads (from aerobic digestion) affect denitrification; additional carbon or anoxic zone retention time may be required to achieve target effluent nitrogen levels
	☐ Additional denitrification results in a net oxygen credit that affects the blowers and diffuser systems
	☐ Additional denitrification results in a net alkalinity credit that affects chemical feed and storage facilities
Biological phosphorus removal	☐ Additional phosphorus loads affect the size of anaerobic zones
	☐ Additional phosphorus loads increases the amount of volatile fatty acids or readily biodegradable chemical oxygen demand required for biological phosphorus removal, which may result in the need for carbon supplementation (acetic acid directly or construction of a fermenter) to achieve effluent target phosphorus concentrations
	☐ Sidestream nitrate loads (from aerobic digestion) must not be recycled to anaerobic zones
Chemical phosphorus removal	☐ Additional phosphorus loads increases chemical demands
	☐ Adding more chemicals for phosphorus removal consumes additional alkalinity, which may affect nitrification
	☐ Adding more chemicals for phosphorus removal produces more chemical sludge, which increases solids loading rates on clarifiers and biosolids processing units

TABLE 9.2   Sludge processing sidestream characteristics (U.S. EPA, 1987).

Source	BOD$_5$, mg/L	TSS, mg/L	Ammonia, mg NH$_3$-N/L	Orthophosphorus, mg P/L
Thickening				
Gravity thickening supernatant	100–1 200	200–2 500	1–30	1–5 (higher if bio P)
Dissolved air flotation subnatant	50–1 200	100–2 500	1–30	1–5
Centrifuge centrate	170–3 000	500–3 000	1–30	1–5
Stabilization				
Aerobic digestion decant	100–2 000	100–10 000	1–50	2–200
Anaerobic digestion supernatant	100–2 000	100–10 000	300–2 000 (higher end for retreated/ advanced processes)	50–200
Incineration scrubber water	30–80	600–10 000	10–50	1–5
Dewatering				
Belt filter press filtrate	50–500	100–2 000	1–1 500	2–200
Centrifuge centrate	100–2 000	200–20 000	1–1 500	2–200
Sludge drying beds underdrain	20–500	20–500	1–1 500	2–200

2.0   SIDESTREAM NITROGEN AND PHOSPHORUS REMOVAL

Sidestream treatment facilities can be small activated sludge systems with or without chemical addition or more advanced proprietary systems. Sidestream treatment processes can be grouped into the following three categories:

- Bioaugmentation processes produce nitrifying bacteria that are subsequently seeded to the mainstream liquid train to support nitrification in the main treatment plant;

- Nonbioaugmentation processes focus on reduction of nitrogen from the high-concentration recycle streams and do not provide a bioaugmentation benefit; and

- Physiochemical processes use chemical addition and physical separation to remove nutrients from the sidestream.

Table 9.3 provides a summary of nutrient removal sidestream treatment processes by category.

For a design example of a sidestream treatment system, the reader is referred to Chapter 17, Section 4.0, of *Design of Municipal Wastewater Treatment Plants* (WEF et al., 2009).

TABLE 9.3 Sidestream treatment processes (BPR = biological phosphorus removal).

Type of sidestream treatment	Process	Advantages	Disadvantages	Reference
Bioaugmentation processes				
Nitration and nitrification	Oxidation of ammonia to nitrite with partial nitrification	Reduced aeration energy by 33% vs. nitrification Reduced chemical demand vs nitrification	Historical problems with process stability (improving)	Chapter 17, Section 3.1 (WEF et al., 2009)
Nonbioaugmentation processes				
Nitration/denitration (including SHARON® and STRASS processes)	Oxidizing ammonia to nitrite then reducing nitrite to nitrogen gas	Produces alkalinity Reduced carbon demand vs denitrification Can achieve 85 to 98% ammonia removal	Supplementation carbon is required Critical control of temperature, aeration, dissolved oxygen, and pH	Chapter 17, Section 3.2 (WEF et al., 2009) Table 8.21 (Metcalf and Eddy, 2003)
Nitration/anammox (deammonification)	Anammox bacteria convert some ammonia to nitrite. Microbes use the remaining ammonia to reduce the nitrite to nitrogen gas.	Reduced aeration energy by 70% vs nitrification Supplemental carbon is not required Reduced aeration (energy savings)	Long acclimation period for anaerobic ammonia oxidizers Critical control of aeration based on pH	Chapter 17, Section 3.2.5 (WEF et al., 2009)
Physiochemical processes				
Ammonia stripping and recovery	Removes ammonia from solution at high temperatures using steam or hot air	Maintain high pH (maintain NH3 rather than NH41) Regular acid washing	High energy, scaling, ammonia emissions require regulations	Chapter 17, Section 3.3.1 (WEF et al., 2009)

(continues on next page)

TABLE 9.3 Sidestream treatment processes (BPR = biological phosphorus removal) (*Continued*).

Type of sidestream treatment	Process	Advantages	Disadvantages	Reference
Chemical precipitation of phosphorus	Phosphate precipitate removed following precipitation	High degree of removal per added metal salt	Effects to BPR processes Higher operation and maintenance costs (chemicals and increased sludge production)	Chapter 17, Section 3.3.2 (WEF et al., 2009)
Struvite precipitation (phosphorus and ammonia)	Controls struvite formation in a fluidized bed or batch reactors	75 to 95% removal of phosphorus 10 to 50% removal of ammonia	Magnesium-limited process	Chapter 17, Section 3.3.3 (WEF et al., 2009)
Calcium phosphate precipitation for phosphorus removal	$Ca_3(PO_4)_2$ crystals are precipitated on fine sand seed crystals in an upflow fluidized bed reactor	No mixing and flocculation required	High energy demand	Chapter 17, Section 3.3.4 (WEF et al., 2009)

3.0 REFERENCES

Metcalf and Eddy, Inc. (2003) *Wastewater Engineering: Treatment and Reuse*, 4th ed.; McGraw-Hill: New York.

U.S. Environmental Protection Agency (1987) Sidestreams in Wastewater Treatment Plants; EPA Design Information Report. *J. Water Pollut. Control. Fed.*, **59**, 54–59.

Water Environment Federation; American Society of Civil Engineers; Environmental & Water Resources Institute (2009) *Design of Municipal Wastewater Treatment Plants*, 5th ed.; WEF Manual of Practice No. 8; ASCE Manuals and Reports on Engineering Practice No. 76; McGraw-Hill: New York.

Water Environment Federation; U.S. Environmental Protection Agency; Water Environment Research Foundation (2012) *Solids Process Design and Management*; McGraw-Hill: New York.

4.0 SUGGESTED READINGS

Qasim, S. (1999) *Wastewater Treatment Plants: Planning, Design and Operation*; CRC Press: Boca Raton, Florida.

Vesilind, P. A., Ed. (2003) *Wastewater Treatment Plant Design*; Water Environment Federation: Alexandria, Virginia.

Chapter 10

Natural Systems

1.0 INTRODUCTION

Natural systems for wastewater treatment include soil absorption, ponds, land treatment, floating aquatic plants, and constructed wetlands. Where sufficient land of suitable character is available, these natural systems can be a cost-effective option for both construction and operation.

The common element in the use of natural systems for wastewater treatment is the significant contribution made by the "natural" environmental components that provide the desired treatment. Typically, these responses by the vegetation, soil, microorganisms (terrestrial and aquatic), and, to a limited extent, higher animal life proceed at their "natural" rates. Design examples and/or procedures are included in this chapter for each system discussed.

Suggested reading material for additional information includes the following:

- *Treatment Wetlands* (Kadlec and Wallace, 2009);

- *Small-Scale Constructed Wetland Treatment Systems—Feasibility, Design Criteria, and O&M Requirements* (Wallace and Knight, 2006);

- *Design of Municipal Wastewater Treatment Plants* (WEF et al., 2009) (Chapter 18, "Natural Systems");

- *Principles of Design and Operations of Wastewater Treatment Pond Systems for Plant Operators, Engineers, and Managers* (U.S. EPA, 2011); and

- *Wastewater Treatment Plant Design* (Vesilind [Ed.], 2003) (Chapter 9, "Alternative Biological Treatment").

2.0   SOIL ABSORPTION SYSTEMS

These systems typically are limited to wastewater flows of approximately 190 m^3/d (0.05 mgd) or less and are described in Table 10.1.

3.0   POND SYSTEMS

The second most prevalent natural system is the wastewater treatment pond. Wastewater treatment ponds can be classified based on their depth and the biological reactions that occur in the pond. Using this classification, the four main types of ponds are described in Table 10.2.

4.0   LAND TREATMENT SYSTEMS

Land treatment is the controlled application of wastewater to land at rates compatible with the natural physical, chemical, and biological processes that occur

TABLE 10.1   Soil absorption systems.

Type of natural treatment	Description	References
Pretreatment (septic)	Typically used to provide primary treatment to remove solids, oil, and grease Additional treatment consisting of anything from a simple outlet screen to a packaged advanced treatment system can be part of pretreatment before soil absorption	Chapter 18, Section 2 (WEF et al., 2009) Chapter 9 (Vesilind [Ed.], 2003)
Typical absorption systems	Series of gravel-filled trenches preceded by a septic tank in which applied wastewater will infiltrate and then percolate through the soil profile	Chapter 18, Section 2 (WEF et al., 2009)
Alternative systems	Used where conventional leach lines cannot function adequately because of adverse site conditions Includes mound systems, at-grade systems, sand-lined beds and fill systems, and evapotranspiration beds. See Table 18.2 in *Design of Municipal Wastewater Treatment Plants* for applicability of each system.	Chapter 18, Section 2, Table 18.2 (WEF et al., 2009) Chapter 9 (Vesilind [Ed.], 2003)
Drip application	Drip tubing is used after pretreatment filtration to apply low loading rates of wastewater at shallow depths for wastewater dispersal in a soil absorption system.	Chapter 18, Section 2 (WEF et al., 2009)

TABLE 10.2   Types of pond systems.

Type of pond system	Description	Typical depth	Typical detention time	References
Aerobic	Relatively shallow ponds mixed by recirculation to maintain dissolved oxygen throughout Typically limited to warm, sunny climates	0.3 to 0.6 m (1 to 2 ft)		Chapter 18, Section 3 (WEF et al., 2009) Chapter 9 (Vesilind [Ed.], 2003)
Facultative	The most prevalent pond type, also referred to as *oxidation ponds;* growth of emergent plants is limited Surface layers of the ponds are aerobic with an anaerobic layer near the bottom Oxygen supplied by surface aeration and photosynthetic algae	1.5 to 2.5 m (5 to 8 ft)	25 to more than 180 days	Chapter 18, Section 3 (see 3.1 for performance and design criteria) (WEF et al., 2009) Chapter 8, Section 8 (Metcalf and Eddy, 2003) Chapter 9 (Vesilind [Ed.], 2003)
Aerated	Can be either partially or completely mixed Oxygen is supplied by mechanical floating aerators or diffused aeration	3 to 6 m (10 to 20 ft)	5 to 30 days	Chapter 18, Section 3 (see 3.1 for performance and design criteria) (WEF et al., 2009) Chapter 8, Section 8 (Metcalf and Eddy, 2003) Chapter 9 (Vesilind [Ed.], 2003)
Anaerobic	Heavily loaded with organics and do not have an aerobic zone Biological activity is typically low when compared to that of a mixed anaerobic digester	2.5 to 6 m (8 to 20 ft)	20 to 50 days	Chapter 18, Section 3 (WEF et al., 2009) Chapter 9 (Vesilind [Ed.], 2003)

on and in the soil. The three types of land treatment systems are described in Table 10.3.

5.0   FLOATING AQUATIC PLANT SYSTEMS

Floating aquatic plants have been used for wastewater treatment in several processes, including upgrading facultative pond effluent. Water hyacinths and duckweed are the most studied and used floating plants, although water hyacinths are a non-native species and may be regulated. Advantages and disadvantages and design criteria for the two are described in Section 5.3 of *Design of Municipal Wastewater Treatment Plants* (WEF et al., 2009).

TABLE 10.3   Types of land treatment systems.

Type of land treatment system	Description	Typical loading rates	Design factors	Expected performance	References
Slow rate	Treatment by percolation through the soil surface runoff typically contained onsite, although rainfall-induced runoff typically allowed to leave site	1 to 2 m/a (3 to 7 ft/yr)	Soil permeability or allowable loading rate for a particular constituent	Refer to Table 18.11 (WEF et al., 2009)	Chapter 18, Section 4 (WEF et al., 2009) Chapter 9 (Vesilind [Ed.], 2003)
Overland flow	Treatment occurs in a thin film on grassy slopes constructed on slowly permeable soil Similar to fixed-film biological treatment systems Significant amount of biochemical oxygen demand, suspended solids, and nitrogen removed Phosphorus, trace elements, and pathogens not removed as well	3 to 20 m/a (10 to 70 ft/yr)	Application rate, slope length, slope grade, application period (refer to Table 18.16 [WEF et al., 2009])	Refer to Table 18.15 (WEF et al., 2009)	Chapter 18, Section 4 (WEF et al., 2009) Chapter 9 (Vesilind [Ed.], 2003
Rapid infiltration	Also known as soil aquifer treatment, wastewater Treated as it percolates through the soil Consists of shallow spreading basins in permeable soils to which wastewater is intermittently applied	15 to 30 m/a (50 to 100 ft/yr)	Nearby groundwater, soil infiltration rate, subsurface flowrate, or biochemical oxygen demand or nitrogen loading rate (refer to Table 18.17 [WEF et al., 2009])	Refer to Table 18.18 (WEF et al., 2009)	Chapter 18, Section 4 (WEF et al., 2009) Vesilind ([Ed.], 2003), Chapter 9

6.0   CONSTRUCTED WETLANDS

Constructed wetlands are designed to treat wastewater using emergent plants such as cattails, reeds, and rushes. There are three primary categories of constructed wetlands: free water surface (FWS); subsurface flow (SSF); and vertical flow. For FWS wetlands, the flow path of the applied wastewater is above the soil surface. For SSF wetlands, the flow runs lateral through the root zone and the media, which ranges from sand to coarse gravel to rocks. For vertical-flow wetlands, the application is either by spray or surface flooding, and the flow path is down through the media and out through the underdrains. Performance and land requirements are further discussed in Section 18.6 of *Design of Municipal Wastewater Treatment Plants* (WEF et al., 2009).

7.0   REFERENCES

Kadlec, R. H.; Wallace, S. D. (2009) *Treatment Wetlands*, 2nd ed.; Taylor and Francis Group: Boca Raton, Florida.

Metcalf and Eddy, Inc. (2003) *Wastewater Engineering: Treatment and Reuse*, 4th ed.; McGraw-Hill: New York.

U.S. Environmental Protection Agency (2011) *Principles of Design and Operations of Wastewater Treatment Pond Systems for Plant Operators, Engineers, and Managers*; EPA-600/R-11-088; U.S. Environmental Protection Agency: Washington, D.C.

Vesilind, P. A., Ed. (2003) *Wastewater Treatment Plant Design*; Water Environment Federation: Alexandria, Virginia.

Wallace, S. D.; Knight, R. L. (2006) *Small-Scale Constructed Wetland Treatment Systems—Feasibility, Design Criteria, and O&M Requirements*; Water Environment Research Foundation: Alexandria, Virginia.

Water Environment Federation; American Society of Civil Engineers; Environmental & Water Resources Institute (2009) *Design of Municipal Wastewater Treatment Plants*, 5th ed.; WEF Manual of Practice No. 8; ASCE Manuals and Reports on Engineering Practice No. 76; McGraw-Hill: New York.

Chapter 11

Disinfection

1.0 INTRODUCTION

Disinfection is the most critical component of wastewater treatment for the protection of public health. Improperly disinfected water and wastewater have been responsible for major disease outbreaks in both the developing and developed worlds. With increasing water reuse resulting from the depletion of water resources, proper disinfection has become even more vital.

Waterborne diseases arise from the contamination of water by any of dozens of potential pathogens including pathogenic viruses, bacteria, or protozoa. A key concept in disinfection design is the concept of the indicator organism or target pathogen, an organism whose concentration serves as a conservative indicator of the presence of other pathogens and thus the success of disinfection or relative safety of the water. Fecal coliform have been used extensively as an indicator organism, although other parameters may be used as an indicator.

Wastewater effluent disinfection can be accomplished through a variety of chemical and physical methods. Common chemicals used for disinfection include chlorine, sodium hypochlorite, calcium hypochlorite, chlorine dioxide, ozone, and hydrogen peroxide. Physical methods include UV radiation, pasteurization, and membrane separation. Principal among these are treatment with chlorine-based chemicals and UV irradiation. Ultimate selection of a disinfection process will depend on several economic and noneconomic factors. Table 11.1 provides a comparison of important disinfectant parameters. For more

TABLE 11.1 Comparison of important properties for common disinfectants.

Characteristic	Chlorine	Sodium hypochlorite	Calcium hypochlorite	Chlorine dioxide	Ozone	Ultraviolet radiation	Hydrogen peroxide
Chemical formula	Cl_2	NaOCl	$Ca(OCl)_2$	ClO_2	O_3	N/A	H_2O_2
Form	Liquid, gas	Solution	Powder, pellets, or 1% solution	Gas	On-site generation	Light	Liquid
Commercial strength, percent	100	12 to 15	70	Up to 0.35	2		35 to 70
Availability/cost	Low cost	Moderately low cost	Moderately low cost	Moderately low cost	Moderately high cost	Moderately high cost	High cost
Deodorizing ability	High	Moderate	Moderate	High	High	N/A*	High
Noncorrosive and nonstaining	Highly corrosive	Corrosive	Corrosive	Highly corrosive	Highly corrosive	N/A	Low
Toxicity	Highly toxic to higher life forms	Toxic	Toxic	Toxic	Toxic	Toxic	Moderately toxic
Safety concern	High	Moderate	Moderate	High	Moderate	Low	Moderate
Stability	Stable	Slightly unstable	Relatively stable	Unstable, must be generated as used	Unstable, must be generated as used	N/A	Stable

*Not applicable.

information, the reader is referred to Table 12.3 of *Wastewater Engineering Treatment and Reuse* (Metcalf and Eddy, 2003) and Table 14.2 of *Wastewater Treatment Plants Planning Design and Operation* (Qasim, 1999).

Suggested reading material for additional information includes the following:

- *Design of Municipal Wastewater Treatment Plants* (WEF et al., 2009) (Chapter 19, "Disinfection");

- *Wastewater Engineering: Treatment and Reuse* (Metcalf and Eddy, 2003) (Chapter 12, "Disinfection Processes");

- *Wastewater Treatment Plants: Planning, Design and Operation* (Qasim, 1999) (Chapter 14, "Disinfection");

- *Wastewater Treatment Plant Design* (Vesilind [Ed.], 2003) (Chapter 11, "Disinfection, Reoxygenation, and Odor Control");

- *Water and Wastewater Engineering: Design Principles and Practice* (Davis, 2010) (Chapter 13, "Disinfection and Fluouridation", and Chapter 25, "Secondary Settling, Disinfection, and Post-Aeration");

- Local and regional codes (i.e., Ten States Standards); and

- *White's Handbook of Chlorination and Alternative Disinfectants* (Black & Veatch, 2010).

Significant factors influencing the action of disinfectants include (1) contact time, (2) concentration of the disinfectant, (3) intensity and nature of physical agent or means, (4) temperature, (5) types of organisms, and (6) nature of suspending liquid. The effects of each of these factors should be considered for each disinfection process. Table 11.2 summarizes common disinfection equations to account for these factors.

2.0   CHLORINATION

Chlorine has been used as the primary disinfectant for wastewater effluents for many years. While the use of chlorine gas may be decreasing, chlorine, whether from bulk hypochlorite or from on-site generation systems, is still being used by a majority of wastewater systems in the United States.

Literature generally indicates that different doses should be used, depending on the type of secondary treatment. The use of literature values tends to result in a conservative design and may result in a large turndown at average flow conditions. Some state design codes are specific on design requirements for the use of chlorine on secondary effluents. These codes should be reviewed by the respective designers to ensure that specific requirements are included in the design of the system. Additional testing may be required to develop chlorine

TABLE 11.2　Equations used to express the rate of kill of microorganisms under different conditions.

Equation no.	Equation*	Description
(11.1)	$N_t/N_0 = 1/(1 + kt_d)$	Die-off in a natural body or treatment unit. The die-off coefficient for different situations (lakes, rivers, ponds, basins) may vary greatly.
(11.2)	$\ln N_t/N_0 = -kt$	The first-order model for die-off with time at a given concentration of disinfectant.
(11.3)	$\ln N_t/N_0 = -kt^m$	Rate of kill may decrease ($m < 1$) or increase ($m > 1$) with time.
(11.4)	$C^n t_p = \text{constant}$	Relationship for a given kill and disinfectant concentration: $n > 1$, contact time is more important than dosage. $n = 1$, the effect of contact time and dosage are about equal.
(11.5)	$C^t N_p = \text{constant}$	Relationship on the initial number of microorganisms and desired reduction level.
(11.6)	$k_T = k_{20}\,\beta^{(T-20)}$	Arrhenuis relationship for increasing kill at higher temperature.

*β = constant found experimentally, which depends on temperature; C = concentration of disinfectant, mg/L; k = die-off coefficient or rate constant; t^{-1}, k_{20}, and k_T are the values at 20 °C and at temperature T °C; m, n, and q = constants obtained experimentally; N_0, N_t = number of microorganisms present initially and at time t; N_p = number of microorganisms reduced by a given percentage kill; t_d = hydraulic detention time, d; and t_p = time required to achieve a constant percentage kill, e.g., $N_t/N_0 = 0.99$.

demand and improve efficiency. Testing has shown that literature values may be conservative, resulting in the use of more chemical than may be needed. Bench-scale tests can assist operations staff in optimizing the chemical-addition system. Typical chlorine dosages for various wastewater sources are summarized in Table 11.3.

There are several ways to control the feed rate of chlorine gas or hypochlorite solutions. These are manual control, automatic-flow proportioning or open-loop control, automatic residual or closed-loop control, or automatic compound-loop control, which combines flow and residual signals to vary the gas-feed rate. Flow proportioning is sometimes referred to as *feed-forward control*, and residual control is sometimes referred to as *feedback control*.

Rapid mixing at the point of chlorine injection is important and can improve disinfection effectiveness. The chlorine contact tank should be tested for obvious signs of short-circuiting, and tracer testing may be done to determine if adequate contact time is provided. *Municipal Wastewater Disinfection Design Manual* (U.S. EPA, 1986) provides some insight to analyzing residence time and distribution curves. Serpentine flow reactors are designed to approach plug-flow conditions, but may contain zones of backmixing (particularly at the entrance zone), short-

TABLE 11.3 Chlorine dosages for proper disinfection of wastewater effluents.

Type of wastewater	Dosage range (mg/L)
Untreated wastewater (prechlorination)	6 to 25
Primary sedimentation	5 to 20
Chemical precipitation	3 to 10
Trickling filter	3 to 10
Activated sludge	2 to 8
Multimedia filter following activated sludge plant	1 to 5
Membranes*	0

*Actual dose requirement for a membrane system depends on the effluent quality and regulatory agency.

circuiting, and dead zones. This type of configuration has been found to be most successful in terms of approaching a plug-flow condition when length-to-width ratios exceed 10:1. A length-to-width ratio of 40:1 or greater is preferred (Metcalf and Eddy, 2003).

Chlorine can be applied either as gaseous chlorine (elemental chlorine, Cl_2), a hypochlorite compound, or as chlorine dioxide. The chlorine present as both hypochlorous acid and hypochlorite ions is defined as free available chlorine or, simply, free chlorine. The percentage available for disinfection changes drastically with respect to pH levels and slightly with respect to temperature, as indicated in Figure 11.1.

In addition to killing pathogens, free chlorine will oxidize many other compounds in wastewater. Demand from competing reactions with inorganic and organic matter increases the dose requirements for a chlorine system. After secondary treatment, inorganic demand will be minimal except for non-nitrifying facilities that have significant ammonia in the effluent. When ammonia is present, facilities may either breakpoint chlorinate or form chloramines. Breakpoint chlorination is the process of using chlorine's oxidative capacity to oxidize ammonia; an approximately 10:1 mass ratio of chlorine to ammonia-nitrogen is required to obtain a strong, free chlorine residual. Facilities that knowingly or unknowingly nitrify most of their ammonia-nitrogen leave little or no ammonia present to form chloramines.

Organic matter exposed to chlorine disinfection has been linked to the formation of hazardous disinfection byproducts (DBPs). The rate of formation of DBPs is dependent on a number of factors including

- Presence of organic precursors,
- Free chloride concentration,
- Bromide concentration,

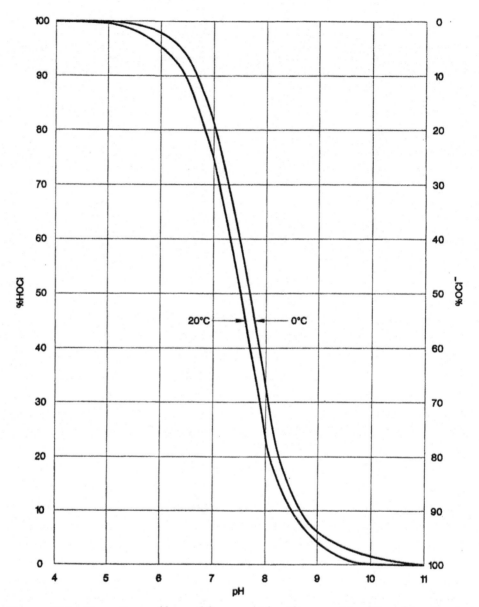

FIGURE 11.1   Percentage of hypochlorous acid with respect to pH and temperature (AWWA, 1973).

- pH, and
- Temperature.

Gaseous or liquid chlorine can be supplied in 45.4- to 68-kg (100- to 150-lb) cylinders, 907-kg (1-ton) containers, and in tank cars. Selection and size of chlorine containers depends on transportation and handling costs, available space, and quantities used. Chlorine storage and handling systems must be designed with full safety considerations because chlorine gas is poisonous and corrosive. The Chlorine Institute provides standards for chlorine-handling equipment and safety procedures. Because of safety requirements and concerns of gaseous chlorine, on-site hypochlorite generation systems are increasingly popular for wastewater disinfection.

3.0   DECHLORINATION

Dechlorination, which is defined as the removal of remaining chlorine, is required in most states to remove the toxic effects of chlorinated effluent. Sulfur dioxide is commonly used for dechlorination. Sulfur dioxide is classified as a nonflammable, corrosive, liquefied gas. In the gaseous state, sulfur dioxide is colorless with a suffocating, pungent odor and is approximately 2.25 times as heavy as air. Liquid sulfur dioxide is approximately 1.5 times as heavy as water. Storage and handling of sulfur dioxide are similar to that of chlorine. In solution, sulfur dioxide hydrolyzes to form a weak solution of sulfurous acid (H_2SO_3). The sulfite ion reacts rapidly with free and combined chlorine. Although the stoichiometric amount of sulfur dioxide required per part of chlorine is 0.9, the actual practice calls for 1:1.

Dechlorination can also be achieved with other compounds such as sodium thiosulfate, activated carbon, or without chemicals but long-term storage. Granular and powdered carbon applications can be combined with a gravity or pressure filter bed. This method is quite expensive, with limited applications where high levels of organic carbon removal are also required.

4.0   ULTRAVIOLET DISINFECTION

Chlorination has been the de facto choice for most wastewater disinfection operations since the early 1900s. Because of the safety and effluent toxicity problems associated with chlorination, UV radiation has become the most common alternative to chlorination for wastewater disinfection in North America. Consequently, the development and application of open-channel, modular systems has reduced the cost of UV disinfection. The costs of the two processes are comparable for new facilities.

The majority of UV disinfection systems currently use an open-channel, modular design. Two principal lamp geometries have been adopted: horizontal, uniform arrays with flow directed parallel to lamp axes, and vertical, staggered arrays with flow directed perpendicular to lamp axes. In-pipe systems also are available.

The main UV parameter is the lamp, and there are three different types of lamps. The characteristics for each of the types of lamps are provided in Table 11.4, which combines Table 12.25 of *Wastewater Engineering Treatment and Reuse*

TABLE 11.4   Typical operational characteristics for UV lamps.

		Type of lamp		
Item	Unit	Low-pressure low-intensity	Low-pressure high-intensity	Medium-pressure high-intensity
Power consumption	W	70 to 100	200 to 500	
	kW		1.2	2 to 5
Lamp current	mA	350 to 550	Variable	Variable
Lamp voltage	V	220	Variable	Variable
Efficiency	%	30 to 40	25 to 35	10 to 12
Lamp output at 254 nm	W	25 to 27	60 to 400	
Temperature	°C	35 to 45	90 to 150	600 to 800
Pressure	mm Hg	0.007	0.001 to 0.01	
Lamp length	m	0.75 to 1.5	Variable	Variable
Lamp diameter	mm	15 to 20	Variable	Variable
Lamp life	hrs	9000 to 13 000	12 000	5000

(Metcalf and Eddy, 2003) and information from *Design of Municipal Wastewater Treatment Plants* (WEF et al., 2009). In the majority of UV-disinfection applications, low-pressure mercury-arc lamps have monochromatic output at a wavelength of 253.7 nm to induce the photobiochemical change in microorganisms. When irradiated by UV light, dimerization of adjacent bases (especially thymine) on nucleic acid strands occurs, rendering the organism inable to reproduce.

Ultraviolet dose is defined as the product of intensity and exposure time provided to a pathogen. The following factors are known to affect the dose provided by UV reactors:

- Lamp intensity,

- Lamp age,

- Sleeve age and degree of fouling,

- UV transmittance of the wastewater, and

- System design.

System efficiency can be optimized by minimizing the effects of the previously listed factors. Electronic ballasts provide variable power input to modulate lamp output. By modulating output, lamps can be operated at less-than-maximum powers and at lower UV intensities. Control of lamp fouling is achieved by a variety of techniques, both manual and automatic. Automated chemical and/or mechanical cleaning can help remove most fouling materials;

however, periodic acid wash cleaning or replacement of the sleeves may still be required. To minimize short-circuiting, computational fluid dynamics modeling is increasingly an important tool for UV reactor design because it can overcome the limitations associated with physical prototyping, which may cause overdesign. The hydraulic behavior of a UV disinfection system is a critical element to ensuring adequate UV disinfection performance. Short-circuiting and variable water levels are two key issues that plague UV systems. Reactor water levels are typically controlled with flap gates or elongated weirs. Elongated weirs have the advantage of no mechanical components and also are potentially advantageous in systems with low overnight flows because they are less likely to allow channel draining than flap gate systems. System control varies from minimal to fully automatic. Fully automatic systems enable system control from a remote location, such as a central operations center. System controls typically provide, at a minimum, system power, system hours, and lamp status indicators. Fully automatic designs can integrate flow and wastewater conditions and pace the UV system by dimming lamps, shutting down banks, or taking channels out of service.

The best design guidance available currently is in *Ultraviolet Disinfection Guidelines for Drinking Water and Reuse* (NWRI and AwwaRF, 2003) and *Wastewater Engineering: Treatment and Reuse* (Metcalf and Eddy, 2003). The following UV system design checklist will help eliminate unforeseen problems during UV design:

(1) Effluent total suspended solids (typically must be less than 20 mg/L);
(2) Peak wet weather, peak dry weather, average design, and minimum initial flows;
(3) Treatment plant design criteria prepared by the regulatory agency;
(4) Specified contact time and corresponding flow condition (peak or average);
(5) Ultraviolet absorbance or transmittance of effluent to maintain the desired level of germicidal effect; color caused by industrial wastes can be serious. Consider floatables (scum, grease, mold, algae, etc.), which may be natural or caused by upstream maintenance;
(6) Equipment manufacturers and equipment selection guide;
(7) Information about existing facility if the plant is being expanded;
(8) Headloss constraints through the unit, as typical designs use close tolerances, approaching 0.63 cm (0.25 in.); additionally, the automatic level control gate requires a minimum of 0.4 m of headloss;
(9) Existing site plan with contours and location of the disinfection system;
(10) Influent and effluent seasonal coliform count for specific flows (annual average, maximum week, maximum month, peak dry weather, and peak wet weather);

(11)   Amount of redundancy required;

(12)   Attitude and capability of operations and maintenance staff toward cleaning the lamps and providing continued operation under adverse conditions; and

(13)   Likely future expansion of the plant and anticipated design challenges such as module size, number of banks, and number of channels.

A key design consideration is good access to the channels (or pipes) for ease of maintenance and especially lamp removal. There also should be adequate space for cleaning and chemical infrastructure, availability and location of the power supply, and provision of emergency power. Lifting devices should be provided to facilitate removal of lamps, modules, and banks. As with other disinfection systems, consideration should be made to limit exposure to UV light and electrical hazards. The reader is referred to Chapter 14, Section 12 of *Wastewater Treatment Plants: Planning, Design and Operation* (Qasim, 1999), for a UV disinfection design example.

5.0   OZONE DISINFECTION

Ozone is a much stronger oxidant (redox potential -2.07 V) than chlorine (redox potential -1.36 V) and is more effective in inactivating viruses and bacteria. Ozonation requires shorter contact times and, because ozone decomposes rapidly in water, there are no harmful residuals that need to be removed after treatment. Ozone is unstable in water; thus, it needs to be generated on-site, which can reduce the safety problems associated with shipping and handling. Ozonation elevates the dissolved oxygen concentration of the effluent. Apart from disinfection, ozone also is effective in reducing odor in wastewater.

Despite its numerous advantages, the capital and operating costs involved with ozone disinfection have made it less popular in the United States compared to chlorination and UV disinfection. Other factors, such as process complexity, operational expertise, toxicity of ozone, concern about bromate formation for waters containing high levels of bromide, and varying disinfection efficiency based on the composition matrix (suspended solids, biochemical oxygen demand, and chemical oxygen demand) have further impeded the use of ozone for wastewater disinfection.

Typical ozone system dosages are listed in Table 11.5 based on Table 12.13 of *Wastewater Engineering Treatment and Reuse* (Metcalf and Eddy, 2003). Various factors affect the dose; key parameters include temperature, pH, inorganic carbon, and organic carbon concentrations. Increasing the temperature will increase the ozone reaction rate in general based on the Arrhenius expression, but will decrease the solubility of ozone in the liquid phase. An increase in pH was found to increase the overall reaction rate of ozone with micropollutants in a deionized

TABLE 11.5   Ozone dosages for proper disinfection of wastewater effluents based on a 15-minute contact time.

Type of wastewater	Dosage range (mg/L)
Untreated wastewater (prechlorination)	15 to 40
Primary sedimentation	10 to 40
Trickling filter	4 to 10
Activated sludge	4 to 8
Multimedia filter following activated sludge plant	3 to 5
Membranes*	0

*Actual dose requirement for a membrane system depends on the effluent quality and regulatory agency.

water matrix. Increasing the inorganic carbon content of the wastewater will decrease the reaction rate. Because wastewater contains a large amount of organic carbon, the importance of its influence on the ozonation reaction needs to be taken into account. The exact role of organic carbon in promoting or inhibiting chain reactions is more complex than inorganic carbon.

The three important components of the ozonation process are the ozone generator, ozone contactor, and ozone-exhaust-gas destruction. Because of the hazardous effects of ozone, proper handling facilities and safety equipment should be provided. Ozone systems that use oxygen also present safety considerations. Oxygen is an oxidant and, therefore, supports the combustion of flammable materials.

6.0   OTHER DISINFECTION METHODS

The majority of disinfection systems in the United States use chlorination or UV disinfection. However, other technologies exist, often either as methods common in other parts of the world or as emerging techniques. These emerging technologies are being considered by designers for incorporation to wastewater treatment plants. Some of these technologies are taken directly from drinking water applications, some are new developments, and others are combinations of conventional physical or chemical unit processes. These emerging technologies are discussed in detail in the reference texts.

7.0   REFERENCES

American Water Works Association (1973) *Water Chlorination Principles and Practices*, M20; American Water Works Association: Denver, Colorado.

Black & Veatch Corporation (2010) *White's Handbook of Chlorination and Alternative Disinfectants*, 5th ed.; Wiley & Sons: Hoboken, New Jersey.

Davis, M. (2010) *Water and Wastewater Engineering: Design Principles and Practice*; McGraw-Hill: New York.

Metcalf and Eddy, Inc. (2003) *Wastewater Engineering: Treatment and Reuse*, 4th ed.; McGraw-Hill: New York.

National Water Research Institute; American Water Works Association Research Foundation (2003) *Ultraviolet Disinfection Guidelines for Drinking Water and Reuse*; U.S. Environmental Protection Agency: Washington, D.C.

Qasim, S. (1999) *Wastewater Treatment Plants: Planning, Design and Operation*, 2nd ed.; CRC Press: Boca Raton, Florida.

U.S. Environmental Protection Agency (1986) *Municipal Wastewater Disinfection Design Manual*; EPA-625/1-86-021; U.S. Environmental Protection Agency: Cincinnati, Ohio.

Vesilind, P. A., Ed. (2003) *Wastewater Treatment Plant Design*; Water Environment Federation: Alexandria, Virginia.

Water Environment Federation; American Society of Civil Engineers; Environmental & Water Resources Institute (2009) *Design of Municipal Wastewater Treatment Plants*, 5th ed.; WEF Manual of Practice No. 8; ASCE Manuals and Reports on Engineering Practice No. 76; McGraw-Hill: New York.

Chapter 12

Solids Management, Storage, and Transport

1.0 INTRODUCTION

Solids management is an important aspect of wastewater treatment design because of the interrelationships between the liquid and solids processes. *Design of Municipal Wastewater Treatment Plants* (WEF et al., 2009) covers the solids generated during sedimentation and/or biological and chemical treatment of raw wastewater. For information on minor residuals streams (e.g., scum, grit, and screenings) and their removal from wastewater, the reader is referred to the chapter on preliminary treatment in *Design of Municipal Wastewater Treatment Plants* (WEF et al., 2009). Sludge is any residual produced during primary, secondary, or advanced wastewater treatment that has not undergone any process to reduce pathogens or vector attraction. Biosolids is any sludge that has been stabilized to meet criteria in U.S. Environmental Protection Agency's (U.S. EPA's) 40 CFR 503 regulations and, therefore, can be beneficially used. *Solids* and *residuals* are terms used when it is uncertain whether the material meets Part 503 criteria. Land application is the process of adding bulk or bagged biosolids to soil at agronomic rates, which is the amount needed to provide enough nutrients for optimal plant growth while minimizing the likelihood that they pass below the root zone and leach to groundwater. Chapter 20 of *Design of Municipal Wastewater Treatment Plants* (WEF et al., 2009) describes federal regulations that designers should take into account and general requirements for landfilling solids. If the treatment plant's solids will be disposed of in municipal solid waste landfills or used as landfill cover material, they must comply with the requirements of 40 CFR 258 (municipal solid waste landfill regulations) rather than with Part 503.

Suggested reading material for additional information includes the following:

- *Design of Municipal Wastewater Treatment Plants* (WEF et al., 2009) (Chapter 20, "Introduction to Solids Management", and Chapter 21, "Solids Storage and Transport");

- *Wastewater Engineering: Treatment and Reuse* (Metcalf and Eddy, 2003) (Chapter 14, "Treatment, Reuse, and Disposal of Solids and Biosolids");

- *Wastewater Treatment Plant Design* (Vesilind [Ed.], 2003) (Chapter 12, "Production and Transport of Wastewater Sludge", and Chapter 16, "Benefit Use and Ultimate Disposal");

- *Solids Process Design and Management* (WEF et al., 2012) (Chapter 7, "Conveyance", and Chapter 20, "Transport and Storage"); and

- *Guide to Field Storage of Biosolids* (U.S. EPA and USDA, 2000).

2.0   SOLIDS MANAGEMENT

2.1   Regulations

Most U.S. states have adopted federal regulations for managing wastewater residuals (40 CFR 503) and some impose even stricter requirements. Biosolids generators are responsible for complying with Part 503. The regulation establishes two sets of criteria for heavy metals (pollutant concentrations and pollutant ceiling concentrations) and two sets of criteria for pathogen densities (Class A and Class B). It also allows for the following two approaches to reducing vector attraction: treating the solids or using physical barriers.

Part 503 labels biosolids either Class A or Class B based on their pathogen levels. Both types have been treated to reduce pathogens and minimize their ability to attract vectors (e.g., rats). However, Class B biosolids still contain detectible levels of pathogens, while Class A biosolids are essentially pathogen-free.

To be considered "Class A", biosolids must meet specific fecal coliform and salmonella limits at the time of use or disposal. Additional requirements are described in Chapter 20 of *Design of Municipal Wastewater Treatment Plants* (WEF et al., 2009).

To be considered Class B, solids must meet at least Class B pathogen requirements before being used or disposed. Solids that do not meet Class B criteria cannot be land-applied, but they may be placed in a surface-disposal unit that is covered daily. If Class B biosolids or domestic septage are land-applied, site restrictions also must be met (see Chapter 22, Section 3.1.6, of *Design of Municipal Wastewater Treatment Plants* [WEF et al., 2009]).

Table 12.1 describes several pathogen treatment processes for both Class A and B biosolids. More details on these processes can be found in Chapter 16 of this handbook.

Vectors (e.g., flies, rodents, and birds) are attracted to volatile solids. Materials with lower volatile solids concentrations are less likely to attract vectors, which spread infectious disease agents. There are 10 options for reducing vector attraction. All biosolids must meet at least one of them before they can be beneficially used.

Part 503's pathogen and vector-attraction reduction requirements are complex. For more information, the reader is referred to U.S. EPA's related guidance documents (especially *A Plain English Guide to EPA Part 503 Biosolids Rule* [U.S. EPA, 1994]), the regulation itself, and the preamble that accompanied the rule when it was originally published in the *Federal Register* in 1993.

There are also requirements for monitoring, recordkeeping, and reporting of biosolids under Part 503 that are discussed in detail in *Design of Municipal Wastewater Treatment Plants* (WEF et al., 2009). Designers should also check with their state regulatory agency because some states have varying and even stricter requirements for solids management.

The National Biosolids Partnership has developed an environmental management system for facilities that produce biosolids intended for beneficial use. The program is designed to help organizations establish good biosolids management practices and become certified for following them consistently.

TABLE 12.1 Pathogen treatment processes.

Pathogen reduction method	Type of biosolids produced
Heat drying	Class A
Digestion	Class B unless modified such as thermophilic anaerobic digestion
Composting	Class A if method meets time and temperature requirements; must monitor for pathogen regrowth
Advanced alkaline stabilization	Class A

2.2   Solids Quantities

The amount of solids generated during wastewater treatment is an important design parameter because it affects the sizing of solids treatment processes and all related equipment. Solids-generation rates also affect the size of liquid treatment processes. Chapter 20 of *Design of Municipal Wastewater Treatment Plants* (WEF et al., 2009) describes ways to estimate quantities. In general, domestic wastewater typically produces about 0.23 kg/m^3 (1 dry ton/mil. gal) of solids. Treatment plants using processes that destroy solids (e.g., digestion or heat treatment) will generate less, and those using chemical addition will produce more. A convenient benchmark for cursory comparisons is 0.25 kg/m^3.

2.3   Solids Characteristics

When designing solids-handling facilities, designers must know the characteristics and volumes of the solids involved. There are several types of solids (e.g., primary, secondary, mixed primary, chemical, and biosolids), and their characteristics depend on many factors (e.g., the percentage of industrial wastes, ground garbage, and sidestreams in wastewater; the use of chemical precipitants and coagulants; process control; peak loads and weather conditions; and the treatment process chosen).

2.4   Pretreatment Options

Solids are removed from primary and sedimentation tanks after being pretreated to facilitate pumping and subsequent handling. The most common pretreatment processes include degritting, grinding, and screening.

3.0   SOLIDS STORAGE

3.1   Liquid Residuals and Biosolids

Storage needs for liquid residuals and biosolids depend on where and why they are being stored. Liquid residuals may need to be stored to equalize flows or provide more operational flexibility. For example, if dewatering equipment is operated periodically, liquid residuals would have to be stored between operating periods.

Although more costly per unit volume than earthen basins, storage tanks can be a good choice when solids volumes are small, land costs are high, or other restrictions make earthen basins infeasible. Some things to consider in the design of storage tanks include mixing, aeration, spill prevention, and odor control. Other storage options for solids and liquid residuals include storage lagoons, aerobic basins, facultative basins, and anaerobic basins.

3.2   Dewatered Cake

Dewatered cake typically is stored somewhere before receiving more treatment (e.g., heat drying) or being hauled off-site for use or disposal. The amount of storage needed depends on what will happen to the cake afterward. Often, biosolids will only be held for a few days or weeks before being treated further or hauled off-site. In these instances, they typically are stored in large roll-off containers, 18-wheel dump trailers, concrete bunkers with push walls, or bins with augurs.

However, if the biosolids will be land-applied or surface-disposed, long-term storage may be required. In these instances, they often are stockpiled on concrete slabs or other impervious pads. When designing long-term storage facilities, engineers need to consider buffering, odor control, and accessibility. They also need to determine whether the storage facility should be open or covered. For more information on calculating storage requirements for land application, the reader is referred to Chapter 21, Section 2.1, of *Design of Municipal Wastewater Treatment Plants* (WEF et al., 2009). For further guidance, the reader is also referred to U.S. EPA and USDA's *Guide to Field Storage of Biosolids* (2000).

Odor control can be an issue with dewatered solids, especially when larger quantities are stored or the solids storage area is relatively close to neighbors.

3.3   Dried Solids

Dried solids typically are stored either on-site or at a land-application site before disposal or beneficial use. They may be stored in stockpiles or silos. Because dried solids contain a significant amount of combustible organic material that can be released as dust, temperature control is important. If silos are used, engineers should design them to promote cooling and maximize heat dissipation. Therefore, tall, narrow silos are better than wide ones. Narrow silos also render fires easier to control. However, if the silo is too narrow, it will make relief venting problematic. If multiple silos are used, there should be procedures to ensure that they are emptied cyclically to avoid exceeding safe residence times. Additionally, designers need to consider the stored product's thermal stability in case a prolonged plant shutdown or silo blockage occurs.

It is critical that dried solids be stored safely. Dried solids have self-ignited on several occasions and, in at least one instance, resulted in the discharge of solids to a surface waterbody. In other instances, the dried particles have caused explosions. Chapter 21 of *Design of Municipal Wastewater Treatment Plants* (WEF et al., 2009) provides explanations of how to consider the critical temperature in the design of storage facilities.

4.0   SOLIDS TRANSPORT

4.1   Liquid Residuals and Biosolids

There are two basic methods for transporting liquid residuals at wastewater treatment plants: pumping and trucking. Residuals typically are pumped on-site and trucked off-site. Liquid residuals typically are transported via tanker trailer trucks. Such trucks typically have nominal capacities ranging from 22 680 to 34 020 L (6000 to 9000 gal).

Pumping systems are an intrinsic part of solids management at wastewater treatment plants. They typically transport solids from

- Primary and secondary clarifiers to thickening, conditioning, or digestion systems;
- Thickening and digestion systems to dewatering operations;
- Biological processes to further treatment units; and
- Degritting facilities to temporary storage areas.

Many types of pumps are available for biosolids, as shown in Table 12.2 from Table 21.3 of *Design of Municipal Wastewater Treatment Plants* (WEF et al., 2009).

Chapter 21 of *Design of Municipal Wastewater Treatment Plants* (WEF et al., 2009) provides the equations needed to design a pump system for liquid residual and biosolids.

4.2   Dewatered Cake and Dried Solids

Modern dewatering operations can produce cake containing 15 to 40% solids or more, depending on the conditioning chemicals and dewatering equipment used. The consistency of such cakes ranges from pudding to damp cardboard, so they will not exit the dewatering equipment by flowing via gravity into a pipe or channel. Instead, they must be transported via the following:

- Positive-displacement pumps;
- Mechanical conveyors (e.g., flat or troughed belt, corrugated belt, or screw augers); or
- Gravity from the bottom of the dewatering equipment into a storage hopper or truck directly below.

Before choosing a cake transportation method, design engineers should analyze various options based on solids-management requirements, site or building constraints, reliability, operations and maintenance, and life-cycle costs. Typical piping headlosses in cake-pumping applications range from 11.3 to 79.1 kPa/m (0.5

TABLE 12.2   Sludge pump application by principle (WEF et al., 2009).

Principle	Common types	Typical applications
Kinetic (rotodynamic) pumps	Nonclog mixed-flow pump[a] Recessed-impeller pump (vortex pump, torque flow pump) Screw centrifugal pump Grinder pump	Grit slurry,[b] incinerator ash slurry[c] Unthickened primary sludge[b,c] Return activated sludge[c,d] Waste activated sludges from attached-growth biological processes[c] Circulation of anaeronic digester[b] Drainage, filtrate, and centrate Dredges on sludge lagoons
Positive-displacement pumps	Plunger pumps Progressing cavity pump Air-operated diaphragm pump Rotary lobe pump Pneumatic ejector Peristaltic pump Reciprocating piston	Waste activated sludge Thickened sludges (all types) Unthickened primary sludge Feed to dewatering machines Unthickened secondary sludges Dewatered cakes[e]
Other	Air lift pump Archimedes screw pump	Return activated sludge

[a]Limited solids capability; useful in larger sizes for return activated sludges. In most other applications, recessed-impeller pumps are more common.

[b]Abrasion is moderate to severe. Abrasion-resisting alloy cast iron is usually specified.

[c]May contain precipitates from aluminum or iron salts added for phosphorus removal.

[d]Particular need for reliable flow meters, for process control, in this application.

[e]Reciprocating piston pumps and progressing cavity pumps only.

to 3.5 psi/ft); design engineers often use these values as a general guideline during preliminary design. Ideally, the final design would keep headlosses below 45.2 kPa/m (2 psi/ft).

Design of Municipal Wastewater Treatment Plants (WEF et al., 2009) provides equations and design considerations to be used to design a pumping system for dewatered solids and conveyors for solids that cannot be pumped, including belt conveyors and screw conveyors.

5.0   REFERENCES

Metcalf and Eddy, Inc. (2003) *Wastewater Engineering: Treatment and Reuse*, 4th ed.; McGraw-Hill: New York.

U.S. Environmental Protection Agency; U.S. Department of Agriculture (2000) *Guide to Field Storage of Biosolids*; EPA-832/B-00-007; U.S. Environmental Protection Agency: Washington, D.C.

U.S. Environmental Protection Agency (1994) *A Plain English Guide to EPA Part 503 Biosolids Rule;* EPA-83Z/R-93-003; U.S. Environmental Protection Agency: Washington, D.C.

Vesilind, P. A., Ed. (2003) *Wastewater Treatment Plant Design;* Water Environment Federation: Alexandria, Virginia.

Water Environment Federation; American Society of Civil Engineers; Environmental & Water Resources Institute (2009) *Design of Municipal Wastewater Treatment Plants,* 5th ed.; WEF Manual of Practice No. 8; ASCE Manuals and Reports on Engineering Practice No. 76; McGraw-Hill: New York.

Water Environment Federation; U.S. Environmental Protection Agency; Water Environment Research Foundation (2012) *Solids Process Design and Management;* McGraw-Hill: New York.

Chapter 13

Chemical Conditioning

1.0 INTRODUCTION

Conditioning is a chemical or thermal treatment used to improve the efficiency of thickening or dewatering processes. Chemical conditioning processes use inorganic chemicals, organic polymers, or both to improve solids' thickening and dewatering characteristics. Typically, chemical conditioning can increase the residuals' solids content from about 1% up to between 15 and 30%. Conditioning not only removes water, but also increases the thickening or dewatering rate significantly by adjusting the chemical and physical properties of solids. Physical conditioning techniques (e.g., thermal conditioning) use heat to condition and stabilize solids and are described in Chapter 17, *Thermal Processing*.

The type and dosage of conditioning agent needed depends on the residuals' characteristics, solids handling and processing before and after conditioning, and the mixing process after agent addition. The efficiency of any conditioning process depends, to a large degree, on the solids' chemical and physical characteristics (e.g., origin, solids concentration, inorganic content, chemistry, storage time, and mixing) before conditioning. To be effective, the conditioning method must be compatible with the proposed methods of solids thickening, dewatering, and ultimate use or disposal.

Theory and additional design considerations for chemical conditioning can be found in Chapters 21, 22, and 25 of *Design of Municipal Wastewater Treatment Plants* (WEF et al., 2009).

Suggested reading material for additional information includes the following:

- *Design of Municipal Wastewater Treatment Plants* (WEF et al., 2009) (Chapter 21, "Solids Storage and Transport");

- *Wastewater Engineering: Treatment and Reuse* (Metcalf and Eddy, 2003) (Chapter 14, "Treatment, Reuse and Disposal of Solids and Biosolids");

- *Wastewater Treatment Plants: Planning, Design and Operation* (Qasim, 1999) (Chapter 18, "Sludge Conditioning and Dewatering");

- *Wastewater Treatment Plant Design* (Vesilind [Ed.], 2003) (Chapter 13, "Sludge Conditioning"); and

- *Solids Process Design and Management* (WEF et al., 2012) (Chapter 8, "Chemical Conditioning").

2.0   INORGANIC CHEMICALS

Inorganic chemical conditioning is principally associated with plate-and-frame filter presses, although they have also been used for belt filter presses. Chemicals typically used are liquid ferric chloride and lime. Compared to polymers, larger doses of inorganic chemicals are required to condition solids, and this affects the volume of solids to be managed.

Less commonly used inorganic coagulants include liquid ferrous sulfate, anhydrous ferric chloride, aluminum sulfate, and aluminum chloride. Other inorganic materials (e.g., fly ash, power plant ash, cement kiln dust, pulverized coal, diatomaceous earth, bentonite clay, and sawdust) have been used to improve dewatering, increase cake solids, and, in some instances, reduce the required dosage of other conditioning agents.

Table 13.1, reprinted from Table 22.3 of *Design of Municipal Wastewater Treatment Plants* (WEF et al., 2009), describes typical dosages of both ferric chloride and lime for dewatering wastewater solids.

3.0   ORGANIC POLYMERS

The organic chemicals used to condition solids are primarily long-chain, water-soluble, synthetic organic polymers. Polyacrylamide, the most widely used polymer, is formed by the polymerization of a monomer acrylamide. Polyacrylamide is nonionic. To carry a negative or positive electrical charge in aqueous solution, the polyacrylamide must be combined with anionic or cationic monomers. Because most solids carry a negative charge, cationic polyacrylamide copolymers typically are the polymers most used to condition biological solids. Polymers are further categorized by the following characteristics: molecular weight (varies from 0.5 to 18 million), charge density (varies from 0 to 100%), active solids levels (varies from 2 to 100), and form (e.g., dry, liquid or solution, emulsion, or gel).

High-molecular-weight, long-chain polymers are highly viscous in liquid form, extremely fragile, and difficult to mix into aqueous solution. Unmixed

TABLE 13.1   Typical dosages of ferric chloride and lime for dewatering wastewater solids (U.S. EPA, 1979a and 1979b) (reprinted from WEF et al., 2009).

Application	Sludge type	Ferric chloride, g/kg[a]	Lime, g/kg[a]
Vacuum filter	Raw primary	20–40	70–90
	Raw WAS[b]	60–90	0–140
	Raw (primary + TF[c])	20–40	80–110
	Raw (primary + WAS)	22–60	80–140
	Raw (primary + WAS + septic)	25–40	110–140
	Raw (primary + WAS + lime)	15–25	None
	Anaerobically digested primary	30–45	90–120
	Anaerobically digested (primary + TF)	40–60	110–160
	Anaerobically digested (primary + WAS)	30–60	140–190
Recessed-chamber filter press	Raw primary	40–60	100–130
	Raw WAS	60–90	180–230
	Anaerobically digested (primary + WAS)	40–90	100–270
	WAS + TF	40–60	270–360
	Anaerobically digested WAS	70	360
	Raw primary + TF + WAS	75	180

[a]All values shown are mass of either $FeCl_3$ or CaO per unit mass of dry solids pumped to the dewatering unit.

[b]WAS = waste activated sludge.

[c]Trickling filter.

polymers in a diluted solution look like fish eyes. As the polymer's molecular weight increases, so does the difficulty in mixing and diluting it.

Unlike the inorganic chemicals discussed previously, polymers have become attractive because they do not appreciably add to the volume of solids to be used or disposed of. They do not lower the fuel value of thickened or dewatered solids. Additionally, polymers are safer and easier to handle and result in easier maintenance than inorganic chemicals, which require frequent cleaning of equipment, typically via acid baths. However, polymers are not completely stable, can plasticize at high temperatures, and are slippery when spilled on floors.

Table 13.2, which combines data from Tables 22.7 and 22.8 of *Design of Municipal Wastewater Treatment Plants* (WEF et al., 2009), describes typical dosages of polymer for thickening and dewatering wastewater solids.

Chapter 22 of *Design of Municipal Wastewater Treatment Plants* (WEF et al., 2009) describes the various process design considerations for conditioning using the following systems:

- Conventional gravity thickening,

- Dissolved air flotation,

- Centrifugal thickening,

TABLE 13.2 Typical polymer dosages for thickening and dewatering.

Application	Sludge type*	Thickening polymer dosage, g/kg	Dewatering polymer dosage, g/kg
Gravity thickening	Raw primary	2 to 4	
	Raw (P + WAS + TF)	0.8	
	Raw WAS	4.3 to 5.6	
Dissolved air flotation	WAS (oxygen)	5.4	
	WAS	0 to 14	
	P + TF	0 to 3	
	P + WAS	0 to 14	
Solid-bowl centrifuge	Raw WAS	0 to 3.6	5 to 10
	Anaerobically digested WAS	2 to 7.2	1.4 to 2.7
	Raw primary		0.5 to 2.3
	Anaerobically digested primary		2.7 to 5
	Raw (P + WAS)		2 to 7
	Anaerobically digested (P + WAS + TF)		5.4 to 6.8
Rotary drum	WAS	6.8	
Gravity belt	Digested secondary	5	
Belt filter press	Raw (P +WAS)		2 to 5
	WAS		4 to 9
	Anaerobically digested (P + WAS)		6 to 10
	Anaerobically digested primary		4 to 7
	Raw primary		2 to 3
	Raw (P + TF)		3 to 6
Vacuum filter	Raw primary		1 to 5
	Raw WAS		6.8 to 14
	Raw (P + WAS)		5 to 8.6
	Anaerobically digested primary		6 to 13
	Anaerobically digested (P + WAS)		1.4 to 7.7
Recessed chamber filter press	Raw (P + WAS)		2 to 2.7

*P = primary, WAS = waste activated sludge, and TF = trickling filter.

- Gravity belt thickening,
- Rotary drum thickening,
- Centrifugal dewatering,
- Belt filter press dewatering,
- Screw press dewatering,
- Rotary press dewatering, and
- Conditioning for drying beds.

4.0   REFERENCES

Metcalf and Eddy, Inc. (2003) *Wastewater Engineering: Treatment and Reuse*, 4th ed.; McGraw-Hill: New York.

Qasim, S. (1999) *Wastewater Treatment Plants: Planning, Design and Operation*; CRC Press: Boca Raton, Florida.

U.S. Environmental Protection Agency (1979a) *Chemical Aids Manual for Wastewater Treatment Facilities*; EPA-430/9-79-018; U.S. Environmental Protection Agency: Washington, DC.

U.S. Environmental Protection Agency (1979b) *Chemical Primary Sludge Thickening and Dewatering*; EPA-600/20-79-055; U.S. Environmental Protection Agency, Municipal Environmental Research Laboratory, Office of Research and Development: Cincinnati, Ohio.

Vesilind, P. A., Ed. (2003) *Wastewater Treatment Plant Design*; Water Environment Federation: Alexandria, Virginia.

Water Environment Federation; American Society of Civil Engineers; Environmental & Water Resources Institute (2009) *Design of Municipal Wastewater Treatment Plants*, 5th ed.; WEF Manual of Practice No. 8; ASCE Manuals and Reports on Engineering Practice No. 76; McGraw-Hill: New York.

Water Environment Federation; U.S. Environmental Protection Agency; Water Environment Research Foundation (2012) *Solids Process Design and Management*; McGraw-Hill: New York.

Chapter 14

Solids Thickening

1.0 INTRODUCTION

Wastewater treatment plants typically use thickening processes to make primary solids or a combination of primary and waste activated solids (combined solids) more concentrated. Thickening reduces volumetric loading and increases the efficiency of subsequent solids-processing steps. Several reliable technologies are available for thickening sludges; each technology differs significantly in process configuration; degree of thickening provided; and chemical, energy, and labor requirements.

Additional design considerations for sludge thickening include sludge pumping, sidestream loadings, operational goals, and maintenance preferences. The reader is referred to Table 14.13 of *Wastewater Engineering Treatment and Reuse* (Metcalf and Eddy, 2003) for a detailed comparison of sludge pumping characteristics. Design Example 14.2 of *Wastewater Engineering Treatment and Reuse* (Metcalf and Eddy, 2003) describes how to calculate headloss in sludge transfer systems. For cost information, the reader is referred to *Process Design Manual for Sludge Treatment and Disposal* (U.S. EPA, 1979) and *Handbook of Estimating Sludge Management Costs* (U.S. EPA, 1985).

Suggested reading material for additional information includes the following:

- *Design of Municipal Wastewater Treatment Plants* (WEF et al., 2009) (Chapter 23, "Solids Thickening");

139

- *Wastewater Engineering: Treatment and Reuse* (Metcalf and Eddy, 2003) (Chapter 14, "Treatment, Reuse, and Disposal of Solids and Biosolids");

- *Wastewater Treatment Plants: Planning, Design and Operation* (Qasim, 1999) (Chapter 16, Section 6, "Sludge Thickening");

- *Wastewater Treatment Plant Design* (Vesilind [Ed.], 2003) (Chapter 14, "Sludge Thickening");

- *Water and Wastewater Engineering: Design Principles and Practice* (Davis, 2010) (Chapter 27, "Wastewater Plant Residuals Management"); and

- *Solids Process Design and Management* (WEF et al., 2012).

2.0   GRAVITY THICKENER

Gravity thickeners function much like settling tanks in that solids settle via gravity and compact on the bottom, while water flows up over weirs. They also provide some solids equalization and storage, which may be beneficial to downstream operations. Gravity thickeners have been applied to several different types of sludges with varying degrees of performance. Table 14.1 shows typical underflow characteristics.

Additional design guidance for gravity thickener physical characteristics can be found in *Design of Municipal Wastewater Treatment Plants* (WEF et al., 2009). For gravity thickener design examples, see Chapter 16, Section 9.1, of *Wastewater Treatment Plants: Planning, Design and Operation* (Qasim, 1999) and Example 14.4 of *Wastewater Engineering: Treatment and Reuse* (Metcalf and Eddy, 2003).

3.0   DISSOLVED AIR FLOTATION THICKENER

In a dissolved air flotation (DAF) thickener, solids and liquid are separated via the introduction of fine gas bubbles (typically air) to the liquid phase. The process forces bubbles to attach to solids particles, making them buoyant. They then rise to the liquid surface, where a skimmer collects them. This process typically is used to thicken poor-settling sludges (e.g., fats, oils, and grease or waste activated sludge [WAS]) (refer to Chapter 23 of *Design of Municipal Wastewater Treatment Plants* [WEF et al., 2009] for additional information).

The main components of a DAF thickener are the pressurization system and DAF tank. The pressurization system has a recycle pressurization pump, an air compressor, an air saturation tank, and a pressure-release valve. Adequate flotation for wastewater treatment plant sludges have been documented using an air-to-solids ratio between 0.02 to 0.06, which can be calculated using eq 16.2 of *Wastewater Treatment Plants: Planning Design and Operation* (Qasim, 1999).

Important design and operation parameters for a DAF system include air to solids ratio, solids loading rate, hydraulic loading rate, and polymer dosage.

TABLE 14.1   Typical gravity thickener underflow characteristics.

Type of sludge	Feed solids concentration, solids, %	Expected underflow concentration, solids, %	Unit solids loading, kg/m^3·d
Separate solids			
Primary (PRI)	2–7	5–10	100–150
Trickling filter (TF)	1–4	3–6	40–50
Rotating biological contractor (RBC)	1–3.5	2–5	35–50
Waste activated sludge (WAS)			
WAS—air	0.5–1.5	2–3	20–40
WAS—oxygen	0.5–1.5	2–3	20–40
WAS—(extended aeration)	0.2–1.0	2–3	25–40
Anaerobically digested solids from primary digester	8	12	120
Thermally conditioned sludge			
PRI only	3–6	12–15	200–250
PRI + WAS	3–6	8–15	150–200
WAS only	0.5–1.5	6–10	100–150
Tertiary sludge			
High lime	3–4.5	12–15	120–300
Low lime	3–4.5	10–12	50–150
Iron	0.5–1.5	3–4	10–50
Other sludges			
PRI + WAS	0.5–1.5	4–6	25–70
	2.5–4.0	4–7	40–80
PRI + TF	2–6	5–9	60–100
PRI + RBC	2–6	5–8	50–90
PRI + iron	2	4	30
PRI + low lime	5	7	100
PRI + high lime	7.5	12	120
PRI + (WAS + iron)	1.5	3	30
PRI + (WAS + alum)	0.2–0.4	4.5–6.5	60–80
(PRI + iron) + TF	0.4–0.6	6.5–8.5	70–100
(PRI + iron) + WAS	1.8	3.6	30
WAS + TF	0.5–2.5	2–4	20–40
Anaerobically digested PRI + WAS	4	8	70
Anaerobically digested PRI + (WAS + iron)	4	6	70

Typical solids loadings are shown in Table 14.2. In addition to these parameters, feed-solids concentration and sludge volume index (SVI) strongly affect DAF performance. For a DAF thickener design example, the reader is referred to Chapter 23, Section 3.6, of *Design of Municipal Wastewater Treatment Plants* (WEF et al., 2009).

TABLE 14.2   Typical solids loadings for DAF thickeners (Metcalf and Eddy, 2003).

Type of sludge or biosolids	Loading, lb/sq ft·hr		Loading, kg/m²·h	
	Without chemical addition	With chemicals	Without chemical addition	With chemicals
Air activated sludge				
Mixed liquor	0.25 to 0.6	Up to 2.0	1.2 to 3.0	Up to 10
Return activated sludge	0.5 to 0.8	Up to 2.0	2.4 to 4.0	Up to 10
High-purity oxygen activated sludge	0.6 to 0.8	Up to 2.0	3.0 to 4.0	Up to 10
Trickling filter humus sludge	0.6 to 0.8	Up to 2.0	3.0 to 4.0	Up to 10
Primary and air activated sludge	0.6 to 1.25	Up to 2.0	3.0 to 6.0	Up to 10
Primary and trickling filter humus sludge	0.83 to 1.25	Up to 2.0	4.0 to 6.0	Up to 10
Primary sludge only	0.83 to 1.25	Up to 2.5	4.0 to 6.0	Up to 12.5

4.0   CENTRIFUGE

Centrifugal thickening is analogous to gravity thickening except that centrifuges can apply a force 500 to 3000 times that of gravity. The increased settling velocity and short particle-settling distance accounts for a centrifuge's comparatively high capacity.

Currently, the solid-bowl (scroll-type decanter) conveyor centrifuges are the most widely used in this application. Process variables that affect thickening include feed flowrate, the centrifuge's rotational speed, differential speed of the scroll relative to the bowl, pond depth, chemical use, and the physicochemical properties of the liquid and suspended solids (e.g., particle size and shape, particle density, temperature, and liquid viscosity). Chemical conditioning is important for centrifuge thickening (refer to Chapter 13 of this handbook or Chapter 22 of *Design of Municipal Wastewater Treatment Plants* [WEF et al., 2009] for more information on polymer requirements).

Table 23.11 of *Design of Municipal Wastewater Treatment Plants* (WEF et al., 2009) indicates how a horizontal solid-bowl centrifuge's capabilities relate to basic rotating assembly size and operating speed at various installations. For a centrifuge thickener design example, the reader is referred to Chapter 23, Section 4.11, of *Design of Municipal Wastewater Treatment Plants* (WEF et al., 2009). Table 14.3 provides actual operating parameters for various horizontal solid-bowl centrifuges.

5.0   GRAVITY BELT THICKENER

Introduced in 1980, gravity belt thickeners represent a fairly recent development in sludge thickening. Gravity belt thickeners are used for thickening poorly settling sludges (i.e., secondary sludge). Chemically conditioned sludge enters through an inlet gate and is dispersed evenly over the moving belt. As a mat of

TABLE 14.3 Reported operational results for horizontal solid-bowl centrifuges (WEF et al., 2009).

Location	Activated sludge type	Feed solids concentration, mg/L	SVI (% VSS)	Feed flow rate, L/min	Thickened solids concentration, %	Solids capture, %	Polymer use, g active polymer/dry kg of solids	Machine size (bowl diameter × length), mm	Bowl speed, r/min	Centrifuge configuration
Atlantic City, New Jersey	Conventional	3 000	100 (60)	1 230	10	95	2.5	740 × 2 340	2 600	Countercurrent
Los Angeles, California, Hyperion	Conventional	4 800–6 000	110–190	2 300–3 000	3.7–5.7 / 3.6–6.0	88–91 / 77–96	None / 0.2–2.2	1 100 × 4 190 / 1 100 × 4 190	1 600 / 1 600	Cocurrent / Cocurrent
	Conventional	4 800–6 000	110–190	2 300–3 000	1.9–7.9 / 1.7–8.2	47–89 / 57–97	None / 0.4–1.4	1 100 × 3 600 / 1 100 × 3 600	1 995 / 1 995	Countercurrent / Countercurrent
Oakland, California, East Bay MUD	High-purity oxygen	5 000	250–400	4 200	7	66	6	1 000 × 3 600	1 995	Countercurrent
Naples, Florida	Conventional	10 000–15 000	70–80	380	6	90–92	None	740 × 3 050	2 000	Countercurrent
Milwaukee, Wisconsin, Jones Island	Conventional	6 000–8 000	80–150 (75)	1 100–1 900	3–5.5	92–93	—	—	1 000	Cocurrent
Littleton, Colorado	Conventional	6 000–8 000	100–300	570–1 100	6–9	88–95	3–3.5	740 × 2 340	2 300	Countercurrent
Lakeview, Ontario (Canada) (PM 75 000)	Conventional	7 560	80–120	840	4.7	77	None	740 × 2 340	2 300	Countercurrent
Lakeview, Ontario (Canada) (XM-706)	Conventional	7 120	80–120	1 350	6.1	65	None	740 × 3 050	2 600	Countercurrent

VSS = volatile suspended solids.

143

sludge builds up over the belt, rows of plows, chicanes, or vans expose the belt area for more water to drain. When treating municipal WAS and biosolids, gravity belt thickeners can produce a material containing 6% solids.

Polymer addition is 1.5 to 5 kg/metric ton (3 to 10 lb/ton), with solids capture efficiencies ranging from 90 to 98%. Additional information and figures regarding polymer dosages are available in Chapter 23 of *Design of Municipal Wastewater Treatment Plants* (WEF et al., 2009). Loading rates are typically normalized per meter of belt width. Hydraulic loading rates may vary from 6 to 16 L/s·m. Solids loading and polymer dosages are summarized in Table 14.4. For a design example, the reader is referred to Chapter 23, Section 5.5, of *Design of Municipal Wastewater Treatment Plants* (WEF et al., 2009).

Gravity belt thickeners are gaining popularity because of their efficient space requirements, low power use, and moderate capital costs. Improvements in both throughput and polymer use are ongoing, and will make this process even more cost-effective. Successful applications of automated polymer adjustment systems using camera color-sensing techniques have been documented to facilitate unmanned thickening operations.

Experience has shown that gravity belt thickeners work well with many types of wastewater solids and are less affected by plant operating problems than many other thickening processes. They typically handle even difficult-to-thicken solids via minor modifications to polymer dose, hydraulic loading rates, and solids loading rates.

If a gravity belt thickener is intended to be used as part of a cothickening process, design engineers should ensure that primary solids and WAS are mixed properly before the material is loaded onto belts. This will eliminate belt blinding caused by grease and debris in the primary solids.

Adding polymer to feed solids is essential to successful thickening when using a gravity belt thickener. It promotes flocculation of solids and release of free water. Without polymer, the belt would blind (because of fine solids filling belt pores) and flood (because of poor water release). Design engineers should

TABLE 14.4   Typical gravity belt thickener performance (reprinted with permission from Ashbrook Simon-Hartley, Houston, Texas).

Type of biosolids	Initial concentration, %	Solids loading, kg/m·h	Polymer dosage, g/kg	Final concentration, %
Primary (P)	2–5	900–1400	1.5–3	8–12
Secondary (S)	0.4–1.5	300–540	3–5	4–6
(50% P)/(50% S)	1–2.5	700–1100	2–4	6–8
Anaerobic (50% P)/(50% S)	2–5	600–790	3–5	5–7
Anaerobic (100% S)	1.5–3.5	500–700	4–6	5–7
Aerobic (100% S)	1–2.5	500–700	3–5	5–6

test various polymers to determine which are the most effective. Cationic (positively charged) polymers typically are chosen because wastewater solids often are negatively charged. However, if the solids contain significant amounts of aluminum or ferric salts (which impart a positive charge), then an anionic (negatively charged) polymer may be better.

Adding higher doses of a less expensive polymer can be more cost effective than using lower doses of a polymer with a high charge strength or molecular weight. As such, design engineers should specify performance requirements based on dollars of polymer per thousand kilograms of solids rather than on grams of polymer per kilogram of solids. During equipment performance tests, manufacturers should choose the polymer so they have full control of, and responsibility for, test results. Afterward, however, design engineers can invite chemical companies to test other polymers.

6.0   ROTARY DRUM THICKENER

A rotary drum thickener (also called a *rotary screen thickener*) basically consists of an internally fed rotary drum, an integral internal screw, and a variable- or constant-speed drive. Both gravity belt and rotary drum thickeners allow free water to drain through a moving, porous media while retaining flocculated solids. In rotary drum thickeners, the rotating drum imparts centrifugal force to separate liquids and solids, while the internal screw transports thickened solids or screenings out of the drum. Similar to gravity belt thickeners, rotary drum thickeners typically incorporate polymer addition to aid sludge thickening performance.

Rotary drum thickeners are most applicable to thickening WAS at small- to medium-sized wastewater treatment plants because the largest unit has a capacity of about 1100 L/min (300 gpm). Its advantages include efficient space requirements, low power use, moderate capital costs, and ease of enclosure, which improves housekeeping and odor control. Typical rotary drum thickener performance is summarized in Table 14.5.

TABLE 14.5   Typical rotary drum thickener performance (WEF et al., 2009).

Type of solids	Feed, % TS[a]	Water removed, %	Thickened solids, %	Solids recovery, %
Primary	3.0–6.0	40–75	7–9	93–98
WAS[b]	0.5–1.0	70–90	4–9	93–99
Primary and WAS	2.0–4.0	50	5–9	93–98
Aerobically digested	0.8–2.0	70–80	4–6	90–98
Anaerobically digested	2.5–5.0	50	5–9	90–98
Paper fibers	4.0–8.0	50–60	9–15	87–99

[a]TS = total solids.

[b]WAS = waste activated sludge.

7.0   COMPARISON OF THICKENING METHODS

A model comparing the cost-effectiveness of various thickening processes rarely applies to all situations because many factors that govern the final decision may be site-specific and more qualitative than quantitative. Such factors include sensitivity to upset, the benefits of achieving the highest possible solids concentration, the quality of operation required, installation size, compatibility with existing thickeners, the effect of downstream processing methods, and var-

TABLE 14.6   Advantages and disadvantages of thickening methods.

Method	Advantages	Disadvantages
Gravity	Simple low operating cost Low operator attention required Ideal for dense rapidly settling sludges such as primary and lime Provides a degree of storage and thickening Conditioning chemicals typically not required Minimal power consumption	High capital cost Odor potential Erratic for WAS Thickened solids concentration limited for WAS High space requirement for WAS Floating solids Biological phosphorus release from WAS*
Dissolved air flotation	Effective for WAS Will work without conditioning chemicals at reduced loadings Relatively simple equipment components	Relatively high power consumption Thickening solids concentration limited Odor potential Space requirements compared to other mechanical methods Moderate operator attention requirements Building corrosion potential, if enclosed Requires polymer for high solids capture or increased loading
Centrifuge	Space requirements Control capability for process performance Effective for WAS Contained process minimizes housekeeping and odor considerations Will work without conditioning chemicals High thickened concentrations available	Relatively high capital cost and power consumption Sophisticated maintenance requirements Best suited for continuous operation Moderate operator attention requirements
Gravity belt thickener	Space requirements Control capability for process performance Relatively low capital cost Relatively lower power consumption High solids capture with minimum polymer High thickened concentrations	Housekeeping Polymer dependent Moderate operator attention requirements Odor potential Building corrosion potential, if enclosed
Rotary drum thickener	Space requirements Low capital cost Relatively low power consumption High solids capture can be easily enclosed	Polymer-dependent Sensitivity to polymer type Housekeeping Moderate operator attention requirements Odor potential if not enclosed

*Phosphorus release may be encouraged if the gravity thickener is incorporated to a nutrient recovery system; WAS = waste activated sludge.

ious personal preferences based on experience. Design engineers should consider all of the thickening alternatives (refer to Table 14.6 of *Design of Municipal Wastewater Treatment Plants* [WEF et al., 2009]). Additionally, a design checklist is provided in Chapter 16, Section 8, of *Wastewater Treatment Plants: Planning, Design and Operation* (Qasim, 1999).

8.0 REFERENCES

Davis, M. (2010) *Water and Wastewater Engineering: Design Principles and Practice*; McGraw-Hill: New York.

Metcalf and Eddy, Inc. (2003) *Wastewater Engineering: Treatment and Reuse*, 4th ed.; McGraw-Hill: New York.

Qasim, S. (1999) *Wastewater Treatment Plants: Planning, Design and Operation*; CRC Press: Boca Raton, Florida.

U.S. Environmental Protection Agency (1979) *Process Design Manual for Sludge Treatment and Disposal*; EPA-625/1-79-011; U.S. Environmental Protection Agency, Municipal Environmental Research Laboratory, Office of Research and Development: Cincinnati, Ohio.

U.S. Environmental Protection Agency (1985) *Handbook of Estimating Sludge Management Costs*; EPA-625/6-85-010; U.S. Environmental Protection Agency, Water Engineering Research Laboratory: Lancaster, Pennsylvania.

Vesilind, P. A., Ed. (2003) *Wastewater Treatment Plant Design*; Water Environment Federation: Alexandria, Virginia.

Water Environment Federation; American Society of Civil Engineers; Environmental & Water Resources Institute (2009) *Design of Municipal Wastewater Treatment Plants*, 5th ed.; WEF Manual of Practice No. 8; ASCE Manuals and Reports on Engineering Practice No. 76; McGraw-Hill: New York.

Water Environment Federation; U.S. Environmental Protection Agency; Water Environment Research Foundation (2012) *Solids Process Design and Management*; McGraw-Hill: New York.

Chapter 15

Dewatering

1.0 INTRODUCTION

1.1 Objectives of Dewatering

Dewatering is the process of removing water from solids to reduce its volume and produce a material suitable for further processing, beneficial use, or disposal. The objective of solids dewatering is to reduce the volume of material and prepare the solids for further processing, beneficial use, or disposal. Reducing the volume cuts subsequent solids-management costs.

Suggested reading material for additional information includes the following:

- *Design of Municipal Wastewater Treatment Plants* (WEF et al., 2009) (Chapter 24, "Dewatering");

- *Wastewater Engineering: Treatment and Reuse* (Metcalf and Eddy, 2003) (Chapter 14, Section 3, "Solids Processing Flow Diagram");

- *Wastewater Treatment Plants: Planning, Design and Operation* (Qasim, 1999) (Chapter 18, "Sludge Conditioning and Dewatering");

- *Wastewater Treatment Plant Design* (Vesilind [Ed.], 2003) (Chapter 14, "Sludge Thickening");

- *Water and Wastewater Engineering: Design Principles and Practice* (Davis, 2010) (Chapter 27, "Wastewater Plant Residuals Management");

- *Solids Process Design and Management.* (WEF et al., 2012); and

- *Design Manual—Dewatering Municipal Wastewater Sludges* (U.S. EPA, 1987).

1.2   Key Process Performance Parameters

All dewatering processes generate two products: a solids cake and a liquid stream that consists of the water removed from the cake and some residual solids. The liquid stream, which has many names (e.g., supernatant, decant, underdrainage, filtrate, and centrate), is often recycled to the head of the wastewater treatment plant as a sidestream. Dewatering process performance is measured by two primary parameters, cake solids content and solids capture rate. These parameters may be used to generate a solids balance around the dewatering device to determine the solids concentration in the recycle stream. When determining solids loading to the dewatering device, the effect of recycled solids should be taken into account. A third important parameter is the cake's bulk density, which is the weight of the cake divided by its volume.

Table 14.41 of *Wastewater Engineering Treatment and Reuse* (Metcalf and Eddy, 2003) and Table 18.2 of *Wastewater Treatment Plants: Planning, Design and Operation* (Qasim, 1999) provide good comparisons of common dewatering methods. For details on polymer and chemical conditioning, the reader is referred to Chapter 13 of this handbook or Chapter 22 of *Design of Municipal Wastewater Treatment Plants* (WEF et al., 2009). In addition to polymer conditioning, many applications use grinders or in-line screening to remove large particles from dewatered cake for improved biosolids drying.

Odor control represents a significant issue to consider with all solids handling equipment, especially dewatering. The likelihood of odor production depends on how the solids were processed and how long they were held and stored before dewatering.

For a general dewatering design example, the reader is referred to Chapter 24, Section 1.10, of *Design of Municipal Wastewater Treatment Plants* (WEF et al., 2009) or Example 14.11 of *Wastewater Engineering Treatment and Reuse* (Metcalf and Eddy, 2003).

2.0   CENTRIFUGES

Centrifuges for dewatering operate much the same as centrifuges used for sludge thickening, although the internal design dimensions for thickening are quite different than for dewatering. Most horizontal solid-bowl conveyor (scroll-type) centrifuges are relatively simple to operate. Operators set the conveyor/ scroll torque to control cake dryness; centrate quality is controlled by changing the polymer dosage. Centrifuges require less operator attention, are easier to automate, and often produce drier cake than other common dewatering equipment. However, they are also typically energy-intensive, noisy, vibrate, and may vent odorous air to the environment. Modern advancements to centrifuges have reduced energy requirements, increased automation, and improved cake solids performance.

Typically, unit loading rates are established by each manufacturer. Because centrifuge manufacturers do not add a service factor, engineers should consider units with 30% higher hydraulic and solids capacity than required.

Table 15.1, adapted from Metcalf and Eddy (2003) and industry experience, provides typical centrifuge dewatering performance for various types of sludge and biosolids. For additional information, the reader is referred to Table 14.40 of *Wastewater Engineering Treatment and Reuse* (Metcalf and Eddy, 2003), which lists typical levels of polymer required for centrifuge dewatering.

3.0   BELT PRESSES

Belt filter presses dewater solids using two or three moving belts and a series of rollers. Akin to the gravity belt thickener, a belt filter press separates water from solids via gravity drainage and compression. After cake is discharged, the part of the belt that was in contact with solids must be washed before returning to

TABLE 15.1   Typical dewatering performance data for solid-bowl centrifuges for various types of sludge and biosolids.

Type of sludge		Cake solids %	Solids capture, %	
			Without chemicals	With chemicals
Untreated				
	Primary	25 to 35	75 to 90	95+
	Primary and trickling filter	20 to 25	60 to 80	95+
	Primary and air activated	12 to 20	55 to 65	92+
Waste sludge				
	Trickling filter	10 to 20	60 to 80	92+
	Air activated	5 to 15	60 to 80	92+
	Oxygen activated	10 to 20	60 to 80	92+
Anaerobically digested				
	Primary	25 to 35	65 to 80	92+
	Primary and trickling filter	18 to 25	60 to 75	90+
	Primary and air activated	15 to 20	50 to 65	90+
Aerobically digested				
	Waste activated	8 to 20	60 to 75	90+

the pressing zones. Figure 15.1 illustrates a belt filter press schematically. Compared to other mechanical dewatering devices, belt presses still have the lowest energy consumption per volume of solids dewatered. Building ventilation and odor-control energy requirements also need to be taken into account when determining the total energy needed for the belt press installation.

Belt press performance data indicate significant variations in the dewaterability of different types of solids or biosolids. Although the press typically can produce a dewatered cake containing 18 to 25% solids when treating a typical combination of primary and secondary solids, many plants produce a cake containing 15 to 18% solids when dewatering anaerobically digested material. The solids capture rate typically ranges from 85 to 95%. Table 15.2 in this handbook and Table 18.6 of *Wastewater Treatment Plants: Planning, Design and Operation* (Qasim, 1999) provide summaries of belt filter press performance with various types of sludge and biosolids. Additional tables with operational data from various installations of belt presses are available in Chapter 24 of *Design of Municipal Wastewater Treatment Plants* (WEF et al., 2009). Ongoing improvements produce higher dewatered cake solids concentrations.

Nominal design hydraulic loading rates for a belt press range from 3 to 4 L/s:m of belt width (15 to 22 gpm/ft of belt width). The maximum hydraulic loading limit is typically 6 to 9 L/s:m of belt width (30 to 45 gpm/ft). Typical solids loading rates range from 150 to 300 kg/m:h (100 to 200 lb/ft:hr) (dry solids basis). A typical maximum solids loading rate is 450 kg/m:h (300 lb/ft:hr).

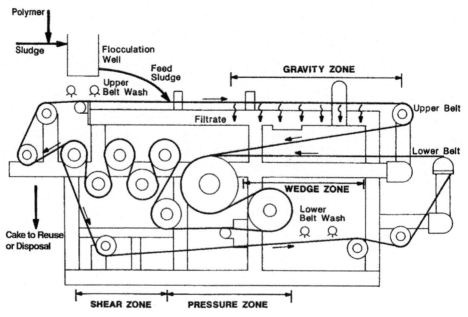

FIGURE 15.1   Belt filter press schematic (WEF et al., 2009).

TABLE 15.2 Typical performance data for a belt filter press.

| Type of sludge | Dry feed solids, % | Loading per meter belt width | | Dry polymer,[a] g/kg dry solids | Cake solids, % | |
		L/min	kg/h		Typical	Range
Raw primary (P)	3–7	110–190	360–550	1–4	28	26–32
Waste activated sludge (WAS)	1–4	40–150	45–180	3–10	15	12–20
P + WAS (50:50)[b]	3–6	80–190	180–320	2–8	23	20–28
P + WAS (40:60)[b]	3–6	80–190	180–320	2–10	20	18–25
P + Trickling filter (TF)	3–6	80–190	180–320	2–8	25	23–30
Anaerobically digested:						
P	3–7	80–190	360–550	2–5	28	24–30
WAS	3–4	40–150	45–135	4–10	15	12–20
P + WAS	3–6	80–190	180–320	3–8	22	20–25
Aerobically digested:						
P + WAS, unthickened	1–3	40–190	135–225	2–8	16	12–20
P + WAS (50:50), thickened	4–8	40–190	135–225	2–8	18	12–25
Oxygen activated WAS	1–3	40–150	90–180	4–10	18	15–23

[a]Polymer needs based on high molecular weight polymer (100% strength, dry basis).
[b]Ratio is based on dry solids for the primary and WAS.

When the drainage system is sized, both filtrate and washwater flows must be included. One 2-m belt press, for example, can discharge between 450 and 950 L/min (120 and 250 gpm) of drainage flow (filtrate and washwater). For a belt filter press design example, the reader is referred to Chapter 18, Section 6, of *Wastewater Treatment Plants: Planning, Design and Operation* (Qasim, 1999).

4.0 RECESSED-PLATE FILTER PRESSES

Solids pumped to the filter press under pressure ranging from 700 to 2100 kPa (100 to 300 psi) force the liquid through a filter medium, leaving a concentrated solids cake trapped between the filter cloths that cover the recessed plates. The filtrate drains into internal conduits and collects at the end of the press. Then the plates separate, and the cake drops via gravity onto a conveyor, collection hopper, or truck.

Pressure filter press systems typically produce cakes that are drier than those produced by other dewatering equipment, typically greater than 35% can be reliably achieved. Typical energy requirements are on the order of 0.04 to 0.07 kWh per kilogram of dry solids processed.

Pressure filtration is affected by several factors (e.g., particle size, specific gravity, and particle concentration). Chemicals (such as ferric chloride, fly ash, and/or lime) may be needed to improve dewaterability. Table 15.3 of this hand-

TABLE 15.3   Typical filter press dewatering performance for fixed volume press.

Type of sludge	Form cycle,[a] minutes	Lime,[b] %	Ferric chloride, %	Other, % as noted	Cake solids,[c] %	Feed solids concentration, %
		Conditioning chemicals				
Raw primary	120	10	5	—	45	5 to 10
Raw primary plus 50% waste activated sludge (WAS)	150	10	5	—	40 to 45	3 to 6
Raw primary plus 50% WAS	150	12	6	—	45	1 to 4
Primary plus trickling filter	120	20	6	—	38	5 to 6
Primary plus ferric chloride (FC)[e]	90	10	—	—	40	4
Primary plus WAS (FC)[e]	180	10	5	—	45	8
WAS	150	15	7.5	—	45	5
Primary plus two-stage high lime	90	—	—	—	50	7.5
Digested primary	120	30	6	—	40	8
Digested primary and WAS	120	10	5	—	45	6 to 8
Digested primary plus WAS (FC)[e]	180	10	5	—	40	6 to 8
Digested primary plus 50% WAS	120	10	5	—	45	6 to 10
Digested primary plus 50% WAS	150	15	7.5	—	45	1 to 5
Raw primary[d]	90	—	—	100 (fly ash)	50	5 to 10
Raw primary plus 50% WAS[d]	120	—	—	150 (fly ash)	50	3 to 6
Raw primary plus 50% WAS[d]	150	—	—	200 (fly ash)	50	1 to 4
Anaerobically digested primary plus 50% WAS[d]	90	—	—	100	50	6 to 10
Anaerobically digested primary plus 50% WAS[d]	90	—	—	200	50	2 to 6

[a]Length of time from initiation of feed to feed pump termination; excludes cake discharge time, which may be estimated at 30 minutes for presses 80 chambers and fewer, and up to 45 minutes for larger presses.

[b]As CaO.

[c]Includes conditioning chemicals.

[d]1600 kPa (225 psig) feed pressure.

[e]Ferric chloride used as coagulant aid in secondary process.

book and Table 18.4 of *Wastewater Treatment Plants: Planning, Design and Operation* (Qasim, 1999) provide typical plate filter press dewatering performance for various feed sludges. The principal design elements include cycle time, operating pressure, number of plates, feed method, type of feed system, layout and access, type of press, mechanical features, and safety.

5.0   DRYING BEDS AND LAGOONS

Drying beds and lagoons use a combination of drainage, evaporation, and time to dewater solids. Both also require considerable area compared to other dewatering methods. Drying beds and lagoons may be problematic if concerns about odors are high.

Drying beds, if well designed and properly operated, are less sensitive to influent solids concentration and can produce a drier product than most mechanical devices. Particularly suited to small facilities in the southwestern United States, they can be used successfully in wastewater treatment plants of all sizes and in widely varying climates. Less common techniques include mechanically assisted solar drying beds, reed beds, or lagoons.

Table 15.4 lists design criteria for sand drying beds. British experience indicates that a minimum of 0.35 to 0.50 m^2/cap (3.5 to 5.5 sq ft/cap) is necessary because of modern changes in solids production and characteristics.

6.0   ROTARY PRESSES

Rotary press and rotary fan press dewatering technology relies on gravity, friction, and pressure differential to dewater solids. Similar to other mechanical dewatering technologies, polymer is added to improve dewatering performance. A slowly rotating drive compresses the sludge against the media (typically a perforated or mesh screen) and filtrate is released. The cake is continuously released through the pressure-controlled outlet.

The hydraulic loading rate is a function of the equipment's size and number of channels. The technology is modular, and the hydraulic loading rate of single-drive units ranges from 0.5 to 15 L/s (7 to 250 gpm). Rotary presses can achieve cake solids and solid capture performance similar to belt presses and centrifuges. Table 15.5 summarizes typical rotary press dewatering performance advantages and disadvantages. The reader is referred to reference literature for similar summaries of advantages and disadvantages for other dewatering technologies. Additionally, Table 15.6 lists performance characteristics of current installations. Building requirements are minimal because rotary presses and rotary fan presses are enclosed and have small footprints.

TABLE 15.4   Design criteria for sand drying beds using anaerobically digested sludge without chemical conditioning (WEF et al., 2009).

Initial sludge source	Uncovered beds		Covered bed area,* m²/cap
	Area, m²/cap	Solids loading, kg/m²·a	
Primary			
Imhoff and Fair (1940)	0.09	134	
Rolan (1980)	0.09–0.14		0.07–0.09
Walski (1976)			
N45°N latitude	0.12		0.09
Between 40 and 45°N	0.1		
S40°N latitude	0.07		0.05
Primary plus chemicals			
Imhoff and Fair (1940)	0.2	110	
Rolan (1980)	0.18–0.21		0.09–0.12
Walski (1976)			
N45°N latitude	0.23		0.173
Between 40 and 45°N	0.18		0.139
S40°N latitude	0.14		0.104
Primary plus low rate trickling filter			
Quon and Johnson (1966)	0.15	110	
Imhoff and Fair (1940)	0.15	110	
Rolan (1980)	0.12–0.16		0.09–0.12
N45°N latitude	0.173		0.145
Between 40 and 45°N	0.139		0.116
S40°N latitude	0.104		0.086
Primary plus waste activated sludge			
Quon and Johnson (1966)	0.28	73	
Imhoff and Fair (1940)	0.28	73	
Rolan (1980)	0.16–0.23		0.12–0.14
Walski (1976)			
N45°N latitude	0.202		0.156
Between 40 and 45°N	0.162		0.125
S40°N latitude	0.122		0.094
Randall and Koch (1969)	0.32–0.51	35–59	

*Only area loading rates available for covered beds.

TABLE 15.5   Rotary press dewatering performance (WEF et al., 2009).

Advantages	Disadvantages
• Uses less energy than centrifuges or belt filter presses • Small footprint • Odors contained • Low shear • Minimal moving parts • Minimal building requirements • Minimal start-up and shutdown time • Uses less wash water than belt filter presses • Low vibration • Low noise • Modular design	• May be more dependent on polymer performance than centrifuges or belt filter presses • Low throughput compared to other mechanical dewatering processes • Screen clogging potential • Need for heavy rated overhead crane to lift and maintain channels • High capital cost

TABLE 15.6   Installation operational performance (TS = total solids; WWTP = wastewater treatment plant; PS = primary solids; and BNR = biological nutrient removal. (WEF et al., 2009).

Facility	Equipment	Facility size ML/d (mgd)	Solids type	Incoming % TS	Discharge % TS
Raiford, Florida, prison WWTP	Rotary fan press	4.2 (1.1)	Extended aeration	1.6–2.5	19–22
Front Royal, Virginia, municipal WWTP	Rotary fan press	12 (3.3)	Thermophilic anaerobic digestion	3.5	25
Fairfield, California, municipal WWTP	Rotary fan press	59 (15.5)	Conventional anaerobic digestion	2	17
Lafayette, Tennessee, municipal WWTP	Rotary press	1.9 (0.5)	Conventional anaerobic digestion	1.0–1.5	25
Portland, Maine, municipal WWTP	Rotary press	75 (19.8)	Thickened PS/WAS	3–6	19–25
Hampton, New Hampshire, municipal WWTP	Rotary press	9.5 (2.5)	Septage/PS/WAS	6–8	26–28
Murfreesboro, Tennessee, municipal WWTP	Rotary press	61 (15)	PS/WAS	0.8–1	12–14
Scarborough, Maine, municipal WWTP	Rotary press	5.3 (1.4)	Thickened PS/WAS	3	28
Ocean City, Maryland*	Rotary press	53 (14)	Conventional aerobic thickened digestion	4.4	35
Aberdeen, Maryland*	Rotary press	7.6 (2)	BNR anaerobic digestion	2.7	23
Salisbury, Maryland*	Rotary press	26 (6.8)	Thickened anaerobic lagoons	2.6	24
Cambridge, Maryland*	Rotary press	31 (8.1)	BNR thickened	2.6	20
Marley-Taylor, Maryland*	Rotary press	23 (6.0)	BNR anaerobic digestion	2.3	19
Broadwater, Maryland*	Rotary press	7.6 (2.0)	BNR thickened	4.5	25
South Central, Maryland*	Rotary press	67 (23)	BNR thickened	3.7	26
SCRWF, Delaware*	Rotary press	23 (6.0)	WAS aerobic digestion	1.9	16.3
Thurmont, Maryland*	Rotary press	3.8 (1.0)	BNR WAS aerobic digestion	1.5	12
La Plata, Maryland*	Rotary press	5.7 (1.5)	BNR WAS aerobic digestion	1.4	16.9
MCI, Maryland*	Rotary press	4.5 (1.2)	BNR WAS thickened	3.3	15.5

*Crosswell et al. (2004).

TABLE 15.7 Screw press operational results summary (WEF et al., 2009).

Facility	Facility information/process[a]	Solids type	Screw press type	Average feed solids (%)	Average cake solids (%)	Solids capture (%)	Typical feed rate (L/m)	Throughput per press (dkg/d)	Polymer dose (gm/dry kg)	Operating schedule	Labor required	Manual cleaning schedule
1[b]	3 ML/d WWTP: OD (SRT = 18–21 d), SC, SH (SRT=3–7 d)	Secondary sludge	Horizontal	4–6	20–45		57–114		11.5	24 h/7 d	8 h/d	
2	7.6 ML/d WWTP: OD (SRT=20 d), SC, SH (SRT=20 d)	Secondary sludge	Horizontal	2–3	15–20		106			16 h/d	1–2 h/week	
3[b]	1.1 ML/d WWTP	Secondary sludge	Horizontal	1.5	30		14–16			24 h/d, 5 d/week	40–50 h/week	Once per week
4[c]		Secondary sludge	Horizontal	1.2	16		13			70–100 h/week		2–3 times per week
5[c]		Secondary sludge	Horizontal	1.2	16		13			150 h/week		Once a day
6	3.8 ML/d WWTP: AS (SRT=24 d), SC, SH (SRT=7–10 d)	Secondary sludge	Inclined	0.07	N/A[d]		38			8 h/d, 5 d/week		
7	17 ML/d WWTP: OD (SRT=2–3 d), SC	Secondary sludge	Inclined	0.5–1	12–17	92	up to 280		7.5–10	24 h/7 d	2 h/d	Once per week
8	7.7 ML/d WWTP: OD, SC, SH	Secondary sludge	Inclined	3.5–4	18–20		up to 150		7.5	8 h/d, 7 d/week		
9	17.8 ML/d WWTP: PC, RBC, SC	Combined primary/secondary sludge	Inclined	2.5	18–30		up to 150	0.0033		2 d/week, 6–8 h/d		Twice per month
10	17 ML/d WWTP: RBC, SC, SH (SRT=2–4 d)	Combined primary/secondary sludge (40%/60%)	Inclined	1.1–1.2	30–40		300–340	0.0066		8 hours Monday, 2–4 hours Tuesday–Friday		Once a month
11[c]	.9 ML/d WWTP: PC, TF, SC, AD	Aerobically digested secondary sludge	Horizontal	1.2	18		26–38			24 h/7 d	8 h/d	Once per week

12	16 ML/d WWTP: PC, AB, SC	Primary/secondary (60%/40%) digested sludge combination	Horizontal	3-4	>18	95	190-378	0.0055	9-11	5 h/d, 5 d/week		Once every 6 months
13	31 ML/d WWTP: BOD removal (SRT=20 d), SH (SRT=1 d)	Aerobically digested secondary sludge	Horizontal	1	15-19	90	95-397	0.0066	8.2	16 h/d Monday-Friday, 8 h/d Saturday-Sunday	Minimal	Once per week
14	9.9 ML/d WWTP: OD (SRT=10 d), SC, AD (SRT=1.5 d)	Aerobically digested secondary sludge	Inclined	0.9	12-14		170			7 h/d, 5 d/week	Operator checks every 1-2 hours	Once per week
15	1.0 ML/d WWTP: AB, SBR, AD (SRT=40 d) sludge	Aerobically digested secondary	Inclined	N/A	22-25		30-34			8 h/d		Once per week
16	6.1 ML/d WWTP	Aerobically digested secondary sludge	Horizontal	0.75-1.0	21-28		22-64			8-12 h/d, 5 d/week	1-2 checks operator by per hour	Once per month
17[c]	83 ML/d	Anaerobically/aerobically digested primary/secondary sludge	Horizontal	3.2	17-21		114					
18	23 ML/d WWTP: PC, OD (SRT=20 d), SC, and (SRT=30-60 d)	Anaerobically digested primary/secondary sludge	Inclined	3-3.5	13-16		90-227			12:00 A.M. to 8-9 P.M. (3 hours downtime/day)	4-6 h/d	

(continues on next page)

TABLE 15.7 Screw press operational results summary (WEF et al., 2009) (*Continued*).

Facility	Facility information/process[a]	Solids type	Screw press type	Average feed solids (%)	Average cake solids (%)	Solids capture (%)	Typical feed rate (L/m)	Throughput per press (dkg/d)	Polymer dose (gm/dry kg)	Operating schedule	Labor required	Manual cleaning schedule
19	3.7 ML/d WWTP: PC, AB (SRT=3.5 d), SC, CCT, DAF, AND (SRT=41 d)	Anaerobically digested primary/secondary (55%/45%) sludge	Horizontal	1	20–24	High	26–30			4 d/week, 10 h/d		Once per month
20[c]		Anaerobically digested primary/secondary sludge	Horizontal	2–4	25		156–312					
21[c]		Anaerobically digested primary/secondary sludge	Horizontal	2	22		163					
22	7.6 ML/d WWTP: PC, AB (SRT=15 d), RBC, SC, SF, UV, AD (SRT=20d)	Aerobically digested primary/secondary sludge	Inclined	2	19–24		106–170			24/7	1 h/d	

[a]PC = primary clarifiers, OD = oxidation ditch, AS = activated sludge, TF = trickling filter, SC = secondary clarifiers, AD = aerobic digestion, AND = anaerobic digestion, SH = sludge holding, DAF = dissolved air flotation, CCT = chlorine contact tank, SF = sand filter, SRT = solids retention time of liquid or solids treatment process, and RBC = rotating biological contactor.

[b]Class A installations with heat/lime process.

[c]Information included for these facilities was provided by the screw press manufacturer.

[d]Facility had only been in service for two weeks at time of survey. Cake solids percentage had not yet been tested.

7.0 SCREW PRESSES

Dewatering is achieved by then squeezing the free water out of the solids as they are conveyed to the discharge end of the screw (either horizontal or inclined) under increasing pressure and friction. The pressure is developed by progressively reducing the available cross-sectional area for the solids or the pitch of the flights. Some applications use an adjustable back-pressure cone to improve dewatering performance. Because screw presses are fully enclosed, ventilation requirements are minimal.

Typical hydraulic loading rates for a horizontal screw press range from 3.8 to 2081 L/min (1 to 550 gpm), depending on the screw press model. Typical hydraulic loading rates for an inclined screw press are between 18.9 and 227 L/min (5 and 60 gpm). The solids loading rate capacity for a horizontal and inclined screw press ranges from 0.91 to 703 kg/h (2 to 1550 lb/hr), and 22.7 to 295 kg/h (50 to 650 lb/hr), respectively, depending on feed solids and equipment parameters.

Solids concentrations in screw press cake vary widely depending on polymer use, solids characteristics, and dewatering application. Table 15.7 provides a summary of a recent survey of existing installations. Unlike many other dewatering systems, screw presses typically are designed for continuous operation; typical operations range from 5 to 7 days per week.

Polymer doses for screw press systems can range from 3 to 17.5 g of active polymer per kilogram of dry solids (6 to 35 lb of active polymer per dry ton of solids), with a typical range of 6 to 10 g/kg (12 to 20 lb/dry ton). As a postpasteurization step, lime and heat may be added to the screw press, which then both dewaters solids and reduces pathogens to produce biosolids that potentially meet the Class A standards in 40 CFR 503.

A summary of the advantages and disadvantages of screw press dewatering is given in Chapter 24, Table 24.9, of *Design of Municipal Wastewater Treatment Plants* (WEF et al., 2009). Additionally, Section 7.4 of *Design of Municipal Wastewater Treatment Plants* (WEF et al., 2009) provides tips for facility layout and design.

8.0 REFERENCES

Crosswell, S.; Young, T.; Benner, K. (2004) Performance Testing of Rotary Press Dewatering Unit Under Varying Sludge Feed Conditions. *Proceedings of the 77th Annual Water Environment Federation Technical Exhibition and Conference* [CD-ROM]; New Orleans, La., Oct 2–6; Water Environment Federation: Alexandria, Virginia.

Davis, M. (2010) *Water and Wastewater Engineering: Design Principles and Practice*; McGraw-Hill: New York.

Metcalf and Eddy, Inc. (2003) *Wastewater Engineering: Treatment and Reuse*, 4th ed.; McGraw-Hill: New York.

Qasim, S. (1999) *Wastewater Treatment Plants: Planning, Design and Operation*; CRC Press: Boca Raton, Florida.

U.S. Environmental Protection Agency (1987) *Design Manual—Dewatering Municipal Wastewater Sludges*; EPA-625/1-82-014; U.S. Environmental Protection Agency: Washington, D.C.

Vesilind, P. A., Ed. (2003) *Wastewater Treatment Plant Design*; Water Environment Federation: Alexandria, Virginia.

Water Environment Federation; American Society of Civil Engineers; Environmental & Water Resources Institute (2009) *Design of Municipal Wastewater Treatment Plants*, 5th ed.; WEF Manual of Practice No. 8; ASCE Manuals and Reports on Engineering Practice No. 76; McGraw-Hill: New York.

Water Environment Federation; U.S. Environmental Protection Agency; Water Environment Research Foundation (2012) *Solids Process Design and Management*; McGraw-Hill: New York.

Chapter 16

Stabilization

1.0 INTRODUCTION

The four most common stabilization processes used in the United States today are anaerobic digestion, aerobic digestion, composting, and alkaline stabilization. Table 16.1 summarizes many of the advantages and disadvantages of these principal stabilization processes.

Suggested reading material for additional information includes the following:

- *Design of Municipal Wastewater Treatment Plants* (WEF et al., 2009) (Chapter 25, "Stabilization");

- *Wastewater Engineering: Treatment and Reuse* (Metcalf and Eddy, 2003) (Chapter 14, "Treatment, Reuse, and Disposal of Solids and Biosolids");

- *Wastewater Treatment Plants: Planning, Design and Operation* (Qasim, 1999) (Chapter 15, "Sludge Stabilization");

- *Wastewater Treatment Plant Design* (Vesilind [Ed.], 2003) (Chapter 15, "Sludge Stabilization"); and

- *Solids Process Design and Management* (WEF et al., 2012) (Chapters 11, 12, 14, 15, and 16).

2.0 ANAEROBIC DIGESTION

Hydrolysis, acidogenesis, and methanogenesis are the three main metabolic steps in anaerobic digestion. The primary products of anaerobic digestion are

TABLE 16.1 Comparison of stabilization processes (adapted from Tables 25.1 and 25.2 [WEF et al., 2009]).

Process	Advantages	Disadvantages	Pathogens	Putrefaction and odor potential[a]
			Degree of attenuation	
Anaerobic digestion	Good volatile suspended solids destruction Net operational cost can be low if biogas (methane) is used Broad applicability Biosolids suitable for agricultural use Reduces total sludge mass Low net energy requirements	Requires skilled operators May experience foaming Methane formers are slow-growing; hence, "acid digester" sometimes occurs Recovers slowly from upset Supernatant strong in ammonia and phosphorus Cleaning is difficult (scum and grit) Can generate nuisance odors resulting from anaerobic nature of the process High initial cost Potential for struvite (mineral deposit) Safety issues concerned with flammable gas	Fair	Good
Advanced anaerobic digestion (many process options)	Excellent volatile solid destruction Can produce Class A biosolids[b] using time and temperature-based batch operations Can increase gas production Can reduce solids retention time	Requires skilled operators Can be maintenance intensive (see "Anaerobic digestion" for other disadvantages)	Excellent[c]	Good
Aerobic digestion	Low initial cost, particularly for small plants Supernatant less objectional than anaerobic Simple operational control Broad applicability If properly designed, does not generate nuisance odors Reduces total sludge mass	High energy cost Generally lower volatile suspended solids destruction than anaerobic Reduced pH and alkalinity Potential for pathogen spread through aerosol drift Biosolids typically are difficult to dewater by mechanical means Cold temperatures adversely affect performance May experience foaming	Fair	Good

Process	Advantages	Disadvantages		
Autothermal thermophilic aerobic digestion	Reduced hydraulic retention compared to conventional aerobic digestion Volume reduction Excess heat can be used for building heat Pasteurization of the sludge pathogen reduction	High energy costs Potential of foaming Requires skilled operators Potential for odors Requires 18 to 30% dewatered solids	Excellent	Good
Composting	High-quality, potentially saleable product suitable for agricultural use Can be combined with other processes Low initial cost (static pile and window)	Requires bulking agent Requires either forced air (power) or turning (labor) Potential for pathogen spread through dust High operational cost: can be power-, labor-, or chemical-intensive or all three May require significant land area Potential odors	Excellent	Good
Lime stabilization	Low capital cost Easy operation Good as interim or emergency stabilization method	Biosolids not always appropriate for land application Chemical-intensive Overall cost is site-specific related to product management costs Volume of biosolids to be managed is increased pH drop after treatment can lead to odors and biological growth in product odorous operations	Good	Good
Advanced alkaline stabilization	Produces a high-quality Class A product Can be started quickly Excellent pathogen reduction	Operator-intensive Chemical-intensive Potential for odors Volume of biosolids to be managed is increased May require significant land area	Excellent	Good

[a]In addition to the stabilization process, putrefaction and odor potential also depend on postprocessing and storage practices.
[b]Refer to the *Standards for the Use or Disposal of Sewage Sludge*, U.S. EPA 40 CFR 503.
[c]For Class A time–temperature processes.

methane (CH_4), carbon dioxide (CO_2), hydrogen (H_2), hydrogen sulfide (H_2S), ammonia (NH_3), phosphorus (PO_4), and residual organic matter and biomass.

Table 16.2 provides typical digester and biosolids characteristics for high-rate digesters.

High-rate digestion is characterized by supplemental heating and mixing, relatively uniform feed rates, and prethickening of solids. Thermophilic digestion destroys more volatile solids and pathogens and produces more biogas. Additionally, thermophilically digested solids have better dewatering characteristics, but can be more costly to implement and operate than mesophilic digestion and can produce a sludge with higher odor levels.

For other variations of anaerobic digestion processes, the reader is referred to Figure 14.29 of *Wastewater Engineering: Treatment and Reuse* (Metcalf and Eddy, 2003) and the following sections (in parentheses) of Chapter 25 in *Design of Municipal Wastewater Treatment Plants* (WEF et al., 2009):

- "Primary-Secondary Digestion" (2.3.3),

- "Two-Stage Mesophilic Digestion" (2.3.5.1),

- "Temperature-Phased Anaerobic Digestion" (2.3.6),

- "Two-Phase (Acid-Methane) Digestion" (2.3.7),

- "Pre-Pasteurization" (2.3.8),

- "Thermal Hydrolysis" (2.3.9),

- "Aerobic Pretreatment" (2.3.10), and

- "Lagoon Digestion" (2.3.11).

Solids disintegration technologies are designed to increase the rate and extent of anaerobic solids digestion by applying external energy to render solids more bioavailable, resulting in more biogas production, increased volatile solids reduction (VSR), and reduced mass of solids for disposal. These processes typically are applied to waste activated sludge (WAS) because it is considered the most difficult to digest. For information on various disintegration technologies that are currently commercially available, the reader is referred to Table 25.9 of *Design of Municipal Wastewater Treatment Plants* (WEF et al., 2009). Table 16.3 of this handbook describes the key components of the anaerobic digester system.

In designing anaerobic digesters, considerations must be made to minimize effects of the buildup of debris, foam, struvite, and vivanite, which are discussed in Chapter 25, Section 2.7.11, of *Design of Municipal Wastewater Treatment Plants* (WEF et al., 2009). For a design example of thermophilic digestion, the reader is referred to Section 2.7.12 of the same chapter.

Anaerobic digesters continuously produce digester gas (biogas). Chapter 25, Section 2.9, of *Design of Municipal Wastewater Treatment Plants* (WEF et al., 2009)

TABLE 16.2 Typical design and operating parameters for anaerobic digestion of wastewater solids in high-rate digesters (adapted from Table 25.4 [WEF et al., 2009]).

Parameter	Typical value	Reference*
Typical loading rate (mesophilic)	1.9 to 2.5 kg volatile solids/m³·d (0.12 to 0.16 lb volatile solids/d/cu ft)	Chapter 25, Sections 2.2.6 and 2.3.2.2 (WEF et al., 2009)
Loading rate (thermophilic)	Pilot test or review existing operations	Chapter 25, Section 2.2.6 (WEF et al., 2009)
Feed cake	4 to 7% solids	Chapter 25, Section 2.3.2.2 (WEF et al., 2009)
Solids retention time (mesophilic)	15 days (to meet Class B requirements)	$\text{SRT}_{\text{min}} = \dfrac{YkS_{\text{eff}}}{K_C + S_{\text{eff}}} - b^{-1}$ Equation 25.3 (WEF et al., 2009) Chapter 25, Section 2.3.2.2 (WEF et al., 2009)
Solids retention time (thermophilic)	Varies with temperature to meet Class A requirements	$D = \dfrac{50\,070\,000}{10^{0.14T}}$ Where D = time (days) and T = temperature (°C) Equation 25.1 (WEF et al., 2009)
Volatile solids destruction (high-rate digestion system)	45 to 55%	$V_d = 13.7 \ln(\theta_d^{\,m}) + 18.94$ Where V_d = VSR (%) and $\theta_d^{\,m}$ = design SRT Equation 25.6 (WEF et al., 2009) Chapter 25, Section 2.7.2.4 (WEF et al., 2009)
pH	6.8 to 7.2	Chapter 25, Section 2.2.10
Alkalinity	2500 to 5000 mg CaCO₃/L	Chapter 25, Section 2.3.2.2
Mesophilic temperature range	35 to 39 °C (95 to 102 °F)	Chapter 25, Section 2.2.8
Thermophilic temperature range	50 to 57 °C (122 to 135 °F)	

(continues on next page)

TABLE 16.2 Typical design and operating parameters for anaerobic digestion of wastewater solids in high-rate digesters (adapted from Table 25.4 [WEF et al., 2009]) (*Continued*).

Parameter	Typical value	Reference*
Volatile acids	50 to 300 mg/L	
Biogas production (range)	0.8 to 1 m³/kg (13 to 18 cu ft/lb) of volatile solids destroyed	$G_v = (G_{sgp}) V_s$ Where G_v = volume of total gas produced [m³ (cu ft)] G_{sgp} = specific gas production, 0.8 to 1.1 m³/kg VRS (13 to 18 cu ft/lb VSR) V_s = VSR [kg (lb)] Equation 25.8 (WEF et al., 2009) Chapter 25, Section 2.2.13 (WEF et al., 2009)
Methane gas content	60 to 65%	$G_m = M_{sgp} [\Delta OR - 1.42(\Delta X)]$ Where G_m = volume of methane produced [m³/d (cu ft/d)] M_{sgp} = specific methane production per mass of organic material (COD) removed [m³/kg COD (cu ft/lb COD)] ΔOR = organics (COD) removed daily [kg COD/d (lb COD/d)] ΔX = biomass produced [kg VSS/d (lb VSS/d)] Equation 25.9 (WEF et al., 2009)
Carbon dioxide gas content	35 to 40%	
Volatile acids	50 to 300 mg volatile acids/L	
Volatile acid:alkalinity	<0.3 mg CaCO₃/mg volatile acids	Bicarbonate alkalinity (mg/L as CaCO₃) = total alkalinity (mg/L as CaCO₃) – [0.71 × volatile acids (mg/L as acetic acid)] Equation 25.22 (WEF et al., 2009)
Ammonia	800 to 2000 mg N/L	

*VSR = volatile solids reduction, SRT = solids retention time, COD = chemical oxygen demand, and VSS = volatile suspended solids.

168

TABLE 16.3   Components of the anaerobic digester system.

Digester components	Purpose	Variations	References
Tank configuration (shape)	Affects operating characteristics, capital costs, operations and maintenance costs	Short cylinder ("pancake") Tall cylinder ("silo") Egg-shaped	Chapter 25, Section 2.7.3 (WEF et al., 2009) Table 14.30 (Metcalf and Eddy, 2003)
Digester cover	Collect gas, reduce odors, stabilize internal temperature, and maintain anaerobic conditions	Floating Fixed Membrane	Chapter 25, Section 2.7.4 (WEF et al., 2009) Figure 14.27 (Metcalf and Eddy, 2003)
Mixing system	Reduce thermal stratification and scum, increase effective volume, keep inorganics in suspension	Mechanical Pumped gas recirculation	Chapter 25, Section 2.7.6 (WEF et al., 2009) Table 14.31 (Metcalf and Eddy, 2003)
Digester heating	Provide suitable conditions for biological activity	Boilers Cogeneration Heat pumps Heat exchangers	Chapter 25, Sections 2.7.7 through 2.7.10 (WEF et al., 2009) Table 14.33 (Metcalf and Eddy, 2003)

covers a wide range of issues with respect to digester gas (biogas) characteristics, gas-processing equipment, gas-handling equipment, and gas beneficial use.

3.0   AEROBIC DIGESTION

Aerobic digestion typically is used at smaller wastewater treatment plants and those that only produce biological solids or WAS. Table 16.4 provides typical digester and biosolids characteristics for conventional aerobic digestion.

Conventional aerobic digestion typically produces Class B biosolids. The Class B biosolids criteria that a conventional mesophilic aerobic digestion system typically is designed to meet are shown in Table 16.5.

Autothermal thermophilic aerobic digestion (ATAD) is an advanced aerobic digestion process that operates at 50 to 65 °C (122 to 149 °F). If sufficient design and operating conditions are provided, the process can be controlled at thermophilic temperatures to achieve greater than 38% VSR and meet Part 503's Class A pathogen requirements. For more information on ATAD, the reader is referred to Chapter 25, Section 3.4.2, of *Design of Municipal Wastewater Treatment Plants* (WEF et al., 2009); Chapter 12, Section 3, of *Solids Process Design and Management* (WEF et al., 2012); and Chapter 14, Section 14.10, of *Wastewater Engineering: Treatment and Reuse* (Metcalf and Eddy, 2003).

For process variations on standard mesophilic aerobic digestion and techniques to optimize aerobic digestion, the reader is referred to Chapter 25, Sections 3.5 and 3.6, respectively, of *Design of Municipal Wastewater Treatment Plants*

TABLE 16.4 Typical design and operating parameters for aerobic digestion of wastewater solids.

Parameter	Typical value	Reference*
Oxygen requirements	1.5 to 2.0 kg O_2/kg (lb O_2/lb) cell mass	$Ri = K (1.67 Si . ms O_a)$ Where Ri = actual aerobic digester oxygen requirements [kg/d (lb/d)] Si = raw wastewater BOD_5 load equivalent to the waste solids under oxidation [kg/d (lb/d)] O_a = oxygen consumed in main aeration basin [kg/d (lb/d)] K = constant equal to 1.0 when main aeration does not nitrify and 1.24 when main aeration does nitrify Equation 25.32 (WEF et al., 2009) Chapter 25, Section 3.3.5 (WEF et al., 2009)
Airflow requirements for oxygen required	0.25 to 0.50 L/m³·s (25 to 30 cu ft/min/1000 cu ft)	Chapter 25, Section 3.3.5 (WEF et al., 2009)
Air required for mixing	0.33 to 0.67 L/m³·s (20 to 40 cu ft/min/1000 cu ft)	Chapter 25, Section 3.3.7.1 (WEF et al., 2009)
Dissolved oxygen level	2 mg/L	Chapter 25, Section 3.3.5 (WEF et al., 2009)
Volatile solids reduction	35 to 50%	Chapter 25, Section 3.3.2 (WEF et al., 2009)
Temperature range	10 to 40 °C (50 to 104 °F)	$(K_d)T = (K_d)_{20°C} q^{T-20}$ Where K_d = reaction rate constant (time) T = temperature (°C) q = temperature coefficient Equation 25.31 (WEF et al., 2009) Chapter 25, Section 3.3.4 (WEF et al., 2009)

Tank volume   40 days at 12 °C (54 °F)

$V = Q_i(X_i + YS_i)/X(K_dP_v + 1/SRT)$

Where

V = volume of the aerobic digester [L (cu ft)]

Q_i = influent average flowrate [L/d (cu ft/d)]

X_i = influent suspended solids (mg/L)

Y = Portion of the influent BOD consisting of raw primary solids (%)

S_i = influent digester BOD_5 (mg/L)

X = digester suspended solids (mg/L)

K_d = reaction rate constant (d^{-1})

P_v = volatile fraction of digester suspended solids (%)

SRT = solids retention time (days)

Equation 25.34 (WEF et al., 2009)

Chapter 25, Section 3.3.6 (WEF et al., 2009)

Detention time   40 days at 20 °C (68 °F)
    60 days at 15 °C (59 °F)

$t_d = (X_i X_e)/(K_d)(D)(X_{oad})(X_i)$

Where

t_d = digester detention time (days)

X_i = TSS concentration in influent (mg/L)

X_e = TSS concentration in effluent (mg/L)

K_d = reaction rate for biodegradable portion of the active biomass (d^{-1})

D = biodegradable active biomass in the influent that appears in the effluent (%)

X_{oad} = percentage of active biomass that is biodegradable in the influent

Equation 25.35 (WEF et al., 2009)

Chapter 25, Sections 3.3.6 and 3.3.7 (WEF et al., 2009)

---

*SRT = solids retention time, BOD = biochemical oxygen demand, BOD_5 = 5-day biochemical oxygen demand, and TSS = total suspended solids.

Table 16.5   Class B biosolids criteria that a conventional mesophilic aerobic digestion system typically is designed to meet.*

Single digester system	Multiple digester system
1. Meet one of the following pathogen-reduction requirements: • 60-day SRT at 15 °C (59 °F) or 40-day SRT at 20 °C (68 °F), or • Fecal coliform density of less than 2 mil. MPN/g total dry solids.	1. Meet both pathogen-reduction requirements: • Fecal coliform density of less than 2 mil. MPN/g total dry solids, and • 42-day SRT at 15 °C (59 °F) or 28-day SRT at 20 °C (68 °F). In this instance, because regulators must approve the process as a PSRP-equivalent alternative, plant operators should demonstrate experimentally that the resulting biosolids both contain low enough levels of microbes and meet one of the vector attraction reduction requirements listed above.
2. Meet one of the following vector-attraction reduction requirements: • At least 38% VSR during biosolids treatment or • A SOUR of less than 1.5 mg/g·h of total solids at 20 °C (68 °F).	
3. Solids also could meet vector attraction reduction requirements if they had less than 15% more VSR after 30 days of further batch digestion at 20 °C (68 °F).	2. Meet one of the following vector-attraction reduction requirements: • At least 38% VSR during biosolids treatment or • A SOUR of less than 1.5 mg/g·h of total solids at 20 °C (68 °F).

*SRT = solids retention time, MPN = most probable number, PSRP = process to significantly reduce pathogens, and SOUR = specific oxygen uptake rate.

(WEF et al., 2009). Finally, for a design example of an aerobic digester, the reader is referred to Chapter 25, Section 3.7.8, of *Design of Municipal Wastewater Treatment Plants* (WEF et al., 2009).

4.0 COMPOSTING

Composting is a biological process in which organic matter is decomposed under controlled, aerobic conditions to convert solids into a soil amendment or conditioner. Composting can be readily used to treat both unstabilized solids and partially stabilized biosolids. Table 16.6 lists the advantages and disadvantages of five composting technologies based on physical facilities, processing aspects, and operations and maintenance.

For design considerations for aerobic sludge composting processes, the reader is referred to Table 14.37 of *Wastewater Engineering: Treatment and Reuse* (Metcalf and Eddy, 2003).

All composting technologies require mixing sufficient quantities of bulking agent with dewatered solids to increase solids content and provide porosity, improve the material's structural properties, and promote adequate air circulation. Bulking agents also provide supplemental carbon to adjust the carbon-to-

TABLE 16.6   Key advantages and disadvantages of composting systems (WEF et al., 2009).

Composting technology	Advantages	Disadvantages
Aerated static pile	• Adaptability to various bulking agents • Flexibility to handle changing feed conditions and peak loads (volume not fixed) • Relatively simple mechanical equipment	• Relatively labor intensive • Relatively large area required • Operators exposed to composting piles • Potentially dusty working environment
Windrow	• Adaptability to various bulking agents. • Flexibility to handle changing feed conditions and peak loads (volume not fixed) • Relatively simple mechanical equipment • Requires no fixed mechanical equipment	• Very large area required • Relatively labor intensive • Operators exposed to composting piles • Dusty working conditions
Vertical plug flow	• Completely enclosed reactors in some systems improve ability to control odors • Relatively small area required • Operators not exposed to composting material	• Single outfeed device per reactor (large reactors), potential bottleneck • Potential inability to maintain uniform aerobic conditions throughout reactor • Relatively maintenance intensive • Limited flexibility to handle changing conditions • Materials-handling system may limit choice of bulking agents
Horizontal plug flow (tunnel)	• Completely enclosed reactors improve ability to control odors • Relatively smaller area required (composting mix compacted) • Operators not exposed to composting material	• Fixed-volume reactors (no flexibility) • Limited ability to handle changing conditions • Relatively maintenance intensive • Materials-handling system may limit choice of bulking agents
Agitated bin	• Mixing enhances aeration and uniformity of compost mixtures • Ability to mix compost (advantage in handling some bulking agents • Adaptability to various bulking agents	• Fixed-volume reactors (no flexibility) • Relatively large area required • Potentially dusty working environment • Operators exposed to composting piles • Relatively maintenance intensive

nitrogen ratio and energy balance. For some commonly used bulking agents and their characteristics, the reader is referred to Table 25.36 of *Design of Municipal Wastewater Treatment Plants* (WEF et al., 2009) and Table 14.38 of *Wastewater Engineering: Treatment and Reuse* (Metcalf and Eddy, 2003).

Materials-balance calculations track the weight and volume of each material through each stage of the composting process. Table 16.7 shows a typical materials balance for 1 dry ton of biosolids (20% solids) in an aerated static-pile process.

TABLE 16.7   Materials balance for 1 dry ton of biosolids in aerated static-pile composting (adapted from Table 25.37 [WEF et al., 2009]).

Material	Volume	Total weight	Dry weight	Volatile solids	Bulk density	Solids content	Volatile solids
Units	m^3 (cu yd)	Mg (ton)	Mg (ton)	Mg (ton)	kg/m^3 (lb/cu yd)	%	%
Biosolids	4.8 (6.3)	4.4 (5.0)	0.9 (1.0)	0.5 (0.5)	949 (1600)	20.0%	53.0%
Yard waste (processed)	8.3 (10.9)	3.0 (3.3)	1.6 (1.8)	1.2 (1.3)	356 (600)	55.0%	70.0%
Wood waste	0.0	0.0	0.0	0.0	297 (500)	60.0%	95.0%
Screened recycled bulking agent	7.6 (9.9)	3.2 (3.5)	1.7 (1.9)	1.6 (1.8)	412 (695)	55.0%	93.0%
Unscreened recycle	0.0	0.0	0.0	0.0	463 (780)	55.0%	88.6%
Mixture	19.6 (25.7)	10.6 (11.7)	4.3 (4.7)	3.3 (3.6)	540 (911)	40.1%	75.7%
Base (recycled bulking agent)	1.1 (1.4)	0.5 (0.5)	0.3 (0.3)	0.3 (0.3)	412 (695)	55.0%	93.0%
Cover (unscreened)	2.2 (2.9)	1.0 (1.1)	0.5 (0.6)	0.5 (0.5)	463 (780)	55.0%	88.6%
Composting losses		0.9 (9.4)	0.4 (0.4)				
Cover (unscreened)	2.2 (2.9)	1.0 (1.1)	0.5 (0.6)	0.5 (0.5)	463 (780)	55.0%	88.6%
Screen feed	16.4 (21.5)	7.6 (8.4)	4.2 (4.6)	3.2 (3.5)	463 (780)	55.0%	74.8%
Recycled bulking agent	8.7 (11.4)	3.6 (4.0)	2.0 (2.2)	1.8 (2.0)	412 (695)	55.0%	93.0%
Curing	7.6 (9.9)	4.0 (4.4)	2.2 (2.4)	1.3 (1.4)	534 (900)	55.0%	58.6%
Curing losses		0.2 (0.2)	0.1 (0.1)	0.1 (0.1)			
Compost to storage	7.3 (9.5)	3.9 (4.3)	2.1 (2.3)	1.2 (1.3)	534 (900)	55.0%	56.9%

Assumptions:

Recovery by screening
- Yard waste   50% by volume
- Wood waste   70% by volume
- Recycled bulking agent   50% by volume
- Pile base   95% by volume

Processing losses
- Losses during composting   10% of volatile solids
- Losses during curing   5% of volatile solids

TABLE 16.8 Typical advanced alkaline stabilization design criteria (Fergen, 1991).

Item	Description or equipment	Parameter	Units	Range of value		Selected design value
				Minimum	Maximum	
Materials	Sludge	Solids	Percent	20	30	25
		Density	lb/cu ft[a]	45	55	50
	Alkaline bulking chemical	Solids	Percent	90	98	95
		Density	lb/cu ft[a]	50	65	65
	Lime	Solids	Percent	90	96	95
		Density	lb/cu ft[a]	55	60	60
	Stabilized product	Solids	Percent	55	65	60
		Density	lb/cu ft[a]	65	75	75
Curing	Technology	Windrow				
	Detention time	Average	Days	3	7	6
		Peak	Days	3	7	4
	Temperatures		°C	—	—	52 to 12 hr
	Pile dimensions	Bottom width	ft[b]	6	14	10
		Mix height	ft[b]	2	3	3
		Top width	ft[b]	4	8	6
		Area/unit length	sq ft/ft[c]	10	33	24
		Pile spacing	ft[b]	—	—	5
	Pile turning		lb/d[d]	—	—	1 (typical)
Odor control	Building air	Number of stages	Number	1	3	1
		Air changes	Number/hr	6	15	12
	Product storage	Number of stages	Number	1	3	1
Storage	Sludge	Days of storage	Days	0	1	1
	Chemicals	Days of storage	Days	5	30	5
	Product	Days of storage	Days	80	180	60

[a]lb/cu ft × 16.02 = kg/m^3.

[b]ft × 0.304 8 = m.

[c]sq ft/ft × 0.304 8 = m^2/m.

[d]lb/d × 0.453 6 = kg/d.

For a design example of composting, the reader is referred to Chapter 25, Section 4.5.11, of *Design of Municipal Wastewater Treatment Plants* (WEF et al., 2009).

5.0   ALKALINE STABILIZATION

Alkaline stabilization processes produce a rich, soil-like product containing few pathogens. The biosolids also have a higher pH, which is desirable at farms with acidic soils. However, alkaline stabilization increases the mass of biosolids to be managed and generates strong ammonia and amine odors that may need to be treated.

Alkaline stabilization is a process in which an alkaline chemical is added to feed solids to raise its pH and adequate contact time is provided. At pH 12 or higher, with sufficient contact time and thorough mixing, pathogens and microorganisms are either inactivated or destroyed. To meet Class B stabilization requirements, the pH of the feed cake–chemical mixture must be elevated to more than pH 12.0 for 2 hours and then maintained above pH 11.5 for another 22 hours to meet vector-attraction reduction requirements. To meet Class A stabilization requirements, the elevated pH is combined with elevated temperatures (70 °C for 30 minutes or other U.S. Environmental Protection Agency-approved time and temperature combinations listed in *Standards for the Use or Disposal of Sewage Sludge* [U.S. EPA, 1999]). As long as the pH remains above 10 to 10.5, microbial activity and associated odorous gases are greatly reduced or eliminated (U.S. EPA, 1979). However, other odorous gases (e.g., ammonia and trimethylamine) may be produced under high-pH and high-temperature conditions. Table 16.8 lists typical advanced alkaline stabilization design criteria.

Typical lime dosages for pretreatment sludge stabilization can be found in Table 14.25 of *Wastewater Engineering: Treatment and Reuse* (Metcalf and Eddy, 2003). For a design example of Class B lime stabilization, the reader is referred to Chapter 25, Section 5.7.4, of *Design of Municipal Wastewater Treatment Plants* (WEF et al., 2009).

6.0   REFERENCES

Fergen, R. E. (1991) Stabilization and Disinfection of Dewatered Municipal Wastewater Sludge with Alkaline Addition. *Proceedings of the 5th Annual American Water Works Association/Water Pollution Control Federation Joint Residuals Management Conference*; Durham, North Carolina, Aug 11–14; Water Pollution Control Federation: Alexandria, Virginia.

Metcalf and Eddy, Inc. (2003) *Wastewater Engineering: Treatment and Reuse*, 4th ed.; McGraw-Hill: New York.

Qasim, S. (1999) *Wastewater Treatment Plants: Planning, Design and Operation*; CRC Press: Boca Raton, Florida.

U.S. Environmental Protection Agency (1979) *Process Design Manual for Sludge Treatment and Disposal*; EPA-625/1-79-011; U.S. Environmental Protection Agency: Cincinnati, Ohio.

U.S. Environmental Protection Agency (1999) *Standards for the Use or Disposal of Sewage Sludge*; Code of Federal Regulations, Part 503, Title 40.

Vesilind, P. A., Ed. (2003) *Wastewater Treatment Plant Design*; Water Environment Federation: Alexandria, Virginia.

Water Environment Federation; American Society of Civil Engineers; Environmental & Water Resources Institute (2009) *Design of Municipal Wastewater Treatment Plants*, 5th ed.; WEF Manual of Practice No. 8; ASCE Manuals and Reports on Engineering Practice No. 76; McGraw-Hill: New York.

Water Environment Federation; U.S. Environmental Protection Agency; Water Environment Research Foundation (2012) *Solids Process Design and Management*; McGraw-Hill: New York.

Chapter 17

Thermal Processing

1.0 INTRODUCTION

Thermal processing methods are a means of producing a marketable product or reducing sludge or biosolids volumes. Economic, environmental, and sociopolitical analyses provide the best basis for deciding whether to use thermal processing methods. The selection of a thermal processing system should recognize new, rapid advancements in dewatering technology. The selection process must weigh the likely effect of present and future regulations on the thermal processing system, associated air pollution control equipment, and the reuse or disposal option. The process should also assess whether the options are flexible enough to accommodate likely regulation changes. Such forethought may prevent installation of a system that becomes obsolete or uneconomical or requires significant modifications to comply with future regulations.

Suggested reading material for additional information includes the following:

- *Design of Municipal Wastewater Treatment Plants* (WEF et al., 2009) (Chapter 26, "Thermal Processing");

- *Wastewater Engineering: Treatment and Reuse* (Metcalf and Eddy, 2003) (Chapter 14, Section 14, "Heat Drying", and Chapter 14, Section 15, "Incineration");

- *Wastewater Treatment Plant Design* (Vesilind [Ed.], 2003) (Chapter 14, "Sludge Thickening, Dewatering, and Drying", and Chapter 15, "Sludge Stabilization"); and

- *Solids Process Design and Management* (WEF et al., 2012) (Chapter 17, "Thermal Drying", Chapter 18, "Thermal Oxidation and Energy Recovery", and Chapter 19, "Other Thermal Processes").

The design and procurement of a thermal processing system often depends on proprietary vendor information, which may not be readily accessible. As a result, a designer should avoid specifying equipment or processes in a manner that may unnecessarily restrict some vendors from bidding on the project. An engineer must set basic requirements such as size of the unit, types of support equipment, and minimum standards for materials.

The following five prevalent thermal processing methods are described in *Design of Municipal Wastewater Treatment Plants* (WEF et al., 2009): conditioning, drying, oxidation, vitrifcation, and biogasification. The regulations that govern particulate and gaseous emissions and emission control technology are also discussed in *Design of Municipal Wastewater Treatment Plants* (WEF et al., 2009), but are not summarized in this handbook. Instead, this handbook focuses on design considerations for the five technologies.

Thermal conditioning is the simultaneous application of heat and pressure to solids to enhance dewaterability without adding conditioning chemicals. During thermal conditioning, heat lyses the cell walls of microorganisms in biological solids, releasing bound water from the particles. This process further hydrolyzes and solubilizes hydrated particles in biological solids and, to a limited degree, organic compounds in primary solids. Conventional mechanical dewatering devices can then readily separate released water from particles as long as the solids have enough fibrous solids for cake structure.

Thermal drying involves heating biosolids to evaporate water, thereby reducing the moisture content further than conventional mechanical-dewatering methods can achieve. Thermally dried biosolids cost less to transport because of the mass and volume reduction that occurs; they also meet Class A pathogen standards and are more marketable than dewatered cake. However, thermal drying processes are more complex and expensive to operate than conventional dewatering methods. Safety concerns and process fundamentals of thermal drying are addressed in *Design of Municipal Wastewater Treatment Plants* (WEF et al., 2009).

Thermal oxidation systems totally or partially convert organic solids into oxidized products (primarily carbon dioxide and water) or partially oxidize and volatilize organic solids via starved air combustion into products with a residual caloric value. *Thermal oxidation* refers to high-temperature oxidation in the presence of excess air. Starved air combustion is thermal oxidation that restricts airflow (oxygen) to produce three potentially energy-rich products: gas, oil or tar, and a char.

Vitrification is a thermal process for converting minerals into glass and has a well-established track record in other industries (e.g., glass furnaces in the glass manufacturing industry and slagging furnaces in coal-fired power generation), but is new to the solids treatment field.

A gasification process uses heat, pressure, and steam to convert solids into a gas composed primarily of carbon monoxide and hydrogen (CIWMB, 2001). Variations in operating temperatures and pressures affect the byproducts, which may be a syngas, char or slag, oils, and reaction water.

Specific thermal processing technologies are described in Table 17.1.

TABLE 17.1   Thermal processing technologies.

Type of thermal processing	Technology	Advantages	Disadvantages	References
Thermal conditioning	Slurry carbonization	Heat energy is recoverable and the product can be used as fuel for manufacturing such as cement kiln	Generates waste stream high in ammonia and organics.	Chapter 26, Section 2.0 (WEF et al., 2009)
Thermal drying	Convection drying systems	Furnace gas can be recycled in rotary drum dryers Low temperatures involved in fluid-bed systems are ideal for energy recovery applications Produces a uniform-sized, spherical pellet well suited to fertilizer applications	Undigested solids can cause problems for dryers. Not designed to be operated as scalping systems. Dust from solids can be an explosion hazard.	Chapter 26, Section 3.3.1.1 (WEF et al., 2009) Chapter 14-14 (Metcalf and Eddy, 2003) Chapter 14 (Vesilind [Ed.], 2003)
Thermal drying	Conduction drying systems	Can be operated as scalping system Produces less exhaust gas than convection drying systems	Some types consume large amounts of power. Dust from solids can be an explosion hazard.	Chapter 26, Section 3.3.1.2 (WEF et al., 2009) Chapter 14-14 (Metcalf and Eddy, 2003) Chapter 14 (Vesilind [Ed.], 2003)
Thermal drying	Belt dryers (emerging technology)	Can recycle process air to improve thermal efficiency Low temperatures involved are ideal for energy recovery applications	Dust from solids can be an explosion hazard.	Chapter 26, Section 3.3.2.1 (WEF et al., 2009)
Thermal drying	Solar dryers (emerging technology)	Can use thermal energy from other treatment processes	Care must be taken and an operation strategy implemented for fire-prevention and explosion hazards.	Chapter 26, Section 3.3.2.2 (WEF et al., 2009)

(continues on next page)

TABLE 17.1   Thermal processing technologies (*Continued*).

Type of thermal processing	Technology	Advantages	Disadvantages	References
Thermal oxidation	Fluidized-bed incinerator	Continuous, automatic operation possible Well suited to large-scale operations	Higher capital and operations and maintenance costs.	Chapter 26, Section 4.2.1.1 (WEF et al., 2009) Chapter 14–15 (Metcalf and Eddy, 2003) Chapter 15 (Vesilind [Ed.], 2003)
Thermal oxidation	Multiple-hearth furnace	Minimal space requirements Easy to operate	Higher capital and operations and maintenance costs, and energy usage. Air pollution and odor problems.	Chapter 26, Section 4.2.1.2 (WEF et al., 2009) Chapter 14–15 (Metcalf and Eddy, 2003) Chapter 15 (Vesilind [Ed.], 2003)
Vitrification	N/A	Glass aggregate vitrified from wastewater solids has multiple construction and industrial applications	New technology to U.S. wastewater industry.	Chapter 26, Section 5.0 (WEF et al., 2009)
Biogasification	N/A	Provides better control of air emissions	New technology to U.S. wastewater industry. Pilot testing is typically required. Expensive process because solids must be heat-dried before gasificiation.	Chapter 26, Section 6.0 (WEF et al., 2009)

TABLE 17.2   Design considerations for thermal processing.

Thermal processing system	Sizing parameters	Emissions and odor control	Other considerations	References
Thermal dryers	Evaporative capacity – Solids concentration – Operating time	Enclose dryer equipment Chemical scrubbers and thermal oxidation Particulate needs to be removed from exhausted air	Storage before and after dryer Water requirements	Chapter 26, Section 3.4 (WEF et al., 2009)
Fluid-bed incinerators	Ignition temperature Reaction time Turbulence with mixing air	Maintain furnace exhaust temperatures above odor-destruction threshold temperature	Gas velocity of bed materials	Chapter 26, Section 4.3 (WEF et al., 2009)

2.0   DESIGN CONSIDERATIONS

Design considerations for each technology are described in Table 17.2.

Design examples for thermal drying and fluid-bed thermal oxidation are provided at the end of Chapter 26 of *Design of Municipal Wastewater Treatment Plants* (WEF et al., 2009).

3.0   REFERENCES

California Integrated Waste Management Board (2001) *Conversion Technologies for Municipal Residuals.* Paper prepared for the Conversion Technologies for Municipal Residuals Forum; Sacramento, California, May 3–4; California Integrated Waste Management Board: Sacramento, California.

Metcalf and Eddy, Inc. (2003) *Wastewater Engineering: Treatment and Reuse*, 4th ed.; McGraw-Hill: New York.

Vesilind, P. A., Ed. (2003) *Wastewater Treatment Plant Design*; Water Environment Federation: Alexandria, Virginia.

Water Environment Federation; American Society of Civil Engineers; Environmental & Water Resources Institute (2009) *Design of Municipal Wastewater Treatment Plants*, 5th ed.; WEF Manual of Practice No. 8; ASCE Manuals and Reports on Engineering Practice No. 76; McGraw-Hill: New York.

Water Environment Federation; U.S. Environmental Protection Agency; Water Environment Research Foundation (2012) *Solids Process Design and Management*; McGraw-Hill: New York.

Chapter 18

Odor Control and Air Emissions

1.0	INTRODUCTION	185	3.0	REFERENCES	188
2.0	DESIGN CONSIDERATIONS	188			

1.0 INTRODUCTION

This chapter is based substantially on information contained in *Control of Odors and Emissions from Wastewater Treatment Plants* (WEF, 2004) and should be the first point of reference. Chapter 7 of *Design of Municipal Wastewater Treatment Plants* (WEF et al., 2009) focuses on characterization, assessment, capture, and treatment of odors and air emissions from various processes at a wastewater treatment plant and on regulations, sampling and measurement, containment, and dispersion modeling. Additionally, emission-reduction strategies are described in chapters specific to the individual process unit in *Design of Municipal Wastewater Treatment Plants* (WEF et al., 2009). The summary information found in this chapter of the handbook is about design considerations.

Suggested reading material for additional information includes the following:

- *Design of Municipal Wastewater Treatment Plants* (WEF et al., 2009) (Chapter 7, "Odor Control and Air Emissions");

- *Wastewater Engineering: Treatment and Reuse* (Metcalf and Eddy, 2003) (Chapter 15, Section 3, "Odor Management");

- *Wastewater Treatment Plant Design* (Vesilind [Ed.], 2003) (Chapter 11, "Disinfection, Reoxygenation, and Odor Control"); and

- *Control of Odors and Emissions from Wastewater Treatment Plants* (WEF, 2004).

Types of odor air emission control techniques are described in Table 18.1.

185

TABLE 18.1 Odor and air emissions control technologies.

Type of treatment	Technology	Advantages	Disadvantages	References
Liquid-phase	Air/oxygen injection	Can prevent odor production Air is readily available source Pure oxygen gas is five times more soluble than air	Liquid oxygen requires special containment vessel	Chapter 7, Section 7.1.1 (WEF et al., 2009) Chapter 15, Section 3 (Metcalf and Eddy, 2003)
Liquid-phase	Chemical oxidation	Chlorine is inexpensive and widely available Systems are relatively simple	Ozone is unstable and must be generated on-site Manganese dioxide (byproduct from potassium permanganate reactions) may be problematic for plants already near manganese limits	Chapter 7, Section 7.1.2 (WEF et al., 2009) Chapter 15, Section 3 (Metcalf and Eddy, 2003)
Liquid-phase	Nitrate addition	Can be used for prevention and/or removal	Reaction for removal is not instantaneous	Chapter 7, Section 7.1.3 (WEF et al., 2009)
Liquid-phase	Iron salts	Fast-acting Commerically available chemicals	Increases solids production of facility May adversely affect UV disinfection equipment	Chapter 7, Section 7.1.4 (WEF et al., 2009)
Liquid phase	pH adjustment	Slight change in pH may be effective enough	Can adversely affect pH-sensitive treatment processes	Chapter 7, Section 7.1.5 (WEF et al., 2009)
Biological	Biofiltration	Reliable Economical	Larger site space requirements Corrosion control is necessary	Chapter 7, Section 7.2.2 (WEF et al., 2009) Chapter 15, Section 3 (Metcalf and Eddy, 2003)

Biological	Bioscrubbers and biotrickling filters	Instead of chemical usage	Not widely used yet in the United States	Chapter 7, Section 7.2.4 (WEF et al., 2009) Chapter 15, Section 3 (Metcalf and Eddy, 2003)
Chemical and physical	Gas-absorption scrubbers	Can be designed to be horizontal for sites with height limitations or vertical for sites with space limitations	Lower odor removal efficiency for crossflow scrubbers	Chapter 7, Section 7.3.1 (WEF et al., 2009) Chapter 15, Section 3 (Metcalf and Eddy, 2003)
Chemical and physical	Dry-adsorption systems	Granular activated carbon has been used for over 100 years and is common	Granular activated carbon can be expensive	Chapter 7, Section 7.3.2 (WEF et al., 2009) Chapter 15, Section 3 (Metcalf and Eddy, 2003)
Combustion emissions control	Thermal oxidation	Achieve high odor removal efficiencies	High capital and operating costs	Chapter 7, Section 7.4.1 (WEF et al., 2009) Chapter 15, Section 3 (Metcalf and Eddy, 2003)
Combustion emissions control	Particulate removal			Chapter 7, Section 7.4.2 (WEF et al., 2009)

2.0   DESIGN CONSIDERATIONS

Before an emissions-control technology can be selected and then sized, the design engineer must define the air flowrate (AFR) of the air or exhaust-gas stream being treated, the loading rate for the pollutant(s) or odorant of concern, and the performance criteria or control efficiency to be achieved.

The primary drivers for determining AFR are ventilation requirements for the process unit or area from which the air is being collected. The designer needs a thorough understanding of the process unit or area to be ventilated, including the temperature, pressure, moisture content, and gas composition of the airflow stream. To treat the exhaust gas from a boiler, engine, dryer, or thermal treatment system, the designer may require a mass and energy balance of the system to obtain the necessary airflow information.

Knowing the maximum pollutant loading affects system sizing while the average pollutant loading affects the life-cycle costs. It is necessary to understand the complexity of odorous air streams from both an olfactometric-character and chemical-composition perspective. The emission-control objectives for criteria pollutants are established through the air quality permitting process. In some instances, a dispersion modeling analysis is required to demonstrate that ambient air quality standards are not being exceeded. Odor-control performance criteria are established to minimize odor complaints or prevent nuisance conditions.

Table 18.1 presents a broad, categorical look at odor control technologies. When selecting technology, the designer should also consider additional required equipment and ancillary systems (such as washwater to keep media moist). Additionally, discussions with manufacturers can indicate ways to offset life-cycle cost with equipment selection that may increase upfront costs.

3.0   REFERENCES

Metcalf and Eddy, Inc. (2003) *Wastewater Engineering: Treatment and Reuse*, 4th ed.; McGraw-Hill: New York.

Vesilind, P. A., Ed. (2003) *Wastewater Treatment Plant Design*; Water Environment Federation: Alexandria, Virginia.

Water Environment Federation (2004) *Control of Odors and Emissions from Wastewater Treatment Plants*; Manual of Practice No. 25; Water Environment Federation: Alexandria, Virginia.

Water Environment Federation; American Society of Civil Engineers; Environmental & Water Resources Institute (2009) *Design of Municipal Wastewater Treatment Plants*, 5th ed.; WEF Manual of Practice No. 8; ASCE Manuals and Reports on Engineering Practice No. 76; McGraw-Hill: New York.

Index

CPSIA information can be obtained
at www.ICGtesting.com
Printed in the USA
BVOW11s0537190816

459274BV00004B/14/P